D0466650

O O N A

O O N A

LIVING IN THE SHADOWS

A BIOGRAPHY
of
OONA O'NEILL CHAPLIN

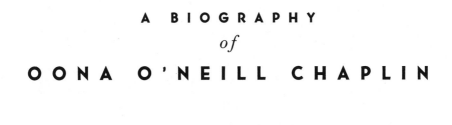

JANE SCOVELL

WARNER BOOKS

A Time Warner Company

Warner Books, Inc., 1271 Avenue of the Americas, New York, NY 10020

Visit our Web site at http://warnerbooks.com

W A Time Warner Company

Printed in the United States of America

First Printing: November 1998

10   9   8   7   6   5   4   3   2   1

Library of Congress Cataloging-in-Publication Data

Scovell, Jane.
      Oona : living in the shadows : a biography of Oona O'Neill Chaplin /
   Jane Scovell.
         p.   cm.
      Includes bibliographical references and index.
      ISBN 0-446-51730-5
      1. Chaplin, Oona.   2. Chaplin, Charlie, 1889–1977.   3. Motion picture
   actors and actresses—United States—Biography.   4. Entertainers' spouses—
   Biography.   5. Comedians—United States—Biography.   I. Title.
   PN2287.C515S36   1998
   791.43'028'092—dc21
      [b]   98-21592
                                                                            CIP

Book design by H. Roberts Design

To:

my children,
Amy, Lucy, and Billy

my friend,
Sidney Sheldon Welton

and

in memory of my mother,
Rhoda Orentlicher Scovell

"It is impossible to please all the world and one's father."

—*Jean La Fontaine*

CONTENTS

PROLOGUE

Oona. What is the root of this magical name? Derived from ancient tongues, *Oona* is a variant of *Una*, which comes directly from the Latin word for "one." Some believe that *Una* is an anglicized version of *Juno*; others suggest that it comes from *uan*, the Irish word for "lamb." If so, it would be a version of Agnes, Oona's mother's name. Although the name is fairly common in Ireland, the double "o" opening is not; those two vowels bestow a visual lift, making Oona lovely to see as well as to say and hear. While Una belongs to others—the actresses Merkel and O'Connor, for example, and the heroine of Spenser's *The Fairie Queene*—Oona has remained the particular property of Eugene O'Neill's daughter and Charlie Chaplin's wife.

O'Neill, America's Nobel Prize–winning playwright, and his second wife, Agnes Boulton, favored the unusual and actively solicited help in naming their two children. Awaiting the arrival of their first child, they received a list of Irish names from a friend, Edmund T. Quinn, and when their son was born, the O'Neills, guided by James Stevens, another friend, selected *Shane Rudraighe.* Shane is Gaelic for "John"; the original Shane Rudraighe was one of the great warrior kings of Ireland. Five years later the couple again referred to Quinn's list, and at the birth of their daughter they once more followed James Stevens's counsel. This time he recommended *Oona*, another resonant complement to *O'Neill*—and with that singular spelling to boot. Oona liked her unique name, although she once heard that it was a form of Winifred and confessed that she "hated that one."

Oona O'Neill was born in Bermuda on May 14, 1925, and died on September 27, 1991, in Corsier-sur-Vevey, Switzerland, where she lived for more than half her sixty-six years and, for more than half of those years, she was the wife of Charlie Chaplin. Because of her lineage and her marriage, this innately private woman was very much in the public eye.

In the late thirties and forties, Oona O'Neill's heyday, Americans idolized goddesses on the silver screen, celluloid Dianae who were as far removed from their worshippers as the moon itself. "If you want the girl next door, go next door," Joan Crawford succinctly put it. Rarely, someone with whom admirers thought they could identify slipped into the frozen climate of celebrity, someone like Oona O'Neill whose unsullied, natural beauty endeared her to a nation ordinarily obsessed with the exotic. A glorified version of the girl next door, Oona wanted to become a movie star. Although she never realized that goal, she still made headlines. Her fame rested on her twin classification as the daughter of a Nobel laureate and the wife of the screen's comic genius. Today, relegated to the amusement section rather than the front page, her name endures as the horizontal or vertical answer to the interchangeable crossword puzzle clues *Wife of Charlie Chaplin/Daughter of Eugene O'Neill.*

Eugene O'Neill was a disaster as a father. He abandoned Oona when she was two years old, saw her for a few brief intervals during her childhood and adolescence, disinherited her when she turned eighteen, and never saw her again. At age eighteen she became the fourth wife of fifty-four-year-old Charlie Chaplin. The May–December alliance was expected to last the requisite six months, but they confounded skeptics by staying together, raising eight children, and remaining, in their words, blissfully happy.

The marriage stood up under powerful trials, including a notorious paternity suit brought against Chaplin at the time of their wedding and, later, during the angst-ridden years of communist witch hunting. In reality, neither of those hazards was the real danger. No, the greatest threat was *time;* three and a half long decades separated them, and they could not make their sun stand still. Considering his well-known boundless agility and energy, Charlie Chaplin did not fare particularly well in advanced age. Fit enough in his early seventies—at age seventy-two he sired a son—by the end of his eighth decade he had markedly weakened. During the last ten years of his life he faded dramatically, but Oona protected him and tended to him from the beginning of the end until the very end. It could not have been easy for a woman barely in her forties to put the brakes on her life and gear down to the snail's pace of an old man. Yet she stood by him, answering those who questioned her total commitment with a quiet, "He was there for me when I needed him; now I must be there for him."

The years passed. Reports about the exiled Chaplins grew more scarce, and the bits and pieces of information which did appear centered on Charlie. He died in December 1977, leaving Oona all but forgotten. Fourteen years later she, too, was gone. At her death, for a brief moment, her name was back on the front pages: *Widow of Charlie Chaplin; Daughter of Eugene O'Neill Dead at 66.*

Cast as a penumbrated figure in the lives of an illustrious father and a celebrated husband, Oona O'Neill Chaplin actually had a complex and compelling story of her own—a life which differs from the one depicted in the superficial headlines of her youth, the deferential captions of her maturity, and even the scandalous suggestions advanced since her death. Rejected and abandoned by her father, she attached herself to another genius and was absorbed by him. Did she give up everything to marry a much older man whose reputation was—to say the least—tarnished, just to spite her father? Or just for money? Was her marriage really perfect? Was she really happy? Was she good to the children, and were they good to her? What about her widowhood? Did she actually hide away? Were there other men? Most crucial, was she able to handle the severance from her father well enough to escape the family strains of alcoholism and melancholia?

Oona's life was a fairy tale without a happy ending, said one of her closest friends, and just like the heroine of a fairy tale, Oona was threatened by an ogre and rescued by a Prince Charming. This is the story of her struggle to break free of the suffocating past.

PART

ONE

one

"BEING IRISH"

Oona O'Neill Chaplin's paternal ancestry has been chronicled and studied in numerous biographical and critical works concerning her husband and her father. In the latter instance, by transforming himself, his father, mother, and older brother into the Tyrones of *Long Day's Journey into Night*, Eugene O'Neill not only created a landmark of American dramatic literature but virtually ensured *his* family's dominance in any future examination of his daughter's life. Given the celebrity status of the O'Neills and the abundance of material on them, it is hardly surprising that Oona's maternal forebears, the Boultons, were accorded a historical backseat. Oona, however, was a product of both houses, and in order to get the full picture, it is necessary to examine her two dynasties. First (and simply because of their accessibility) a look at the notable O'Neills, whose story, up to James O'Neill's breakthrough as a theatrical star, follows a classic American immigrant pattern.

Oona's paternal great-grandparents, Mary and Edward O'Neil (the name is Gaelic for "champion"), fled from Ireland in the mid-nineteenth century to escape the devastating effects of the Great Potato Famine. Edward brought his wife and children to America, where they settled first in Buffalo, New York, and then in Cincinnati, Ohio; during this time a second "l" was added to the family name. Edward O'Neill did not do well in the new world. His two oldest sons took off almost immediately, leaving James, born in 1846 in Kilkenny, Leinster, as the oldest male child in a household that included five younger sisters. Always homesick, unable to support his brood, and fearful of dying in a strange country, Edward abandoned his family and returned to Ireland while his wife struggled on as a charwoman. James O'Neill, himself forced to work at the age of ten for fifty cents a week, never forgot those early years of humiliating poverty. Indeed, despite his future affluence he never let his wife and sons forget, either. Young James gravitated to the stage, worked long and hard as an apprentice, and overcame his biggest hurdle, a thick brogue. In an era when declamatory actors like the raging Edwin Forrest were yielding to more subtle stage performers like the subdued, but no less dramatic, Edwin Booth, the handsome, gifted, and appealing James O'Neill emerged as a bona fide matinee idol with unquestionable potential.

Oona's paternal grandmother, Mary Ellen Quinlan, was born in New Haven, Connecticut, in 1857 and grew up in Cleveland, Ohio. She too was the offspring of Irish immigrants; unlike the O'Neills, her parents, Thomas and Bridget Quinlan, prospered. Her father had a successful career in real estate and became part owner of a liquor and tobacco shop. Actors from the nearby Academy of Music frequented Quinlan's establishment, and before long the proprietor struck up a friendship with one of the troupers, Jimmy O'Neill. O'Neill soon was introduced to Quinlan's only daughter, fourteen-year-old Mary Ellen, or Ella, as she preferred to be called. Ten years younger than James O'Neill, Ella developed a teenage crush on the good-looking and personable young man, whereas he viewed her as a sweet child, someone to be gently teased but not amorously pursued. Shy and modest, Ella exhibited personality traits that might have led her into religious life—like many Catholic girls, she briefly flirted with the idea of taking the veil.[1]

At the age of forty Thomas Quinlan, a teetotaler, suddenly began drinking heavily, jeopardizing his health. He fell ill with tuberculosis and died while his daughter was still in school. Always a daddy's girl, the grief-stricken Ella immersed herself in her studies, music in particular, and proved talented enough to receive a gold medal for her achievements at the piano. After graduation from St. Mary's Academy in Indiana, an institution renowned for educational excellence, Ella overcame her mother's objections and moved to New York City. There, almost immediately, she renewed her acquaintance with James O'Neill, now a principal of the Union Square Stock Company. Ella had been dreaming of him since their first meeting; now he fell for her and soon proposed. Despite similarities in their Irish Catholic backgrounds—just as she had thought of taking the veil, he once had considered wearing the collar—the outgoing, earthy actor and the shy, ladylike musician were oddly matched. What brought them together was a powerful mutual passion and Ella's unconscious desire to replace her beloved father. Convent-bred and conventionally raised, Ella Quinlan should have married an upstanding solid citizen, either a prosperous businessman or a professional, the kind of husband who would have sheltered and coddled her. She *should* have married such a man, but she did not. She married an actor, an alliance her father surely would have frowned on, for although Thomas Quinlan had enjoyed Jimmy O'Neill's company, it is doubtful that he had fancied the itinerant performer as a son-in-law. His widow, Bridget, certainly expressed her misgivings about having James as a son-in-law.

The wedding of James O'Neill and Ella Quinlan took place on June 14, 1877, in St. Ann's Church on East Twelfth Street in New York City. Ella, who had a taste for luxury in clothes, wore an exquisite and expensive satin and lace wedding gown, which in future times came to symbolize her lost youth and innocence. Often Ella would take it out and ruminate over her past life, a process that became so difficult and tear-filled she eventually put the gown away for good. Eugene O'Neill brilliantly used this remembrance in the closing scene of *Long Day's Journey into Night* when, in a drug-induced haze, the character Mary Tyrone meanders about the stage cradling her tattered wedding dress in her arms and talking of happier days.

Drawn into the theatrical life by her husband's profession and associations, Ella's convent-based sensibilities soon were buffeted. She was vastly different from the worldly ladies with whom James O'Neill previously had kept company. One of them, the actress Louise Hawthorne, committed suicide after losing his affections, and still another, Nettie Walsh, swore that James had married her. Walsh sued the actor right after his wedding, making Ella's adjustment to her new life that much more difficult. The case was dropped, but not before Ella Quinlan O'Neill had been thoroughly shamed and disenchanted. Hurt followed hurt. She claimed, for example, to have learned of her husband's predilection for alcohol on their honeymoon. Although James O'Neill definitely imbibed, heavy social drinking was the norm for men of that era, particularly men of the theater, and despite the frequency of his drinking and the volume consumed, he seemed quite capable of holding his liquor—a skill neither of his sons inherited.

Not only did O'Neill's drinking upset his wife, but his profession itself proved an ongoing obstacle. Acting still was considered less than respectable, and following her marriage Ella's

social standing took a nosedive. Former friends and classmates gave her the cold shoulder. She had no place to go except into her husband's flamboyant world, and as Ella took her place beside him, the security of a solid home life yielded to a succession of hotel suites in scattered cities. She always accompanied her husband on the road yet would not deign to spend time sitting around theaters waiting for him. Consequently she spent many hours alone in nondescript hotel rooms. James O'Neill revered his wife and, all too aware that he had married above himself, suffered guilt pangs for subjecting this gentle woman to the harsh vicissitudes of the actor's life.

Shortly after the Nettie Walsh lawsuit was resolved O'Neill took Ella to San Francisco, where they remained for almost two years, possibly the happiest of their married life. Soothed by the genteel atmosphere of the Bay City, Ella relaxed and even found herself drawn to some of her husband's associates. On September 28, 1878, in the home of one of those friends, she gave birth to their first child, James Jr. Five years later in a St. Louis, Missouri, hotel, their second son, Edmund, was born.

Ella attempted to properly care for her children and to continue being her husband's traveling companion as he settled into his acclaimed portrayal of Edmund Dantes in a dramatization of Dumas's *The Count of Monte Cristo*. The play was a mixed blessing. Through it O'Neill latched on to a perennial source of income, but the promise of his youth was essentially squandered on a potboiler. In the opinion of contemporary critics and his fellow actors, had he not confined himself to the Chateau d'If, James O'Neill might have become one of the theater's immortals, someone whose name would have been said in the same breath as Edwin Booth (in America) or Sir Henry Irving (in England). However, since his fear of poverty compelled him to stay with a role that made money, his fame and fortune came out of a role he grew to loathe. The public's insatiable appetite for Dantes, the actor complained, kept him from undertaking the

classic roles of the theater and forever mired him in melodrama. In one sense he was correct—he was only giving the public what it wanted, yet he too was at fault. A dedicated actor often elects to take on a superior role for less money simply to stretch his abilities. James O'Neill was unwilling to make the sacrifice; he could not tear himself away from a proven meal ticket to fully explore his talent, and that frustration no doubt contributed to his thirst. In later years the elder O'Neill gave vent to his discontent again and again, all within earshot of his impressionable son Eugene. In Eugene's view, by capitulating to the pit his father took the easy way out, something the younger O'Neill vowed he never would do. His aspirations always would exceed his grasp; anything that came easily would not be worth the effort. Ironically, after enacting the Count for more than 4,000 of the estimated 6,000 performances he gave in his lifetime, James O'Neill did try to wean himself and his audiences away from Dumas and into other dramas. By then it was too late. He had lost the spark; the vaunted potential had been dashed against the walls of the Chateau d'If.

Although he toured for most of the year, James O'Neill maintained a hotel apartment in New York City where Ella stayed with the boys. Their passion undimmed, the couple could not stand to be apart for long, and Ella regularly left the children in the care of her mother and a nursemaid to join James on the road. The physical desire to be with him temporarily overcame her maternal instincts, but those conjugal visits were marked by guilt as well as ardor. Wife? Mother? In a dilemma similar to the one her granddaughter Oona would face in future years, Ella, the good Catholic girl, was torn between the two demanding roles of wanting to be at her husband's side and wanting to look after her children. Decisions usually were made in favor of the former, for not only did James need her, she herself could not bear the separation.

On a western tour in the winter of 1885, James wrote and

begged Ella to come to him. Squelching her misgivings, she agreed, and leaving Jamie and Edmund with her mother and the nurse, Ella went to Colorado. During her absence Jamie came down with measles and passed it on, in a far more virulent form, to his infant brother. Word of the boys' illness was sent to their parents in Denver, and the frantic mother made plans to catch the first train east. O'Neill, bound to the tradition of "the show must go on," had no choice but to remain. Just before Ella left town, a telegram arrived announcing Edmund's death. Alone and wracked with grief, she made the long trip back even as her husband put aside his personal agony and again stepped onto the stage as Edmund Dantes.

Within months of his son's death, and after two and a half years of playing the Count of Monte Cristo, James bought the rights to the drama and took control of the production. Now working for himself, the actor raised his interpretation to a new level of fervor; his increased efforts paid handsomely, netting him some $25,000 per year. The joy in realizing that he was becoming a rich man was mitigated somewhat by Ella's behavior; she never could fully let go of her lost child or of the part she felt that she had played in his death. Blaming herself for leaving Edmund, Ella still would cry out for her infant son a quarter of a century later.

In the mid 1880s Bridget Quinlan moved to New London, Connecticut, to live with her sister, and during frequent family visits to see his mother-in-law, James O'Neill found himself drawn to the quiet New England sea town. He purchased property on Pequot Avenue, and that residence became the O'Neills' summer home and the setting for *Long Day's Journey into Night*. Although only a summer citizen, Ella came to regard New London as home, especially since little Edmund was buried there. Having a place to call home, however, was not enough to alleviate her grief. In 1887, in an effort to lift her spirits, O'Neill took Ella on a grand tour of Europe. Whatever pleasure that trip might have afforded was shattered when they returned to discover that Bridget Quinlan had died. At this, Ella was thrown deeper into heartache and despondency. With her father and mother gone, James remained her sole bulwark and she became increasingly dependent on him. Trying to bolster his wife, O'Neill decided that with Jamie enrolled at boarding school Ella needed someone else to occupy her time—that is, another child. At first she resisted, arguing that no one could replace Edmund. In time she yielded with the hope that the newborn would be a girl, a daughter who would not replace the lost boy but, rather, be her mother's comfort and darling. The darling comfort turned out to be Eugene Gladstone O'Neill.

Born on October 16, 1888, the O'Neills' third son weighed a phenomenal eleven pounds. His head was exceptionally large, which prompted one of Ella's more outspoken cousins to declare that Eugene would "either be an idiot or a genius!"[2] Apprised of the baby's imminent arrival, James, on the New England theatrical circuit in his sixth consecutive tour of *The Count of Monte Cristo*, raced home between appearances in Brockton and Fall River, Massachusetts, to attend his wife. Whether he arrived in time for the actual birth is not known; it is known that he stayed for only a day and then immediately returned to the road.

While her husband continued to triumph on the stage, Ella suffered at home, and morphine was prescribed to ease her postpartum pain. In those days the indiscriminate administering of drugs was an accepted practice; despite the dire predictions of certain watchdog groups, most physicians relied heavily on them. Ella Quinlan O'Neill found bottled comfort, became hooked without realizing it, and within a short time was addicted. She blamed James for her plight, arguing that he had put her in the hands of a second-rate doctor in order to save money. In all probability had Ella given birth to Eugene in a fashionable private residence instead of a small family hotel on the corner of Broadway and Forty-third Street, and had she been looked after by a high-ranking physician rather than the hotel's on-call doctor, she still would have been provided with morphine. Deeply concerned and somewhat helpless in the face of Ella's urgent need, James coped by doing his best to cover up. He would take the train to New York City after Saturday evening performances and would stay for the weekend in order to keep an eye on Ella.

During one of James's weekend visits, Eugene was baptized and christened at Holy Innocents Church on West Thirty-seventh Street. His name was derived from Eoghen, a famous figure of Irish lore; however, the loyal Irish nationalist James O'Neill made a slight error in translation—Eoghen is Gaelic for Owen, not Eugene. The name Gladstone was bestowed in homage to the British prime minister, whose efforts for Irish home rule endeared him to Hibernians but did nothing to advance his career in England. O'Neill's fierce love of the Auld Sod was handed down to his son, and being Irish, Eugene O'Neill later maintained, was what explained him the most.

In the early weeks and months of Eugene's life, while his mother flowed in and out of awareness, he was looked after by Sarah Sandy, an English nanny. The diminutive nursemaid remained with the family for seven years, leaving when the boy was enrolled at boarding school. Apparently Sarah Sandy was a mixed blessing; although she was a loving, constant presence, her taste for the macabre—she regaled Eugene with horror stories and took him to museums featuring hideous wax figures of murderers and various grotesques—definitely had an adverse effect on the impressionable child. Not an unkind person, Sarah Sandy added a touch of the terrifying to her charge's childhood. Eugene was nervous, and the jittery upside-down, inside-out quality of the O'Neills' life, the travel, the hotels, the theaters, all served to advance his nervousness. The rootless nature of his existence, combined with the ghoulish bent of his nursemaid, produced in him such a terrible fear of the dark that he suffered constant nightmares. To help the boy, James O'Neill reached back to his Irish peasant roots for a remedy: when the night terrors came, he would offer his son a glass of water mixed with a few drops of whiskey. Eugene later claimed that he believed this act of comfort predisposed him to spirits and in some way led to his alcoholism. Although ancient remedies can indeed wreak havoc, in this instance O'Neill's problems more likely stemmed from his family's fly-by-night existence—his father's endless touring and the equally disturbing touring of his mother's mind—than from the sprinkling of a few whiskey drops in his drinking water.

During Eugene's infancy and throughout his young adulthood, Ella O'Neill wallowed in depression and drugs and remained icily out of reach. The boy's love and need for her went unanswered. As a result of that lack and the nomadic existence he was forced to lead, the future playwright shouldered his way through a lifetime of what he termed "hopeless hope."[3] By his own admission he was a person who never felt at home, always felt like an outsider, and always was "a little in love with death." The bleakness seems to have been relieved only through books. First, Sarah Sandy read to him and then helped him learn to read by himself. He poured his heart and soul into mastering the words and became an ardent and devoted reader; books, in fact, became one of the two great loves of his life, the other was the sea. Indeed, so considerable was his enthusiasm for the water that O'Neill more than once declared that he wished he had been born an amphibious creature rather than a man.

Eugene spent eight to nine months of the year touring with his parents. That life, as his mother had learned before him, proved far more rigorous than glamorous. In at least one instance it was downright calamitous. Nutrition sometimes was sacrificed to expediency; meals were grabbed on the run between performances and/or cities, so Eugene's diet suffered. He came down with rickets, a bone disease resulting from a vitamin D deficiency frequently seen in poor children. Once the disease was discovered it was successfully treated. Still, the idea that he had been subjected to such a degrading illness remained an embarrassment all his life. Fortunately the summers in New London provided a welcome, if not a complete, respite from life on the road. At the Connecticut shore Eugene knew where he would be from one day to the next and took solace in the soothing monotony of sameness. Those summers notwithstanding, the playwright later bluntly declared that he had no youth. Caught between his powerful father and his fearful mother, Eugene O'Neill grew up gloomy.

Once he reached school age, Eugene's days on the road ended. Sent to Mount St. Vincent-on-Hudson in Riverdale, a boarding school run by the Sisters of Charity, he was introduced to the formal teachings of Catholicism. In the sixth grade, about to receive his first Holy Communion, he took some of his classmates to see his father on stage. Informed of their whereabouts and incensed that the boys had stepped into the nefarious realm of the theater, one Sister of Charity showed no mercy and refused to allow the miscreants to receive communion. The punishment hit hard; clearly his father was involved in something disdained by the Church, and though Eugene had done nothing wrong the sins of his father were visited upon him.

In 1900 Eugene left Mount St. Vincent and enrolled in the De La Salle Institute in New York City, first as a day student and then as a boarder. Two years later he transferred to Betts Academy in Stamford, Connecticut, and was graduated from that institution in June 1906. During his days at Betts Academy, Eugene spent time with Jamie, who magnanimously introduced his younger brother to the wicked ways of the world. Later Jamie would brag that Gene learned sin more easily because his big brother paved the way. Eugene was accepted at Princeton and upon entering that august university chose to concentrate on drinking rather than studying. Although he was intelligent enough to handle the college curriculum, O'Neill was not emotionally mature enough to fit in. His tendency to take himself seriously earned him the nickname Ego. Suspended for two weeks for unruly behavior (i.e., drunkenness), he made known his intention to withdraw from the university at the end of his freshman year.

Following Eugene's defection from academia his father arranged for him to work at the New York–Chicago Supply Company, a mail order house selling inexpensive jewelry in which James O'Neill had invested money. Employed, if not exactly gainfully, Eugene palled around with college chums from Princeton and other Ivy League schools. At this time he met Kathleen Jenkins, an attractive, socially connected young woman. In 1909 she became his wife. Within weeks of their wedding Eugene took off on a gold-mining expedition, leaving behind a girl he barely knew who, by this time, was carrying his child.

Eugene Gladstone O'Neill Jr. was born in May 1910 while his father was in British Honduras. A few weeks after his son's birth Eugene returned to the States and, making sure that Kathleen was not present, went to her mother's house to see his infant son. He held the boy in his arms, cried, handed the infant back to the grandmother, and left for good. Later the playwright told his namesake that he was forced into the decision. What else could he do? Not only was he a twenty-one-year-old drop-out with no means of supporting a wife and child, but his parents had been against the marriage from the beginning and wanted it annulled. Confused and depressed, O'Neill called this the lowest moment of his life and tried to end his agony in an unsuccessful attempt at suicide. Eugene and Kathleen subsequently were divorced, and the former was put under no obligation to pay alimony or child support. Kathleen Jenkins married a second time and her husband, George Pitt-Smith, raised O'Neill's son as his own; Eugene Pitt-Smith did not even learn of his true parentage until he was eleven years old, at which time he took back his birth name.

With the marriage to Kathleen officially over, Eugene returned to the bosom of his family. To keep him busy, James made his son an assistant manager of his theatrical company, a job which consisted of hanging around the entrance to the theater to make sure no one got in without a ticket. Soon enough, Eugene bolted and went off to sea. He landed in Buenos Aires, where his seemingly aimless debauchery continued. In truth, all that Eugene O'Neill experienced during this time became fodder for his artistic soul. Returning to New York in 1911, the twenty-three-year-old ne'er-do-well, as his father termed him, headed for familiar stamping grounds—Jimmy the Priest's waterfront café. Then, in 1912, O'Neill shipped out to sea for a final voyage as an able-bodied seaman, a title that meant almost as much to him as his later designation as Nobel Prize laureate. Upon his discharge O'Neill returned to the family and along with his brother toured with their father's hoary *Monte Cristo* show. One story has it that Eugene, pressed into undertaking two minor roles in the Dumas opus, was accosted by his father after the young man's first stage appearance. "Sir," said the senior O'Neill, "I am not satisfied with your performance." To which his son answered, "Sir, I am not satisfied with your play."[4]

The O'Neills returned to New London for the summer of 1912, the exact time setting for *Long Day's Journey into Night*. For years Ella's boys had known of their mother's addiction (really, just about everyone knew), and the worst part for Eugene was the damning suggestion that it was his fault, that the pain of bringing him into the world had coerced her into drugs. Living through it was hell, but later O'Neill the artist would use O'Neill the son's guilt to great advantage in his dramas. That summer the O'Neill boys hung around together. Jamie, ten years Eugene's elder, already was in the grip of a hopelessness that far eclipsed his younger brother's despair. A hapless drunkard, both charming and cynical, kindly and nasty, Jamie never did amount to anything. James Sr. eventually took great pride in Eugene's accomplishments and frequently bragged about his younger boy even as he denigrated his elder son. As Eugene's achievements increased, Jamie continued to do nothing and succeeded only in becoming morbidly attached to his mother, an alliance which culminated in his accompanying her corpse on a train ride from Los Angeles to New York. That horrific episode resulted in Jamie's return to raging alcoholism and became a moving theme of his brother's play *A Moon for the Misbegotten*.

During that central summer of 1912 Eugene worked for a newspaper, wrote poetry, and contracted tuberculosis. TB, the *white plague*, was believed to be hereditary and so highly contagious that sufferers were set apart like lepers. Moreover, devout Irish Catholics attached a tragic spin to consumption by assuming that God visited it upon sinners. Bedridden, tended to by a nurse, cut off from his companions, and aware that both his grandfathers had died of the disease, Eugene understandably was terrified. His father, fearful lest Ella, in her perpetually weakened condition, contract the illness, arranged for Eugene to enter the Gaylord Farm Sanatorium in Wallingford. Watched over and cared for as he had never been before, O'Neill used the five-month stay to great advantage, especially in reading; at Gaylord he discovered the works of Strindberg, which had a most profound influence on his own dramas. Friends said that Eugene O'Neill went into Gaylord a boy and came out a man. O'Neill himself said that he was reborn within the sanatorium's confines.

Early in June 1913 Eugene returned to New London and immersed himself in serious reading—from Aeschylus to Nietzsche, from Shakespeare to Ibsen—and began the serious business of writing plays. During these years of training his father was by turns tight-fisted and generous. For example, while he would not wholly subsidize Eugene, granting him a mere ten dollars a week allowance, he did pay for the publication of *Thirst*, the first collection of Eugene's plays. Eager to pursue his career, Eugene entered George Baker's renowned drama workshop at Harvard in the fall of 1914. There, according to a fellow student, he "stood out like an oyster in a lunchroom stew."[5] O'Neill finished the term at Harvard, returned to New York, and rented a room in Greenwich Village. The aspiring playwright supplemented his allowance by selling bits and pieces of his own writing to magazines and newspapers and by working on screenplays for the fledgling movie industry. He also spent quite a bit of time with his brother at the latter's favorite watering hole, the Columbian Saloon.

Jamie, now a confirmed alcoholic, befriended whores and drunks and pipe-dreamed of becoming a newspaperman. He loved his younger brother yet could not help but be envious of Eugene's obvious talent, and that filial resentment inspired more drinking. Like his brother, Eugene drank; but unlike Jamie, his drinking was not continuous. Eugene would work intensely, then would go on sprees and recover, and then, racked with guilt, return to his work. Years later, when he could no longer balance the drunkenness and sobriety, he stopped drinking completely because it interfered with his creative process. Eugene O'Neill was an artist first and then a drinker. Jamie O'Neill was simply a drinker.

In the summer of 1916 Eugene made his first trip to Provincetown, Massachusetts, where he shared an oceanside shack with a friend. Like Greenwich Village, although on a far smaller scale, the picturesque town at the tip of Cape Cod had become an artists' colony. It was here that *Bound East for Cardiff* premiered at the Wharf Theater, marking the first O'Neill drama to be staged as well as the beginnings of the Provincetown Players. Unable to serve his country in the First World War because of his fragile health, Eugene concentrated on his work and his drinking. In 1917 the Provincetown Players established themselves on Macdougal Street in Greenwich Village and, at O'Neill's insistence, called their New York venue the Playwrights' Theater. From the onset the plucky little company—which included writers Terry Carlin, Susan Glaspell, George Cram "Jig" Cook, Hutchins Hapgood, Neith Boyce, Wilbur Daniel Steele, William Zorach, and John Reed, and set designer Robert Edmond Jones—achieved national recognition. Among its offerings were O'Neill's one-acters, *In the Zone*, *Ile*, and *The Long Voyage Home*.

Striking in appearance, the lean and wiry O'Neill had inherited his father's Black Irish looks. Distinguished from their fair-skinned, light-haired countrymen, the Black Irish are said to be descendants of shipwrecked sailors washed up on Ireland's shores during the Spanish Armada debacle. The fact that he was an Irishman who did not look like the majority of Irishmen provided another deviation from the norm for the man who never felt he belonged. (Charlie Chaplin, an Englishman by birth, also was distinguished from that fair-skinned race by *his* dark coloring, which was variously attributed to his being Black Irish, a Gypsy, or a Jew.) Women were very attracted to Eugene O'Neill and he responded, but in a diffident rather than active manner. Characterized as affectionate more than sensual, he often was the pursued, not the pursuer. Although O'Neill had many casual affairs during this period, he seemed to have been genuinely enamored of Louise Bryant. Louise was the lover of John Reed at the same time that she took up with Eugene, and when she ran off and married Reed, O'Neill was left in the unwelcome role of unrequited suitor. Small wonder the abandoned, dejected playwright immediately gravitated toward a woman who bore a remarkable resemblance to Louise. Her name was Agnes Boulton.

two

"THIS IS GENE O'NEILL"

Without doubt the O'Neills loom as the dominant force in Oona's history, yet her maternal line was not lacking in aesthetic and intellectual substance. James O'Neill was an artist of the theater; Edward W. "Teddy" Boulton, Oona's maternal grandfather, also was an artist, a credible if minor painter. The Boultons, a shipping family, had left England and settled in Philadelphia. Teddy turned his back on commerce, choosing instead to attend the Pennsylvania Academy of Fine Arts. He studied under Thomas Eakins, who, according to Boulton lore, considered E. W. Boulton his most promising student. Attractive, affable, and talented, Teddy got along splendidly with Eakins and worked with him in and out of the studio. He served as a model for Eakins's oil canvas *Cowboys in the Badlands* and the related study, *Sketch of Edward Boulton,* and he assisted the artist in casting the death mask of Walt Whitman. When Eakins was dismissed from the Academy because of his "improper" use of the nude model, Teddy joined with him in founding the Art Students' League of Philadelphia and was elected the League's first president. E. W. Boulton made friends easily, but like most artists he had difficulty making a living. While he never was able to provide richly for his family, the kindly artist was characterized by his children as a man of compassion and understanding. His dour future son-in-law, the playwright, would use him as a model for the professor father in *Strange Interlude*.

On a trip to London Teddy Boulton met his future wife, Cecille Williams. Oona's maternal grandmother was the daughter of Robert Williams, a scholar of classics at Oxford, and Florence Harper, a young woman who taught piano. Robert's parents had not been pleased with his choice of a partner; they had higher hopes for their son and wanted him to marry someone rich and prominent. Despite the opposition, Oona's great-grandfather chose to marry the woman he loved. Agnes Boulton knew and admired her Grannie Williams, but all that remained of her grandfather was a few photographs and a yellowed clipping from a 1902 edition of the *Freelance*, an English weekly, which told of the death of "Bob Williams, that mad scholar, once of Christ Church Oxford, then fellow of Merton who coached Lord Rosebery for the Oxford schools."[1]

The tall, commanding Grannie Williams had been brought up in the Church of England; then one day she discovered a Catholic missal left by a departed Irish servant. Believing this was an act of God meant especially for her, she read the book, called on a Jesuit priest, and become a convert. Her seventeen-year-old-daughter, Cecille, went along with the conversion and was a devout Catholic when she married E. W. Boulton. Unlike Ella and James O'Neill, the Boultons were not united in religious belief; but to please his bride, Teddy, a protestant, consented to be married in the Catholic Church. Though he never evinced much interest in his wife's religion, he did not interfere when Cecille chose to raise their four daughters in the faith. The first, Agnes, was born in England in 1891 and brought to America as a child. Along with her younger sisters, Barbara, Margery, and Cecil, she was educated in convent schools.

Teddy and Cecille Boulton took up residence at various times in London, Philadelphia, New York, and Connecticut, but their primary residence was in the seaside town of West Point Pleasant, New Jersey. There, in 1892, Teddy purchased a rambling two-story house at the corner of Herbertsville Road and Hall Avenue. While the family lived in other places, this dwelling, affectionately dubbed "Old House," became a haven for three generations of Boultons. Built in 1860, Old House was situated next to a grove of pine trees that stood between the house and the Manasquan River. A series of individual coal stoves, attended to daily, provided heat. Water was supplied by a noisy windmill, but the house was not wired for electricity until 1918.[2] The Boultons' West Philadelphia mansion was sold after Great-Aunt Agnes, Aggie's namesake, died and the contents were shipped to New Jersey. Much of the heavy walnut furniture was incorporated into the decor of Old House, and Aggie was given her great-aunt's ornate Victorian bed. Anything that could not be used was stored in the barn, where it remained for years. Aggie remembered seeing unpacked cartons of books from the Boultons' extensive library stacked in the attic.

After Cecille married Teddy and went to America, Grannie Williams, now in her sixties, had moved into a London club composed of intellectuals and free thinkers. The convert Catholic got caught up in further religious/philosophical pursuits and became an active member of the Theosophist Society (founded in 1875 by Helena Petrovna Blavatsky). Grannie Williams bombarded her daughter in New Jersey with letter after letter expounding on the musings of Mme Blavatsky and a Mr. Sinnet, and she urged Cecille to avail herself of the literature available at the Oriental Esoteric Society in Washington, D.C. Just as she had been led into Catholicism, Cecille Boulton again followed her mother's lead and looked further eastward. She began ordering books from the Oriental Esoteric Society's circulating library, for which service she only had to pay return postage. The volumes arrived each month and ranged from the *Upanishads* to Meyer's *Survival of the Human Personality after Death*. Like her mother, young Agnes read the books avidly; Cecille favored the life-after-death component; Aggie was captivated by everything, particularly the philosophy of Yoga. Aware of her daughter's intense interest, Cecille bought a copy of *Hatha-Yoga, the Science of Health* and gave it to Agnes so that she "could learn how to take care of herself." Steeped in the philosophy, Agnes Boulton decided that she was destined to became a practitioner, an Adept. To that purpose she pledged herself to the teachings and created a discipline which she kept secret from her parents and her sisters. She explained in her memoir, *Part of a Long Story* (1958), that she never thought about her discipline during the day; she read and pondered during the night. Throughout her childhood and adolescence Aggie eagerly absorbed knowledge from any and every available source.

Around this time Cecille's sister, Margery, arrived from Europe for a visit. Married to the Italian poet Francesco Bianco, Margery was a successful author of children's books, some of which were illustrated by the renowned, Arthur Rackham. Aggie was immediately taken by her aunt's ready intellect and her extravagant dress. Even more, Agnes was impressed with the Indian *jibbah* her aunt wore around the house and envisioned herself in similar garb. "I felt that a jibbah would be more appropriate for my dedicated life than a middy blouse."[3]

Among her father's acquaintances was a Mr. Clark, a Baptist minister whose keen and surprising mind greatly impressed the artist. Mr. Clark was interested in watercolor painting, Teddy's medium, and Teddy guided him in this pursuit. On his frequent visits to the Clark home, Teddy sometimes brought Agnes along.

She sat and listened intently as her father and the minister and his wife discussed philosophy, especially Kant. One evening Mr. Clark read from the German philosopher's works, and Aggie, struck by the words, wanted to know more. She asked if she could borrow the book and later remembered her hurt indignation when Mr. and Mrs. Clark laughingly told her she would never understand it. Yet something must have struck the minister's wife because suddenly she stopped laughing, left the room, and returned carrying her personal copy of Kant. She presented it to Agnes, telling her that she could keep the volume for as long as she wanted. That baffling book, said Aggie, played a large part in her discipline for becoming an Adept. During the next months she rose at 3 A.M., put on her bathrobe, and sat at a table by the window reading Immanuel Kant. When he proved too tough to handle, she relaxed with Mr. Sinnet's *Esoteric Buddhism*. At the time of this ardent search for the meaning of life, Agnes Boulton was thirteen years old. Her impassioned thirst for knowledge, the eagerness with which she devoured books, matched Eugene O'Neill's—and both strains would go directly to their daughter.

Teddy Boulton's art along with Cecille's avid interest in religion and literature influenced, in varying degrees, all their daughters. The sisters were lively and attractive. Barbara, two years younger than Agnes, had been a painfully shy child who hid in the closet whenever a visitor appeared. At age fifteen she affected an upswept hair style and refused to change it. Agnes noted that with her pompadour and lordly profile, Barbara looked like George the Third of England. Cecil was a talented caricaturist, and the youngest sister, Margery, was thought to resemble portraits of Lady Hamilton. As for Agnes, the family joke had it that she looked like Great-uncle John Boulton. Uncle John must have been a handsome man, for Agnes was a stunning woman. Slim and well proportioned, she had a long face dominated by high cheekbones and large brown eyes over a straight, prominent nose and generous mouth. A mole

on her chin occasionally can be seen in unretouched photographs.

Definitely free thinkers, Teddy and Cecille Boulton's bo-
hemian ways did not endear them to their New Jersey neighbors.
Cecille shocked many of them by smoking in public and showed
an equally upsetting unconventionality in other areas. An oil
painting of an artist's studio, allegedly by Eakins, was in the
Boulton family's possession for years and passed down
through her mother to Oona. In the center of the painting a
nude woman presents her front to the artists sketching her,
and her back to the viewers of the painting. According to Aggie
the au naturel model was none other than Oona's grandmother, Cecille Williams Boulton.

After graduating from high school, perhaps following in
her father's footsteps, Agnes studied art at the Philadelphia
School of Industrial Arts. Presently she had a change of
heart—she would be a writer, not a painter. Immediately she
began to write—successfully. At age sixteen she sold her first
short story and within a few years was supporting herself by
writing popular fiction for pulp magazines and literary pieces
for prestigious publications. Two of her works were selected
for an annual collection of Best Short Stories, and until the end
of her life she was always involved in some sort of writing
project. Just before the outbreak of the First World War, Agnes
went to England to visit with Grannie Williams. During this
time she said that she met and married a war correspondent
named Burton who was later killed while on assignment in
Belgium, leaving the widowed Agnes to bear his child, Barbara. Her war-shrouded union remained a mysterious interlude throughout Agnes Boulton's life. Although she assumed
the name of Burton for a while, no marriage record was ever
found and no one in the Boulton family seemed to have any
information about Mr. Burton, including his first name.

*   *   *

In 1917 Agnes was living on a farm in Cornwall Bridge, Connecticut, and at the same time her parents were living in nearby Woodville. At age twenty-four, a widow (apparently) with an infant daughter, Agnes had returned to her writing to sustain herself and Barbara, and to help out her parents as well. Leaving her little girl in the care of the Boultons, Agnes made frequent trips into New York City to consult with magazine editors and to visit friends often remaining in the city for weeks at a time. On one of those trips Agnes stayed at the Brevoort Hotel in Greenwich Village and made arrangements to get together with a friend, Christine Ell. A huge, homely woman, Christine was one of the more flamboyant Village characters of the day; she even served as a model for O'Neill's oversized, generous-spirited farm girl, Josie, in *A Moon for the Misbegotten.* Christine proposed that Aggie join her at the Hell Hole, the back room of the Golden Swan saloon at the corner of Sixth Avenue and Fourth Street in Greenwich Village. Aggie arrived at the barroom ahead of her friend, took a seat at one of the tables in the dimly lit room, and removed her coat.

While awaiting Christine's arrival Aggie noticed a dark-eyed man wearing a thick seaman's sweater under his jacket seated against the wall in a corner of the room. He kept looking her way with a somber expression that she found unnerving. She did not recognize him, yet something in his gaze, something she found both "sad and cruel," gave her the sense that he knew her. After Christine arrived and joined Agnes, the dark man rose and, staggering slightly, came over to their table. Up close, Agnes saw that he was quite young and that his hands trembled slightly; he also was a bit tight. "This is Gene O'Neill," Christine said by way of introduction. O'Neill sat down and joined them. Later another man wearing a bowler hat and a black and white checked suit with a carnation in the buttonhole stormed into the back room and with a loud "What ho!" headed right for Aggie's table. The nattily dressed gentleman was Jamie O'Neill making his usual, boisterous entrance. Jamie slipped into a chair, and soon the four of them were laughing and chatting—that is, *three* of them were. Eugene listened more than he talked. Jamie turned his full attention to Agnes Boulton and began to flirt. She noticed Jamie's playful come-ons less than she did Eugene's displeasure at his brother's advances. The two men went off for drinks at the bar, and in their temporary absence the two women discussed them.

Christine told her friend that Gene was a playwright and though he usually remained indifferent to women, he obviously had fallen for Aggie. Eugene, she further confided, possessed a "sorrow which wasn't a secret," and Jamie had a "secret which he would not allow to become a sorrow." The young Ms. Ell's offhand comment tapped into the O'Neill brothers' core; each carried within himself an immutable sadness, but Eugene brandished his sorrow like a sword (or more aptly, a pen) whereas Jamie endeavored to ignore his anguish by washing it away. When at last the quartet left the Hell Hole, Eugene shook off his brother's request to join him and chose instead to walk Agnes back to her hotel. They stood in front of the Brevoort, and though Aggie could not recall what he said before she wished him a good night, she never forgot his final words. Looking directly at her, O'Neill said in low, sure tones, "I want to spend every night of my life from now on with you. I mean this. Every night of my life."[4]

O'Neill was entranced by Agnes Boulton's beauty, her intelligence, her shy, womanly manner, and of course, her resemblance to Louise Bryant. In less than a year they would be married, and in that alliance the O'Neill and Boulton families would merge. Illustrious and intriguing as many members of both of Oona's families were, basically they were minor figures. James O'Neill and Teddy Boulton were the hottest contenders for lasting fame, but James never became an Edwin

Booth and Teddy never became a Thomas Eakins. Like them, the other Boultons and O'Neills were of their era and not for all time. Only one of Oona Chaplin's forebears rose above the crowd, defined his time, and changed the face of American drama. Only one, Eugene Gladstone O'Neill, was a genius.

three

A BROKEN ALONENESS

he courtship of Oona's parents did not exactly run smoothly. Things rarely do when you are dealing with either a genius or an alcoholic, and almost never when you are dealing with both. The morning after their meeting at the Hell Hole, Christine Ell telephoned to ask Aggie how she and Eugene had gotten along, and also to invite her to an upcoming party at which O'Neill would be present. Agnes went, specifically to see him; but in the crowded room Eugene O'Neill was nowhere in sight. At last he arrived. Curiously, considering his dramatic declaration at their recent parting that he wanted to spend every night for the rest of his life with her, he completely avoided her. Aggie walked over to him, said hello, and added, "Remember me?" O'Neill looked at her vaguely, ignored her query, and politely stated, "It's quite a party." Then, catching sight of a friend across the room, O'Neill called out, "It's a cold night—good night for a party! The iceman cometh!"[1] and, turning on his heels, walked away and joined the crowd.

Watching from a distance, Aggie saw O'Neill surreptitiously help himself to the contents of a bottle concealed in his coat. Unaware that his actions were being noticed, the playwright took swig after swig. With liquor firing his veins, O'Neill then pulled a chair over to the fireplace, placed it before the mantel above which hung a large clock, climbed up, and cried out, "Turn back the universe. And give me yesterday." Repeating the chant, he opened the clock face and ceremoniously pushed back the second hand. Climbing down, O'Neill continued to ignore Aggie and instead directed his attention toward Nina Moise, an old friend.

When the whispering about Eugene's outburst began, someone suggested that the "yesterday" he referred to meant the times spent with Louise Bryant. Gene was upset, one partygoer theorized, because of Aggie's resemblance to his lost love. That evening, regardless of the actual motivation, O'Neill's bizarre antics were generated by his ferocious drinking. Agnes chose to overlook his behavior and later stated that from the first she had seen through his ugly actions into his soul. Morose, ironic, somber, romantic, tender, and childlike, Eugene O'Neill held himself apart from others and remained a stranger in the midst of friends. Agnes, like many other women, viewed him as an irresistibly romantic figure, a kind of contemporary Childe Harold, a prisoner of his own dark mind.

When the two of them met for the third time, again at the Hell Hole, Aggie felt as strong an attraction coming from O'Neill as she herself felt toward him. She also sensed that he was trying to avoid connecting, which made him all the more intriguing. Their meetings escalated. In the many evening walks they took through the quiet streets, she found herself fascinated by this strange, mad, great person. Their romance seesawed back and forth with Aggie balancing, on the one hand, the offensive slights and outbursts that arose from his drinking, and on the other hand, his many expressions of infatuation. One evening he poured out his heart. Crying that he wanted her "alone, in an aloneness broken by nothing," he asked her to go with him to Provincetown after Christmas. She agreed.

In the weeks before their departure for Cape Cod, Aggie checked out of the Brevoort and into a small apartment on Waverly Place along with another writer friend, Dorothy Day (who later would cofound the Catholic Workers Union and become an ardent advocate of social justice). O'Neill still maintained a dingy room at the Golden Swan yet spent more and more time with Agnes. Friends learned of her intention to follow him to Provincetown, and most were not thrilled with the arrangement; a few expressed deep concern. One of them, Mary Pyne, had known the playwright for years and cautioned Aggie that no matter what Gene said, he probably was still in love with Louise Bryant, who had gone off to Russia with John Reed. The clever Louise, predicted Mary Pyne, would return and snap her fingers and O'Neill would run back to the pleasure of being mistreated. Such warnings did not register; Eugene had assured Agnes that Louise meant nothing to him anymore, and she believed him.

Just prior to the couple's intended departure for Provincetown, Louis Holladay, a close friend of O'Neill's, committed suicide. Shaken, O'Neill immediately made for the Hell Hole, where he drank himself into oblivion. In the aftermath of Holladay's suicide the playwright's usual bitterness softened, especially toward Agnes, who claimed that at this point, O'Neill suggested they get married. She held back, preferring to wait until things were calmer.

In December 1917 Eugene and Agnes headed for Provincetown, where they rented a small, stove-heated studio and spent the winter. The self-styled bachelor could move about as it pleased him; Aggie, however, had considerations—specifically her daughter, Barbara. Because they were often separated for long periods, Agnes kept up with the girl's activities through communications from Cecille Boulton. Although Cecille wrote that Barbara was doing fine and did not seem to miss Agnes at all, it would have been presumptuous for Aggie to assume that her absences would not affect her child. All told, Agnes Boulton appeared to be less interested in her daughter's well-being than in her own—or, perhaps, than in Eugene O'Neill's. She established a pattern as an absentee mother, and though she never deserted her children, she continued to slip away from time to time.

That winter Eugene and Agnes, content in each other's presence, worked together harmoniously, he on his dramas and she on her stories. In the early spring when O'Neill learned that *In the Zone* had been sold to the Keith-Orpheum vaudeville circuit, the promise of financial security and his need for Agnes prompted him to propose marriage again. Agnes accepted, and on April 12, 1918, they were married in Provincetown by (in the groom's words) "the most delightful, feeble-minded, God-helpus, mincing Methodist minister that ever prayed through his nose."[2] Scoffing aside, O'Neill confessed that while listening to the sweet sincerity of the marriage service, he found himself wishing that he, like the minister, could believe in a gentle God. Now man and wife, the O'Neills returned to their work; he labored on *Beyond the Horizon*, she produced pulp fiction.

Not long after the wedding Eugene received a letter from Louise Bryant. As predicted, Louise had returned from Russia and wanted him to see her in New York, immediately. He wanted to go out of friendship, he said, but Agnes would not have it. "Fine," she informed her bridegroom; "see Louise, but not in New York City. Let her meet you halfway, in New Bedford." Informed of the alternate plan, Louise, as Aggie anticipated, indignantly dismissed the idea. Agnes won that day, and for lack of fanning, the spark between O'Neill and Louise eventually died. Although she went on to another advantageous marriage after Reed died, ultimately Bryant's luck ran out. The beautiful, vivacious Louise would die penniless and alone in a squalid Paris hotel room, remembered, if at all, as someone who was once linked to John Reed and Eugene O'Neill.

In the spring Eugene and Agnes O'Neill journeyed back and forth to New York City from Provincetown. Aggie made no references in *Part of a Long Story* to any visits with her daughter on these occasions. On one trip, while Eugene attended rehearsals of his *Rope* at the Playwrights' Theater, the couple stayed at the Garden Hotel, a dingy place in which Jamie had been living, across from Madison Square Garden. O'Neill was edgy about being away from his writing; in fact, his main objective during his New York stay was to get back to Provincetown and his work. However, he soon lost himself in a monumental drinking binge and forgot where he was, let alone where he wanted to go. True to form, O'Neill was drinking because he was not writing. Thus his return to Provincetown and work became an imperative. In a bad state of humor and nerves, he, along with Aggie and Jamie, boarded the train for Massachusetts. When the trio arrived in Provincetown, Eugene immediately took to his bed with barely a memory of the trip from Boston. For a while the O'Neill brothers continued their carousing, downing Tiger Piss, a cheap, lethal concoction of raw alcohol. Then, with his work awaiting him, Eugene began the painful process of sobering up.

Always aghast at the extent of her husband's drinking, Agnes O'Neill now found herself imbibing more than she ever had before. Like her husband, Aggie was shy and alcohol relaxed her inhibitions; unlike him, she was not a despondent drunk. Indeed, while under the influence she became outgoing and flirtatious rather than withdrawn and angry. Agnes drank, but her craving paled in comparison with her husband's savage thirst. Ironically, although Aggie tried to get O'Neill to stop, he gave up alcohol only after leaving her. At the age of thirty-eight he quit and, save for a few early setbacks, stayed sober until the day he died. Agnes continued to drink for the rest of her life.

In the summer of 1918 Cecille and Teddy Boulton returned to Old House, bringing Barbara Burton with them. Aggie still had made no move toward having Barbara join her. The notion of a child being around her poet-genius husband seemed absurd, and especially so after Aggie learned that Eugene already was a father. She had told him about her child prior to their wedding, but he had no more interest in Barbara or in Aggie's previous marriage than he had in Eugene Jr. or his own first marriage. The ground rules were clear: he wanted Agnes alone. Although she kept busy with her writing, and although she may not have been fully aware of her role, Agnes's main function was to serve Eugene O'Neill, see to his physical and emotional needs, and create the necessary ambiance in which he could go about his business. Everything was geared to his work, for only in writing could he find any peace. "Writing," he said, "is my vacation from living."[3] Howsoever Agnes might have viewed her role as his wife, O'Neill was very clear about what he wanted; and as long as it was forthcoming, he was satisfied.

For the next year Agnes and Eugene O'Neill lived in Massachusetts, Connecticut, New York, and New Jersey. Late in November 1918 they moved into Old House for the winter, and Aggie literally kicked out her parents, her sisters, and her daughter so that O'Neill could write without distractions. Teddy rented a cottage in Point Pleasant and took a job at a hardware store to pay the rent. Along with the other Boultons, he stayed out of Aggie and Eugene's way. At Old House as everywhere, O'Neill's moods continued to swing; he could be loving and gentle one minute and nasty and brutal the next. He sometimes got roaring drunk and reeled along the deserted streets early in the morning, shouting at the top of his lungs. Point Pleasant citizens were scandalized at having the miscreant playwright in their midst, and a few took action. On one of his drunken forays into New York City, O'Neill had returned with a stray dog that became part of the household and whose yelps filled the night air. To show their contempt a small group of locals slit the dog's throat and threw the carcass on the lawn at Herbertsville Road. It could have been a scene from one of O'Neill's plays. Much as he disliked the scene, O'Neill stayed at Old House through that winter and then returned with Aggie to Provincetown. Eugene O'Neill would never again set foot in Old House, the place his daughter always referred to as *home*.

Once, at a party given in New York by the Provincetown Players, Agnes got into a conversation with one of the actors in the company and O'Neill took offense. Furious at her for paying attention to another man, the drunken playwright went up to his wife and, without saying a word, slapped her across the face with the back of his hand. Later he was penitent and begged her forgiveness. She felt pity for him, viewed him as sick, and took him back. He was an abuser, but he was also her love. Two days after the party a sober Eugene took Agnes to meet his parents at their suite in the Prince George Hotel. Ella and James O'Neill were delighted with their daughter-in-law and could not have been more welcoming. Like Gene's first wife, Kathleen, Aggie was attractive, well mannered, and well bred. However, Aggie had been raised a Catholic, and that made a big difference to the devout Ella and James. By this time Ella O'Neill had overcome her drug addiction and Agnes saw no symptoms of substance abuse. Aggie genuinely liked her mother-in-law, and so taken with Agnes was Ella that she convinced her husband to provide Eugene with the funds to buy a proper home for his young bride. Always condemned by his family for his stinginess, James O'Neill generously bought the property in Provincetown that Eugene ached to own—Peaked Hill Cottage, a former Coast Guard station.

In January 1919, while at Peaked Hill, Agnes discovered that she was pregnant. The news was not exactly heartening. How could it be? In his declaration of love to her, in his impassioned "I want you and you alone" statement, her husband had declared that he wanted their aloneness unbroken. Children made him uneasy; he did not understand them and did not know how to act with them. Knowing his attitude, Agnes did not immediately inform O'Neill of her condition; rather, she waited until the next day. His first reaction was that the doctor had made a mistake; then he lapsed into silence and went off to his work. Unable to discern his feelings, Agnes was miserable. Later that day the situation eased when the O'Neills' cat, Happy, gave birth and, together, Eugene and Agnes looked after their pet. Comfortably assisting in the procedure, O'Neill sang sea chanteys to the laboring Happy. Three kittens were born and promptly christened Whiskey, Blow, and Drumstick by the attending playwright. At the end of this shared interlude, to her great relief, Eugene took Agnes in his arms and kissed her devotedly. Somehow the birthing of the three kittens had cut through Eugene O'Neill's indifference, or so his wife believed.

Putting aside his anxieties at becoming a father again, O'Neill managed to be properly considerate of Aggie during the ensuing months and, in May, took her to Provincetown to await the arrival of their child. During the last months preceding the birth, Eugene O'Neill experienced a kind of unparalleled happiness. Agnes described him as "tall and brown and tender and smiling, working all morning, lying for hours in the sun, absorbing life and courage and hope from the sea." She too "felt strong and well and happy; full of a sort of creative joy and well-being, a physical at-oneness with life and nature, with the sea, the sand, the dunes and the ever-changing sky."[4]

In late August Cecille Boulton arrived at the Cape to help her daughter through the final stretch of pregnancy. Unfortunately the due date was inexact, and Mrs. Boulton had to leave before her grandson arrived. Shane Rudraighe was born on October 30, 1919, in the former Coast Guard shack that had been purchased by his grandfather. After the doctor left, Agnes lay in bed with her "little Black Irishman" beside her. O'Neill approached, pulled up a chair, and sat there holding her hand and looking tenderly at the baby. "It'll be *us* still, from now on," he said. "Us—alone—but the three of us.—A sort of Holy Trinity."[5]

The trinity conspicuously overlooked the existence of both Eugene O'Neill Jr. and Barbara Burton, and the blessed trio itself broke up abruptly when Eugene left to attend to business in New York. Away from his wife and newborn son for months, his letters to Agnes expressed his longing for her and included kisses for his son whom he professed to love—in his own fashion.

In the five years between the births of their son and daughter, Eugene O'Neill took his place in the literary world while Agnes juggled roles as wife, writer, and mother. Since she could not fill all those roles at the same time, a nursemaid was hired for Shane. Just as Sarah Sandy had influenced Eugene O'Neill's young life, Mrs. Fifine Clark, known affectionately as "Gaga," became a dominating force in Shane's. Her penchant was not so much for the terrifying stories and horror shows which Sarah Sandy had preferred as it was for maintaining her position in the household. Much as she loved Shane, Gaga was not above using him. If he did not follow orders or if she and Agnes had one of their recurrent spats, Mrs. Clark threatened to leave. Evidently Mrs. Clark's dramatic "I quit!" episodes occurred with shameful frequency, and her threats, along with his parents' indifference, regularly rocked the boy's confidence and reduced him to tears. O'Neill once told his friend Elizabeth Shepley Sergeant that he did not know how to talk to children and that he could not have any kind of connection with his son until the boy grew up. Later, Elizabeth Sergeant visited the O'Neills in Bermuda and found that O'Neill indeed shunned the boy almost completely. In Sergeant's opinion, Agnes did not pick up much of the slack.

With his parents otherwise occupied and with Gaga busy with household chores, Shane often was on his own and could be found wandering along the edge of the sea at a time when most children would have been called in by their parents. Ms. Sergeant discovered him sitting alone on the dock late one afternoon and invited him to come into the house, where she promised to read to him. Starved for attention, the boy responded with eager delight;[6] unhappily, such soothing moments were sadly lacking in Shane's young life. Living with his parents' detached indifference and the frightening possibility of his adored nursemaid's imminent departure, Shane Rudraighe O'Neill grew up on emotional quicksand.

Even though his parental performance continued spotty, Eugene O'Neill's literary output remained steady. By the mid-twenties much attention was being given to the writer of acknowledged successes such as *Beyond the Horizon, Anna Christie, The Emperor Jones,* and *The Hairy Ape.* He received a Pulitzer Prize for *Beyond the Horizon* and *Anna Christie;* later he would be awarded two more, for *Strange Interlude* and *Long Day's Journey into Night.* O'Neill's financial situation improved as his plays brought in money, but he continued to alternate between periods of abstinence and periods of rampant alcoholism. As always, he had to stop drinking in order to work, and the struggle made his efforts to write painful and conflicted. Other conditions worked against his productivity as well. Over the course of a few frigid winters, O'Neill discovered that the quality of his writing seemed to decline during the cold months; consequently the playwright made plans to take his family to Bermuda in the winter of 1925. O'Neill had gone on the wagon specifically to expedite work on *The Great God Brown*, but when Agnes announced that she was pregnant again he returned to the bottle and stayed under the influence for the rest of that year—the year in which Oona was born.

Eugene, Agnes, Shane, and Gaga took up residence in a secluded wooden cottage on Bermuda's south shore. Nearby, a smaller cottage, Crow's Nest, served as Eugene's work house. Both dwellings were modest, but each had grand views of the sea. In April, when Agnes was in her eighth month of pregnancy, Eugene transferred the family inland to a solid old house called Southcote. Originally Agnes had planned to have her child in the hospital; Southcote, however, was considerably more substantial than Peaked Hill, where Shane had been born, so she decided to have the baby at home. During the last weeks of Agnes's pregnancy Maude Bisch, a neighbor in Bermuda, was a great source of comfort to the expectant mother and an unexpected source of the same for the father-to-be. Eugene suffered from insomnia, and Mrs. Bisch, a trained nurse, provided him with paraldehyde.

While awaiting the birth of his third child, O'Neill wrote playful letters to friends explaining that he was certain Agnes was carrying twins because she was so big, and further, that he and Aggie had decided that "in order to mitigate the chances of the child devoting its entire life to serious drinking, it had better be born outside the U.S."[7]—an insensitive comment considering the havoc alcohol had wreaked on O'Neill and his family. Unenthusiastic about having any more children, O'Neill declared that if it had to be, let it be a female; he began to refer to the expected heir as a she, almost as though by saying it, he would make it so. On May 13 Agnes and Eugene took a long walk along the shore. At one point Eugene went for a swim. Agnes watched admiringly as her husband cut through the waves with precise ease. If only he could apply that clean precision, that unclouded joy, to other areas. By now he was in the middle of the binge that had begun after completion of *The Great God Brown*. Nothing, not even his plays, seemed to be entirely what Eugene O'Neill hoped for, and he always surrendered to his gloom by picking up a bottle. On this occasion, though, his depression and drinking might have had more to do with Oona's impending arrival than with the finishing of his play. Another child? Why? He did not want children, period!

four

"IT'S A GOIL!"

Early on the morning of May 14, Agnes went into labor and, less than a half hour after the doctor arrived, gave birth to an exceptionally beautiful, dark-haired, dark-eyed infant girl. O'Neill sent a telegram to his friend Kenneth Macgowan announcing the arrival: "It's a Goil. Allah be merciful. According to indications will be first lady announcer at Polo Grounds. Predict great future grand opera. Agnes and baby all serene."[1] Eugene O'Neill was impressed by his newest offspring—according to Agnes, the only very little baby whose appearance he ever liked. In the beginning Oona satisfied her father simply by being what he wished for—a girl—and further enhanced her position by being something else that meant a great deal to him—physically attractive. Inasmuch as he could be pleased by an infant, Oona pleased him, but not enough to keep him around. This time, though, Aggie did pick up the slack. Insisting that she had felt alienated from Shane because Gaga took over, she would not be put off her motherly role again; let Gaga keep her distance and let her husband drown himself in liquor, she would drown herself in the care and feeding of Oona.

Whether or not Aggie's maternal assertions were carried out to their fullest, Oona's later behavior (as opposed to her brother's) suggests that she probably did have the unconditional devotion of her mother during the very important early stages of development. Eugene O'Neill may have paid as little attention to his daughter as he did to his son, but in the first months of her life Oona was coddled by Agnes, which seems to have put her on more solid emotional ground than Shane. It was enough to imbue her with certain lifelong character traits—for example, a cool tenacity—which her brother dramatically and tragically lacked. Despite his pride in his daughter's gender and appearance, Eugene O'Neill did not alter his behavior and continued to drink heavily. Agnes, deeply offended that he would not make the effort to sober up for her and their newborn, alternated between feeling sorry for him and resenting the way his alcoholism clouded her joy at Oona's birth.

Late in June the O'Neills made ready to return north for the summer—this time with a change of destination. Deeming Peaked Hill too primitive for their infant daughter, they were headed for more suitable lodgings in Nantucket. The family decamped and went first to the LaFayette Hotel in New York City. A week later Eugene sent Agnes and the others on to Nantucket, while he remained in the city to look after his theatrical affairs. Away from home, Eugene wrote frequently to Agnes and in his correspondence generally comes across as an extremely needy husband and caring father. His early letters invariably ended with loving wishes to Shane; once Oona arrived, the expressions of devotion expanded to include the little girl, with whom he still appeared to be quite taken. "I'm

damn lonely," he wrote to his wife; "I miss you like the devil—
and I miss Oona over on the couch. I really love her! Never
thought I could a baby!"[2] Pretty, affectionate, and doted upon,
Oona somehow managed (directly or indirectly) to perk up her
father's usual sour outlook. (Flora Merrill, a newspaper reporter who interviewed O'Neill in New York and found him to
be a delightful conversationalist, wrote that she was sure that
he was an ideal play-fellow for his little daughter. Ms. Merrill
missed the mark on that point; *play* was an operative word for
Eugene O'Neill only as a noun.)

In February 1926 the O'Neills moved into the main house
of Bellevue, an impressive estate on some twenty-five acres in
Paget Parish, Bermuda. Eugene was pleased not only with the
house but even more so with its relatively low rent of $150 a
month. As he grew older O'Neill's attitude toward money became increasingly reminiscent of his father's; in many ways
the playwright proved even more tight-fisted than the man
whose stinginess he decried. A photograph taken during this
Bermuda stay shows Eugene, Agnes, and Oona together. On
the right, Oona is being held by an unseen person, no doubt
Gaga. Agnes stands in the middle, her eyes fixed on her husband. He is in profile and gently smiling down at the baby girl,
whose gaze is directed up at him. For that brief recorded in-
stant, Oona was the recipient of her father's tender attention.
However, as he proved over and over, that attention could not
be diverted for any meaningful length of time from his art. If
his genius was to remain incorruptible, he could not make
room for playing daddy. Eugene O'Neill, the neglected child,
had grown up to neglect his own children.

O'Neill liked Bellevue well enough to seriously consider ex-
tending his lease for the next few years and was about to do
so when another place caught his eye. Instead of renting Bellevue he purchased Spithead, a two-hundred-year-old house situated by the waters of Little Turtle Bay. The simple two-story

residence made of native stone had not been occupied for years, and the interior was badly in need of repair. Spithead offered a commanding view of the ocean on the one hand and dangerous flooring on the other. O'Neill remarked that although Spithead was just a shell of a house, it was a very fine shell. Part of its mystique had to do with its provenance—the house had been built by a buccaneer, Captain Hezekiah Frith, and had been both his home and the repository for his ill-gotten gains. Said to be inhabited by the ghosts of the pirate captain and his son, Spithead's romantic aura pleased O'Neill to such an extent that he endured the agony of renovations with unaccustomed composure. Spithead was repaired and restored at a cost of $20,000; among the improvements, a tennis court and concrete dock were built. While the repairs were made to the main house, the family crowded into a large cottage on the property. As O'Neill labored at his work in the master bedroom, nearby the pandemonium of construction mingled with the noise of romping children.

During his abbreviated stay as father-in-residence, O'Neill spent very little time in the company of his children. On one occasion Agnes was called away to look after her ailing father (like his son-in-law, Teddy Boulton suffered from the white plague), leaving Gaga and her husband in charge. Right after Aggie left, Eugene wrote that Oona had gotten into bed without protest, called wonderingly and beseechingly for her mother a few times, and then drifted off to sleep. A day or so later Shane and Oona went down to the beach for a swim. With Eugene watching, Shane immediately plunged into the waves, leaving behind a baby sister who, unable to keep up, had to content herself to wade in the shallow water. O'Neill's letters contained many tender observations and were replete with assurances that the children were doing fine. Everything on those written pages indicated that he was a caring and concerned parent proudly describing his children's everyday activities. But that was on paper. Despite sporadic spurts of attention, what took precedence never was in doubt.

Just one incident concerning Eugene O'Neill Jr., with whom his father lately had become reacquainted, provides ample evidence of O'Neill Sr.'s paternal coolness. Young Gene fractured his skull in a biking accident and was confined to a Long Island hospital, where he remained in critical condition for five weeks. When apprised of his son's plight O'Neill arranged for a specialist, offered to pay for everything, and told Kathleen Pitt-Smith to send him a collect night letter every day to let him know the boy's condition. O'Neill provided money and medical care and requested daily updates, yet although he was as close as New York City, he never once went to Long Island to visit his severely injured son. Eugene O'Neill's muse came first, and he readily affirmed that his flesh-and-blood progeny were not as meaningful to him as the characters in his dramas. His real children had to fend for themselves while he concentrated on his children born of inspiration.

In the summer of 1926 the O'Neills moved into Loon Lodge, a two-story log cabin on Loon Lake in Belgrade Lakes, Maine. Eugene Jr. and Barbara Burton arrived for a portion of the summer, and with everyone gathered under one roof, O'Neill commented that they constituted a "fat family."[3] Soon enough the playwright wanted to skim the fat. The walls of the lodge were thin and Eugene could hear everything that was going on, and since what was going on often emanated from the children, he became more and more frustrated. Eugene Jr. was sixteen; Barbara, eleven; Shane, six; Oona, fourteen months. Struggling with *Strange Interlude*, O'Neill felt that his slow progress was at least partly attributable to the children. "Perhaps I could do with less progeny about," he wrote to his friend Kenneth Macgowan. "I was never cut out, seemingly, for a pater familias and children in squads, even when indubitably my own, tend to get my goat."[4]

Realizing that her husband was frustrated in his attempts to create, and knowing that he needed complete solitude when he worked, Aggie took the advice of a friend and had a one-room shack built far enough away from the lodge (i.e., the children) to ensure his tranquillity. The solution was semi-successful. Yes, O'Neill got his work done, yet at the same time he remained aloof and uncomfortable. The love and kisses lavishly bestowed via the mail evaporated when his children actually were in his presence. He was with them when *he* could spare the time, not necessarily when *they* wanted or needed to be with him. In this residence of a creative genius, "Shh, Daddy's working" was raised to the highest degree of caution. Young as she was, along with her siblings Oona had to heed the warning and keep her distance. Most often she played down by the water. A little rubber bathtub on legs had been set up and she would sit by herself while her big brothers and sister romped in the water. Not far away, her father and her mother were at their respective work.

That summer at Loon Lake, Eugene O'Neill renewed his acquaintance with the actress Carlotta Monterey, whom he had briefly met some five years earlier when she joined the cast of *The Hairy Ape* as a last-minute replacement. Now the elegant and vivacious Carlotta would step into his life, permanently.

Carlotta Monterey was born in December 1888 to Nellie and Christian Tharsing of Oakland, California, and was christened Hazel Neilson Tharsing. Within five years Nellie walked out on her husband, placed her daughter with an aunt, Mrs. John Shay, and went to make her living in San Francisco, where she ran boardinghouses and took on a series of well-to-do lovers. Hazel lived with the Shays until she was thirteen, and although her mother visited on frequent occasions, the

Shays really were her family. Hazel attended Catholic school and then went to Europe to train for the stage. She spent five years in Paris and London, completing her theatrical training at Sir Herbert Beerbohm Tree's Academy of Dramatic Arts, now known as the Royal Academy. Returning to America, Hazel assumed the theatrical name of Carlotta Monterey, went on the stage, and advanced herself through three marriages, numerous affairs (one with the popular stage and movie star Lou Tellegen), and a shrewd liaison with a wealthy benefactor. During her second marriage to Melvin Chapman Jr., Carlotta produced her sole child, Cynthia. Within a year of Cynthia's birth Carlotta deposited the child with her grandmother, Nellie, and went back on the stage and into a third marriage—this time to Ralph Barton, a well-known caricaturist for the *New Yorker* magazine. After that marriage was terminated Carlotta Monterey journeyed to Maine in the summer of 1926 to visit her friend Elizabeth Marbury, a wealthy theatrical producer and author. At a social gathering at Ms. Marbury's home, the playwright and the actress re-met.

Years before, Charlie Chaplin, Ralph Barton's good friend, had expressed a belief that Carlotta Monterey "wanted to be all-sufficient to a man of genius, to cut him off from everybody and minister to his genius, while she herself shone in reflected glory."[5] At their first meeting some five years earlier the actress had taken an immediate dislike to O'Neill; she had thought he was self-centered and rude because he failed to thank her for going into *The Hairy Ape* with barely a rehearsal. But in the summer of 1926 she saw him in a different light. O'Neill was a genius she could nurture, and the prospect proved irresistible. Women had always pursued the handsome, brooding playwright, but none possessed the single-mindedness of the self-assured, attractive Carlotta Monterey. Although they were drawn to each other for many reasons, the most obvious involved his need to be totally cared for and her need to totally care for him. Both were indifferent as parents. His callous treatment of Oona and his sons could be said to have been predicated on his needs as a creative artist, the actress's disdain for her own child had no apparent justification. Carlotta Monterey was a perfectionist; when her rather plain daughter did not live up to her exacting standards, she was banished.

O'Neill watched Carlotta in action and admired her ease in social situations. Even more appealing, she evinced genuine interest in his plays—by now Agnes had had enough of all the theater talk. Although she was more intelligent than Carlotta, Aggie did not possess the actress's bearing and poise, and, more damning in the eyes of her husband, she never completely reconciled herself to his greater gift. She wanted recognition for her own work.

For a while Carlotta and both O'Neills became part of the Maine social scene, which was presided over by a number of prominent personalities including Ms. Marbury and Elizabeth Arden, the cosmetics entrepreneur. Ms. Arden maintained a farm for her thoroughbred horses in Belgrade Lakes which was staffed by employees of her beauty salons. Friends and acquaintances were invited to the farm, where they were pampered with facials, massages, manicures, and hairstyling. Arden kept a guest book, and among those who signed in during the summer of 1926 were three visitors. Eugene O'Neill wrote his name in his characteristic tight, tiny hand; Agnes Boulton O'Neill wrote in a more expansive yet contained style; and below their names, Carlotta Monterey inscribed hers in a large, lavish script. (A handwriting analyst would have had a field day comparing the signatures.) Elizabeth Arden eventually turned her farm into a ladies spa, and the Belgrade Lakes Maine Chance flourished until the early seventies when a fire destroyed the house and its contents, including the yellowed guest book with its telltale trio of signatures.

Agnes O'Neill remained unaware of her husband's growing attraction toward Carlotta. Later she acknowledged her
mistaken belief that Carlotta was not smart enough to interest Eugene. The children were more prescient. Sensing that
something was happening, Gene Jr., Barbara, and Shane talked
among themselves about the beautiful lady in the skimpy
bathing costume who seemed to fascinate their father.

Summer ended, and with Eugene Jr. and Barbara already
dispatched to their respective schools, the rest of the O'Neills
left for Bermuda. Despite the clamor and tumult of Spithead's
renovations, Eugene worked steadily on *Strange Interlude.* In
March 1927 the family moved into the refurbished main
house. By that time Eugene O'Neill conspicuously turned
away from Agnes, Shane, and Oona.

Aware that Agnes was suffering burnout from his increasing needs, O'Neill had found a woman who could validate his
emotional pain—something his mother never had been able to
do and something that Agnes had tired of doing. Eugene
O'Neill, the creative artist, realized that his salvation lay with
Carlotta the caretaker. O'Neill truly loved Agnes and probably
was faithful to her during their eight-year marriage, at least,
until Carlotta came along. At this point he presumably succumbed. Later he denied having had sex with the actress, and
Agnes believed him—then again, she never thought he was attracted to Carlotta in the first place.

In November 1927 O'Neill returned to New York City, settled into a suite in the Hotel Wentworth, and attended to his
theatrical duties—the pending productions of two of his plays,
Strange Interlude and *Marco Millions.* Confused and agonized
over his personal life, he began seeing Carlotta. Once she responded sensitively to his repeated avowals that he needed her,
the final decision was made. Torn between his loyalty (guilt)
toward his wife and children and his growing passion (need)
for Carlotta, O'Neill confessed all to Agnes. He intensely de-

sired Carlotta but did not want to break up his marriage. He even suggested that Carlotta join them in a ménage à trois, a solution Aggie immediately vetoed. Whatever effect his defection had on the others, the choice was absolutely right and necessary for Eugene O'Neill. Carlotta legitimized his work, his pain, his sobriety, his existence, and he would remain with her for the rest of his life. First, though, he had to break from Agnes. She had never believed that he would leave her and had not paid attention to the warning signs. O'Neill wrote from New York City in the fall of 1927 urging her to join him, but she stayed in Bermuda, thus allowing his affair to flourish. Despite her intelligence Agnes did not understand the depths of O'Neill's need, and she mistakenly believed that his love and loyalty to her and the children would triumph over his infatuation with Carlotta. In truth, Eugene O'Neill's infatuation was his work and whatever it took to keep him writing. He was waiting for something to happen, something to get him out of what had become an untenable situation, and something did happen—Carlotta Monterey. By January 1928 O'Neill had determined to marry Carlotta. All he needed was a divorce, which he thought would be immediately forthcoming. He was wrong. Despite the fact that he and Agnes had agreed at the onset of their marriage that neither would stand in the other's way if either wanted out, when the possibility became an actuality and Eugene asked for the divorce, Agnes did stand in the way.

In February 1928 Eugene and Carlotta departed for England on an extended trip abroad. Agnes received a telegram from the *New York World* asking about the divorce—her first inkling, she later maintained, of O'Neill's intent. Shane received a letter in which his father, in attempting to explain why he was leaving, spoke of living life according to one's personal truth. This can make life sad, O'Neill commented, "but you are not old enough to know what that feeling is—and I hope to God you never will know, but that your life will always be simple and contented!"[6] The fact that O'Neill could even think that his son's life, already complicated by his father's neglect and desertion, could ever be content is another example of the playwright's utter lack of understanding for his flesh and blood. O'Neill ended his letter with protestations of love for Shane and Oona and a plea for them never to forget their Daddy. A desperate attempt to assuage his guilt, O'Neill's letter was more an exercise in self-pity and senseless cruelty than an expression of parental love. His reign as distant father-in-residence officially over, Eugene O'Neill began his second regime as permanently absent father to a bewildered eight-year-old son and an uncomprehending two-year-old daughter.

five

LITTLE ORPHAN OONA

At first O'Neill maintained haphazard contact with his children through the mail; the infrequent letters were addressed to Shane, who was asked to relay messages of love to his baby sister. These secondhand communications hardly satisfied Oona's need to see her father. Too young to be completely aware of what had happened, she was aware enough to miss his customary cameo appearances in her life. She looked for him in vain, spoke of him as soon as she could talk, and by the age of three was poring over magazines and newspapers looking for pictures of him. Immediately recognizing the much photographed playwright, she would stab at the image on the page with her little fingers and cry out, "Daddy! Daddy!" Again and again she implored, "Will he come back and live with us, Mummy?" On one occasion after a demanding wail of "I want him!" she proceeded to weep so uncontrollably that she could not be consoled. Finding it extraordinary that her daughter had such a strong memory of someone who, by this time, had been gone for a year, Agnes penned a letter to O'Neill beseeching him to pay some attention to his little girl. If he would not see her in person, the least he could do was write to her with some regularity. Failing that, it might be kinder for him to stop all correspondence and withdraw completely, thus allowing Oona to forget him. Agnes later told O'Neill biographer Louis Sheaffer, with whom she became quite friendly, that for reasons of her own she never mailed that letter.[1] Yet her suggestion that O'Neill stop tantalizing his daughter was well taken. If he had made a clean break, it would have been easier. With the prospect of his coming back erased, the memory of him would have faded. Oona's hope, however, was kept alive because her father could not bring himself to the point of total abandonment. His genius required that he be free of his children in order to do his work, but complete disassociation from Oona and Shane was too reprehensible an action even for him to take—both because of his guilty conscience and because of the way it would look to others. He needed provocation to justify a final break, and for the moment he did not want to be forgotten, just gone.

As soon as Oona could write she sent simple messages of her own, but most of the early correspondence came from Shane. Along with his little sister, he eagerly awaited the intermittent replies. O'Neill kept up a sporadic communication; if one could overlook the fact that he was substituting written words for hands-on care, those letters can be viewed as rather charming. He wrote all the right things and was chatty and loving—on paper. Avowing that he missed them tremendously, O'Neill told Shane and Oona that he thought of them every day, usually when he was lying in bed just before going to sleep. He wanted to hear news of what they were doing. Eager to please, Shane complied by describing their daily life in detail, making small occurrences into major episodes. Informed by his son that Oona had recovered from a rash, O'Neill solemnly replied that he was relieved to hear the news; "Sores don't look very good on anyone and they completely spoil a lady's complexion."[2]

Everyday thoughts and descriptions filled O'Neill's letters and always, in all his correspondence, he expressed the desire to be with them. "I want to see you so much that I feel like taking the first boat to America—but I have such important business to attend to over here that I have to stay for a while longer," he wrote from England in January 1929. In a letter to Oona he enclosed some recent pictures of himself and, explaining that he kept a picture of her in his workroom, told her that she in turn could look at his photograph and think of him. "I love you very much, Don't forget me!" the letter ended. The content was laden with fatherly affection, yet how much nourishment could a letter and some photographs provide for the not yet four-year-old? And although he declared that only unavoidable circumstances prevented him from being with her, no matter whether he was as far away as Shanghai, China, or as close as New York City, for almost three years he never appeared before her—to look at her, to hug her, or to speak to her. Words, not deeds, were his priority.

Eugene and Agnes also corresponded for a time; she kept him abreast of the children's activities, and he told her about his dealings in the theater. When he made it clear that Carlotta had taken her place and that he wanted a divorce, the letters stopped. Aggie still forwarded the children's mail to him, but she and he no longer were in touch.

Desperately desiring to squelch the nagging twinges of culpability and to get on with his life, O'Neill wanted the divorce over and done with. Naively anticipating that Aggie would abide by their original marital agreement, he was flabbergasted when she would not be railroaded into action. Her reason was simple: she was holding out for a better settlement, which, considering that she had children to raise, was not out of line. Stubbornly refusing to accept his inadequate offers, she pressed O'Neill for more. He became increasingly irate at Agnes's stance, and yet her obduracy actually suited his purpose—now he had something to latch on to to justify his actions. In his eyes she was behaving abominably; by not letting him go she was preventing his genius from flourishing.

Within a short time hatred rather than guilt became Eugene O'Neill's motivation for seeking a speedy end to his marriage. He went at it rabidly by smearing Aggie's character with every bit of mud he could dredge up, including the mystery of her first husband. No marriage certificate existed, no one in the Boulton family ever mentioned Agnes's marriage as a fact of the past, and in O'Neill's opinion Aggie never had been married to Mr. Burton or anyone else; as he saw it, the whole business was a cover-up for a child born out of wedlock.[3] He let it go because it meant nothing to him and he did not want to hurt Barbara Burton. Now, eager to supply himself with ammunition for the divorce, O'Neill substituted his own plot. He decided that Aggie had had her first child by a Polish farmer who lived near her parents' farm in Connecticut and who was, incidentally, her mother's lover. Calling the affair a nice mess, O'Neill sarcastically commented, "And people think my *Desire under the Elms* is too sordid to be real!"[4] Having thus dealt with the past, he turned to the present and accused Agnes of being a drunk as well as a wanton woman and of having had numerous affairs. Agnes Boulton was indeed no saint—she may not have married a Mr. Burton, she did drink, she was negligent with her children, and she may have had flirtations—but Eugene O'Neill was the deserter. Unable to accept responsibility for his actions, O'Neill industriously crafted a script in his favor by casting himself in the role of the beleaguered gentleman.

Decrying and denouncing Agnes, he wrote furiously to his lawyer, Harry Weinberger. His correspondence grew increasingly acrid and threatening as he threw up a smoke screen of invective in order to smother his conscience. Weinberger counseled O'Neill to ease up, advising his client that newspapers eagerly sought stories about the messy divorces of the famous. To illustrate, Weinberger cited the sensational headlines during the recent divorce of Charlie Chaplin and his second and much younger wife, Lita Grey. Among other degenerate exploits, Chaplin was accused of demanding oral sex, an act defined in the California Penal Code as illegal, even between married couples, and punishable by imprisonment of some fifteen years. O'Neill pooh-poohed Weinberger's comparison and protested that unlike Chaplin, who he believed was guilty of every form of perversion with young girls, he himself had nothing to hide. How it must have galled O'Neill fifteen years later when the man he deemed guilty of every form of degeneracy became his son-in-law!

Despite his lawyer's cautioning, Eugene O'Neill continued to regard his own far-from-exemplary behavior and actions as unavoidable. Repeatedly he recounted in his letters to Weinberger all the things he had done for Agnes and her family. He had given money to Teddy Boulton; he was paying Barbara Burton's school tuition; and while he did not wish to hurt (again!) the girl's feelings, he did not feel that Barbara should be his dependent. Moreover, he was furious at Agnes's demand that Oona and Shane receive more money from him than Eugene Jr. did. Spurred on by the narcissism of his genius, the underlying remorse which he could not bear to recognize, and the comforting fact that he had found provocation to sever his ties with Aggie, O'Neill continued to inveigh against her. Blaming everything on his estranged wife, he howled that he hated the memory of Agnes Boulton and hoped never to see her or hear of her again.

After much wrangling and negotiating, and after O'Neill had left for Europe with Carlotta, Agnes at last agreed to the divorce. She suggested getting one in Connecticut but was convinced by Harry Weinberger that Reno, Nevada, was a better choice; less attention would be given by the press because the agreement and details could be kept secret. In order to obtain the divorce she had to establish residency in Nevada for three months, a long time to be away from her children. Shane and Barbara were at boarding school in Lenox, Massachusetts, but the nearly four-year-old Oona was very much at home. With her father gone and her mother not exactly hearthbound, Oona was very much in need of attention.

Once O'Neill made clear his intentions regarding Carlotta, Agnes did not stand still regarding male companionship; she became intimately involved with James J. Delaney, a newspaper man. Exactly when and where Agnes met him is not known, although it probably occurred following O'Neill's defection and most likely at a literary-social gathering. Jim Delaney started out as a reporter on the *Albany Knickerbocker Press,* was promoted to city editor, and then became political editor of the *Albany Times-Union* and assistant chief of the International News Service in Albany. Sometime in the early twenties he left for New York City, where he worked for the *New York Sun* and did freelance writing. Delaney and Agnes shared a common interest in creative writing. He functioned as an in-house editor, helping and encouraging her in her literary efforts. Intelligent, attractive, and amiable, Delaney liked children and was considerate and thoughtful with Barbara, Shane, and especially Oona. He stepped into the littlest O'Neill's young life and, although he never could fill the void left by her father, became an above-average surrogate.

During Agnes and Eugene's separation, the playwright lived openly with his lover, Carlotta; however, his estranged wife was not granted that privilege. A man could consort but a woman could not, and had Aggie's affair been made public it could have been used against her in the courts. Despite the double standard, James Delaney did move in with her—but not exactly. In the backyard at Herbertsville Road stood a small, two-story cedar shed, large enough for an adult to sleep in, and it was here that James Delaney evidently dwelt. In later years Aggie had the shed redone into a dollhouse for Oona. The extraordinary dwelling included near professional touches, tongue-and-groove fittings, a Dutch door, double-hung windows with window seats below, and built-in shelves. Shane O'Neill's daughter, Sheila, vividly recalled playing in the remodeled shed many years later when she and her sisters and brother visited their grandmother.

In March 1928 Agnes set off for Reno and settled into her headquarters for the next ninety days, the Monte Cristo Ranch. Going to Reno for a divorce was a common procedure at the time, and residences were established that specifically catered to a clientele of waiting women. Professedly dude ranches, they actually were holding places for potential divorcees who spent their days desperately attempting to stave off boredom by reading, horseback riding, listening to the radio, gossiping among themselves, flirting with male staff members, and in Agnes Boulton O'Neill's case, trying to work. Claire Boothe Luce drew a trenchant picture of one such residence in her play *The Women*.

Back at Old House, Oona was being looked after by Gaga Clark, Aggie's sister Cecil, and Jim Delaney. Gaga Clark was in poor health (she died five days after the O'Neill divorce was granted) and thus could do very little; nor was Cecil Boulton much help, either. Single, unemployed, and for both those reasons, cranky, Cecil apparently got it into her head that her absent sister's lover had his eye on her. Nervous about the presence of an unattached male, she was antagonistic toward Delaney, Gaga, and Oona. A power struggle developed between Cecil and Gaga, and both sent letters of protest to Aggie. Cecil was incensed that the housekeeper, a servant, was sitting at the dinner table with them. When Aggie replied suggesting that Mrs. Clark dine in the kitchen, Delaney immediately answered that if that happened he would join Gaga.

Jim Delaney's actions as well as his letters indicate that he was a decent man—with a particular problem. A binge drinker and subject to bouts of alcoholism, Delaney had gone on the wagon for his stint as protector of Agnes's household, vowing that his sobriety would continue once she returned. He dearly loved Agnes Boulton O'Neill, and part of the reason that he was willing to move in with her family was his belief that once she was divorced she would marry him. This belief helped him to stay dry as well as get through the hard times in that house of women. With Gaga sick and Cecil slightly gaga, the main responsibility of Old House fell to him. He ably filled the role of Aggie's factotum and looked after her property, her finances, and her family.

Barbara and Shane were at home only during school breaks, so most of Delaney's care was focused on Oona. In daily letters he kept Agnes abreast of her daughter's progress. Oona was an unusually well-behaved child, and Delaney reported that he rarely resorted to the chief weapons of his disciplinary program—the threat of taking her thumb out of her mouth, or not letting her ride in the car with him. In the beginning Oona missed Agnes terribly and was understandably concerned. Why not? Her father had left and never returned; and while she had the security of Gaga's, Cecil's, and Delaney's presence, she must have had deep-seated fears. Would her mother, like her father, disappear for good? Jim Delaney had to keep up morale on two fronts, at home and in his reports to the absent mother. Delaney played down Oona's anxieties to keep Aggie from worrying. His letters described Oona's cheerful side rather than recording any plaintive cries or need for her mother. His correspondence echoed Cecille

Boulton's letters of ten years earlier in which Aggie's mother had written that little Barbara was doing just fine.

One of Oona's biggest thrills was receiving letters from Aggie. Always expressing the hope that there would be "mails from muvver,"[5] she insisted on accompanying Delaney on his trips to the post office. Sometimes she would dictate a letter and Delaney would set down every word, including the symbols for hugs and kisses and love. Delaney often read his own letters from Agnes to Oona, substituting sentences for the ones actually written so as to make their content apply only to the little girl. He did his best to entertain her and to keep up her spirits, but at the same time his own spirits often needed lifting. He, like Oona, missed Agnes dreadfully. However, while his *thoughts* were constantly on Agnes, his focus stayed on her tiny daughter. He showered attention on her and included her in most activities—she even stood at his side while he did repair work on the house. He set up two gardens, one for him and one for her, and they competed to see whose would bloom first—hers, thanks to some deft transplanting by Gaga. Oona, the father-starved child, basked in the attention of a man who delighted in her company, who played with her, hugged her, comforted her, and loved her, and also like her, fiercely desired to be reunited with Aggie. "I guess Oona does come pretty close to loving me, now," wrote Delaney. "I come as close as I can to loving her for two reasons: she means so much to you, and she constantly reminds me of you. Every time I paint a shutter or a rung on the porch rail Oona asks: What will Muvver say when she sees that. When she sticks a new piece of dry grass in her garden she asks the same question. She can't know how her question fits my own thoughts. Yet, sometimes, I think she does."[6]

Meanwhile, Agnes kept at her writing and sent her work in progress to Jim Delaney. He did some blue penciling and returned the story along with tactful comments that his marks were merely suggestions, not corrections. He could not resist pointing out, however, that her spelling was as bad as ever.

Agnes reached her sixth week in Reno, the halfway point of her required stay. The time had passed slowly and was made even more burdensome by her concerns over finances and the situation at home. Barbara had come down with the measles after returning to school, and certain that Oona would also be stricken, Aggie hounded Delaney with advice about what to do when that happened. "She hasn't a damn thing, believe it or not," Delaney finally wrote in exasperation. Agnes was frustrated at being too far away to do anything, and Jim Delaney was equally frustrated because he had to placate the nervous mother as well as deal with the domestic situation. He usually handled everything with equanimity, but after one squabble among the ladies he wrote in frustration, "I do wish to God that Gaga or Oona could stand a beating; if they could I would give it to them tonight."[7]

That spring the weather was particularly bad on the East Coast and the rains kept the occupants of Old House housebound. "No sun for eight days," Delaney moaned. "I have been trying so long to pick up Gaga's and Oona's hopes for better weather that now I am beginning to feel the need of someone to jack my own up. Because of our seemingly endless days of confinement Oona, I believe, is growing bored with me. Even such hot numbers as *O by Jingo* and *Won't You Come Over to My House* don't seem to have the old appeal for her."[8] Storm after storm ravaged the coast until, at last, the first dry day dawned. Delaney celebrated the event by making Oona a new swing, with a comfortable wooden seat to replace the old rope swing, which, complained Oona, was too sharp and hurt her bottom.

Oona's birthday was approaching, and she could not stop talking about it. How big would she be when she got to be four? she demanded of Delaney. Her daughter had grown, he boasted to Aggie, and never looked so well as she did now. Not only was her health great, he was teaching her new words all the time and her vocabulary was increasing by leaps and bounds. When they sat down to meals, she chatted on and on about "the Ritz Carlton, highbrows, lowbrows, groceries, one-arm joints, etc." It was at one of those dinners that, Delaney reported, "Oona solemnly declared that she wanted to grow up to be one of the very best people."[9]

Oona's presents began to arrive. Aggie sent her an Indian doll, and her father sent a book of children's stories along with a large unbreakable doll from FAO Schwarz in New York. Gaga told Delaney that O'Neill's gifts probably had been picked out and purchased by the lawyer Harry Weinberger. Oona had heard from her father twice since her mother's departure. In April she received a letter and a check for $25, and in May she received a postcard from France.

On May 13 Delaney took Oona and Gaga to Asbury Park to purchase party favors and decorations for the birthday celebration. Oona promised to give him as much of her cake as he wanted, but not half of it, and also told him that he could "petend" it was his birthday too, but that he could not take her presents the way she took his on his birthday. Feted and pampered though she was, Oona O'Neill celebrated her fourth birthday with neither parent present.

At the end of May, Agnes moved from the ranch full of women to the Hotel Golden in Reno and continued to occupy her time by waiting, writing, and occasionally going for horseback rides. By then Oona had Delaney literally counting the days until her mother's return. On the last weekend of the month, the Akron blimp flew over Point Pleasant and Jim Delaney took Oona outside to watch. He told her beforehand of the dirigible's enormity, but when they viewed it Oona began to cry. The Akron was not *that* big, she complained, and realizing that he had overdone his description, Delaney understood her disappointment. Oona was expecting something the size of the state of New Jersey, he wrote to her mother, adding that perhaps the imagining such *big* things came from having a daddy who wrote fourteen-act plays. Much taken by Oona's flirtatious forthrightness, Delaney reported that, among others, Oona had gone after the grocery delivery man. Occasionally friends of Delaney would drop by, and one of them, a young man named Ray, caught Oona's fancy. "Oona has made a definite victim of Ray," wrote Delaney; "her womanish wile is so pronounced as to be almost unbelievable. Ray—this will make your mother's heart jump—predicts she will be married when she is sixteen." Calling her a chip off the old block, Delaney laughingly warned Agnes never again to try and tell him that "there is nothing to this heredity bunk. Oona is, in the vernacular, a wow!"[10]

In her mother's absence Oona reigned supreme, and James Delaney jokingly cautioned Agnes that when she returned there would be a showdown—one of them would have to knuckle under. "I have told Oona it undoubtedly will be she who will have to bend the knee and that she had better prepare for the end of her reign. Of course it really will be between Oona and 'Muvver' to decide by battle, who is to abdicate. One of you must. Oona has established herself as absolute mistress of the house. Nor are there any but her subjects (I should say slaves) present. A visitor becomes a slave as soon as he crosses the threshold. Everything, and everybody is hers."[11]

On July 3, 1929, Agnes Boulton O'Neill was granted a divorce from Eugene Gladstone O'Neill on grounds of desertion. Provisions in the separation agreement regarding Shane and Oona granted the father and mother equal control, equal rights of visitation, and sole custody at various times. No arrangement would be allowed to interfere with the children's health, welfare, or schooling. O'Neill insisted that one clause call for Shane and Oona to enter at age thirteen a first-class American preparatory boarding school chosen by mutual agreement. Agnes had to pay all school and college fees if her alimony were at least $8,000; if not, O'Neill had to pay. She received $6,000 a year plus additional amounts that would vary according to O'Neill's income. Whatever he made, however, the top figure she could receive was $10,000, and this would be possible only if O'Neill's income were $30,000 a year.

When at last Agnes returned to Point Pleasant, Oona was thrilled and so was Jim Delaney. Over and over, he had expressed the belief that this was to be his and Aggie's big year. Big it was, in terms of Agnes's getting her divorce, but not in terms of their relationship. Agnes came back from Reno free from Eugene O'Neill the husband, but beholden to Eugene O'Neill the provider of alimony and child support. Although she loved Jim Delaney he was not a man of income, and she needed alimony more than she needed a legal mate. Marrying him would have meant sacrificing financial security, something she would not do. Heartbroken, the disconsolate suitor turned to the obvious. On August 26, 1929, the *New York Times* reported that J. J. Delaney, an Albany newspaperman, had been arrested for drunk driving and that only the intervention of the divorced wife of Eugene O'Neill, who paid his fine and the damages, saved him from going to jail.

Although marriage was out of the question, Agnes O'Neill and James Delaney stayed together for a few more years. He continued to treat Oona like a daughter, and she remained completely at ease in his presence. A visitor at Point Pleasant recalled the seven-year-old Oona calling downstairs one evening to say goodnight and concluding with "Jimmy, kiss Mother good night for me."[12] A decade after the O'Neill divorce, Jim and Aggie, no longer lovers, remained on friendly terms. Not until the mid-forties, when she began seeing the man she eventually would marry, did Aggie end their relationship. For Delaney there never would be anyone else. Agnes was the love of his life. Nor did his feelings toward Oona change. He called her his "little gel," and even after she moved a continent away and became Mrs. Charlie Chaplin, he continued to regard her in a fatherly fashion.

In 1942 Delaney joined the Office of War Information and in 1948 was named chief of the copy desk section of the State Department's international press and publications division. While on a trip to Los Angeles in the late forties, he telephoned Oona asking to see her. She wanted to invite him over, but Charlie Chaplin said no. Furthermore, he told Oona that he did not want her to have any contact with Delaney. Chaplin gave no reason—most likely he was keeping unwanted (by him) personages from Oona's past out of her present. Oona felt terrible yet was unable to go against her husband's wishes. She turned away her childhood paladin and never heard from him again.

On March 20, 1950, James J. Delaney, recently returned from an official trip to Singapore for the State Department, died, after a brief illness, at the age of fifty in Sibley Hospital in Washington, D.C. He had never married. Among the tributes received by the Delaney family in Albany was a large floral arrangement from Mr. and Mrs. Charles Chaplin.

six

"A HAND LIKE A PRUNE"

Eugene O'Neill and Carlotta Monterey were married on July 22, 1929, in Paris. From that date nearly two years would pass before Oona saw her father again. On May 17, 1931, the O'Neills returned to New York City, and that summer Shane visited with his father in a house Carlotta had rented in Northport, Long Island. At nearly twelve years of age Shane was deemed old enough for the O'Neills to handle; Oona, at barely six, was not. In the fall Eugene and Carlotta moved into the Hotel Madison on East Fifty-eighth Street, and at long last arrangements were made to bring Oona into the city to see him. Oona was curious and excited about meeting him again and at the same time felt "horribly shy." Ushered into the hotel suite along with her brother, she was pleased that the gentle and handsome man who greeted her turned out to be her father. She also was relieved that O'Neill and his wife, whose imperious manner frightened her, concentrated on talk-

ing to Shane. O'Neill brought out a music box he had purchased in Europe and, turning the key, played the tune for his
little daughter. She was enchanted.

Later the lyrical mood of the visit turned slightly discordant.
Carlotta saw fit to serve kidneys for lunch—at least that is what
Oona recalled her serving. (Doubting that even Carlotta Monterey could have shown such a complete misunderstanding of
children and/or their appetites, Oona later wondered if she had
remembered correctly.) Nevertheless, whatever the food, it was
inappropriate, definitely a dish that Oona would not have eaten
under normal circumstances. She rose to the occasion, though,
and despite her strong aversion ate slowly and cautiously and,
just to be polite, even took more when Carlotta offered seconds.
After the meal the two adults and two children went for a ride
through Central Park in O'Neill's chauffeur-driven Cadillac.
Shane sat up front next to the driver while Oona sat in the back
between her father and Carlotta. A fur-lined robe had been
thrown over the laps of the backseat occupants, and as the automobile moved along the conversation flowed between Eugene,
Carlotta, and Shane. The topic of discussion was the brand-new
car and how much O'Neill enjoyed owning it. The playwright,
so miserly with his family, had a taste for personal luxury, and
the Cadillac was his latest indulgence. As the car bounced over
rough cobblestone road, Oona's thoughts turned to the beef kidneys. At the memory her stomach, too, began to turn. She dared
not say anything, held back as long as she could, then, without
a word, proceeded to throw up all over her father, her stepmother, the fur-lined robe, and the upholstery. The car was
pulled over to the curb and the passengers leaped out. People
strolling in the park stopped to watch the chauffeur attempt to
clean up the mess as Carlotta tried to comfort the shaken little
girl. Oona remembered her stepmother crying out grandilo-
quently, "GOOD GOD, CHILD! Why didn't you SAY SOME-
THING?! We could have stopped the car. You must have KNOWN

you felt sick!" Carlotta bemoaned the desecration of her husband's new automobile, yet she did not totally crush her trembling stepdaughter. "It's not her fault; she felt sick," Carlotta said in Oona's defense, "but why didn't she SAY SOMETHING!"[1]

O'Neill himself was not unduly upset by the accident; somewhat anxious about seeing Oona after so long and concerned at what she would be like, he in fact was quite pleased with his youngest child. "Oona is very much O'Neill in spite of the environment she's been up against, and a nice shy quiet little girl," he wrote to his son Eugene.[2] Three decades later, in a letter to Louis Sheaffer, Oona described that first visit with her father as "funny." Making light of her own discomfort, she remembered feeling awfully sorry for her brother.[3] Five and a half years older than Oona, Shane had a tough time adjusting to his parents' divorce. Although Oona's feelings may have gone deeper than anyone realized, Shane's agony was easily read and not easy to placate, especially since he received little in the way of support. Emotionally wobbly even when Eugene and Agnes were together, Shane never got on his legs after they split up.

Despite his own vulnerability Shane was a hero to his little sister in those early years, the big brother whom she looked up to and relied on. Shane, after all, was the link to their father; he got to see him before she did, and he got the letters from him. Oona's half siblings played lesser roles. Barbara Burton was not an O'Neill and not a regular member of the household until Agnes and Eugene were divorced, by which time she was away at boarding school for most of the year. Barbara, at least, was a viable figure in Oona's life, whereas Oona's contact with her other half sibling, Eugene Jr., was even more limited than her contact with their father. Fifteen years older, Gene Jr. had little reason to keep up with his kid sister, especially after their father turned against her. Oona and her half-brother shared a few summer visits and then never saw each other again. In later years O'Neill favored his first-born for at least two reasons: Gene Jr.'s mother never asked for financial support, and the junior O'Neill's scholastic brilliance pleased his father. Eugene O'Neill Jr. became an esteemed classicist, an instructor at Yale University and a lecturer at Princeton University, and co-editor of *The Complete Greek Drama* with Whitney J. Oates, still the standard in the field. Eugene Sr. basked in the glory of his son's achievements and accepted him because of those accomplishments. The relationship between O'Neill and his academically successful first child grew stronger as the bond between O'Neill and his underachieving Boulton children weakened.

In the years following the divorce, Agnes and the children moved around a bit. Old House was home base, but they stayed at Spithead in the summer and made occasional trips to Connecticut and to Jim Delaney's cabin in Westport, New York. Because Aggie thought Shane would fare better under the discipline of the Sisters of Charity than he would in public school, he was enrolled in Saint Peter's Parochial School in Point Pleasant, New Jersey. Once her son reached high school age, Agnes looked into various elite boarding schools. She and Shane visited a few and then chose Lawrenceville School, which was not only prestigious but close by; moreover, Shane liked the school and wanted to go there. O'Neill thought Lawrenceville too much of a stretch academically, and he proved to be correct. Shane was in deep trouble by the start of his second term, but when the headmaster wrote to O'Neill suggesting that a little interest in his son's progress might ease the situation, O'Neill, in poor health and busy with his plays, had word sent that he would accept no future communications from the school, that everything had to be handled through his lawyer. Agnes took matters into her own hands and arranged for Shane to transfer to the Florida Military Academy in St. Petersburg. Shane did no better in Florida and was again transferred to another prep school, this time in Colorado.

Failing to make the grade once again, he returned to the East Coast.

Oona was sent to a convent school but did not thrive in the parochial atmosphere. She became very serious and quiet and developed a *fainting complex* which began, Oona said, when she *conveniently* swooned at a morning mass. From then on she associated fainting with incense and needed only a "whiff of the stuff" to send her out of church. Ultimately Oona gave up going to church, which, in her opinion, "probably was what it was all about in the first place."[4] Organized religion, in fact, would not figure much in her future.

Oona next attended the Ocean Road Public School in Point Pleasant. Over a half century later, Walter Hance, a classmate in the fifth and sixth grades, still remembered her although he confessed to having been more taken with Oona's close friend—blond, blue-eyed Helen Mauer, whose fair beauty stood out against Oona's dark good looks. Did O'Neill's position as America's foremost playwright mean anything to her grammar school chums? Walter Hance did not think so; he, for instance, was far more impressed by the fact that Helen Mauer's father was an engineer on the Upper Manasquan River Bridge than by Oona's father being a famous writer.[5]

In the fall of 1938 Agnes sent Oona to the Warrenton Country School in Warrenton, Virginia, the heart of hunt country. Oona roomed with Grace Penington and four other girls. Grace and her older sister, Olivia,* immediately struck up a friendship with Oona. According to Grace, unlike most of the rest of the students, the Peningtons and Oona were avid readers and intellectually curious. The three girls spent a good deal of their free time together—often they would climb into a

---

*Grace Penington spoke at length to the author, but at her request the sisters' real names have not been used.

boat, row out to the middle of a nearby pond, and after pulling up oars, drift around in the idling craft reading plays aloud.

Advertised as a school where "French was the language of the house," Warrenton's academic program was, according to Grace Penington, third-rate, and the atmosphere was decidedly un-Gallic. "We were supposed to speak French at certain hours, and we did, but no one corrected our pronunciation and we had no idea how to say anything in the right manner," recalled Grace. "It was just a lot of words and we struggled along until the French speaking time ended. I dare say very few actually wound up with a command of the language. I know I didn't, and from what I was told, neither did Oona."

The big event for the Virginia horsey set was the Gold Cup Race, an annual steeplechase which Warrenton girls were encouraged to attend. Oona and the sisters planned to go together. When they met up at the bus stop they were amused to discover that without consulting each other, all three had rejected the purple and green school uniform and cape and donned instead an identical outfit: a beige, ribbed cotton suit with a short jacket and flared skirt—the so-called cricket suit from the bastion of proper garb for the social set, Best's department store. The girls reached the race site and wandered among the various booths, one of which—a fortune-teller's tent—greatly intrigued Oona; she was eager to have her palm read. The sisters, unwilling to spend the money, held back as Oona marched into the tent. She emerged almost immediately. When asked what the fortune-teller had predicted, Oona threw back her head and laughed. "She said I had a hand like a prune and she couldn't read it. She couldn't tell me anything about the future."

The Peningtons were only at Warrenton for a year. "My mother visited the school and was unimpressed with what was going on," Grace remembered. "Among other things, we weren't allowed to go home for Thanksgiving because the big hunt was on, and Warrenton girls were expected to be there and act as hostesses for the visiting riders. Mother was shocked by this, maybe more by the school's standards. She spoke fluent French, herself, and was appalled at the way my sister and I were learning it." Mrs. Penington was so dissatisfied with Warrenton that she withdrew her daughters at the end of the second term and enrolled them in Manhattan's prestigious Brearley School. Their friendship with Oona O'Neill, however, continued. That summer they were invited to visit in Bermuda. "We never discussed our family situations," said Grace, "but I'm sure Oona knew that our parents were separated. We were with our mother that summer, and so she was included in the invitation. My mother was a writer and probably Agnes O'Neill enjoyed having a fellow author around. I remember that she showed Mother a novel she was working on—it was called *Tourist Strip*, and it was about an automobile trip to Florida. I don't think it was ever published."

The Peningtons spent an enjoyable six weeks at Spithead. "Life was very romantic in Bermuda in those days," said Grace. "You were taken around in horse-drawn buggies and there were all sorts of dances and get-togethers. Olivia and I went to them, but we weren't very successful with the boys and *struggled* with our image. Oona tried to help. She was always telling us what to wear and insisted that our hemlines were far too long. 'Get your skirts above the knees!' she'd say. We were pretty hopeless when it came to fashion—and to boys, too. Oona was popular and very social but in that shy, slightly sorrowful way of hers. She was flirtatious and yet, I have to say, underneath the playfulness you sensed an unhappiness. If something came up that she didn't want to discuss, she wouldn't deal with it; she'd just put her head down like an ostrich. Sometimes we'd be talking and she'd just get up and go into her bedroom and shut the door. And that was that. I was young, but I thought it was dangerous to bottle yourself up so much. Another thing I remember, even though you knew Oona read a lot and that somewhere she was smart, she didn't express herself very well. If you asked her opinion about a book or a play, she'd say, 'it's swell' and go on to something else. She just didn't verbalize her opinions or her feelings, at least at that time."

That summer Mrs. Penington told Agnes that she was taking her daughters out of Warrenton and urged her to do the same with Oona. Oona went back for her sophomore year, but in the fall of 1940 she was transferred. "I'm sure that it was my mother who influenced Agnes's eventual decision to enroll Oona in Brearley," said Grace Penington. "Oona was a grade ahead of me, and once she got into the social whirl at Brearley, we were not as close as we had been at Warrenton. But she was always kind to my sister and me. Considering that she was so popular and we were such dorks, we should have been jealous of her. Honestly, I think it's a tribute to Oona that we never were."

Oona O'Neill changed schools; Eugene and Carlotta O'Neill changed residences. Barely six months after they moved into a duplex apartment on Park Avenue, they made plans to build a twenty-two-room house on a piece of land O'Neill had purchased in Sea Island, Georgia. The house was constructed and called, at Carlotta's suggestion, Casa Genotta—a combination of Gene and Lotta, their names for each other. In 1932 nine-year-old Oona wrote and asked if she could pay them a visit. Carlotta, who handled O'Neill's affairs, wrote back that it was not a good time and issued a vague rain check. When it came to dealing with Oona, O'Neill usually deferred to Carlotta or, if he actually answered himself, sidestepped any requests to see him. Reluctance often was reflected in his replies and letters, which included declarations such as "I am so proud of being the father of a such a fine girl" and inevitably ended with such statements as "It is all right for Shane to visit here in the summer, because he is so much more grown than you, but I am afraid the sudden change to this climate would not be a good thing for you until you are a little older."[6] Over and over Oona received the brush-off, and though she persevered the rewards seem to have been few. In an interview in the *New York Daily News* of October 25, 1942, Oona said that she visited Sea Island several times as a little girl but remembered little of those occasions save that it was damp. Much later, when discussing the past with Louis Sheaffer, she did not mention those visits at all.

In 1937 Carlotta and Eugene O'Neill relocated to Costa Contra, California, and on a mountainside overlooking the San Ramon Valley, thirty-five miles from San Francisco, they built a home that they called Tao House. Although her father had moved a continent away, Oona continued to importune him for an audience and eventually made two pilgrimages to Tao House. Before his daughter's first visit, Eugene O'Neill received the Nobel Prize in literature. Oona wrote at least three separate times asking to come and see him, yet O'Neill, in March 1939, wrote that he had not heard from her in so long that he could not imagine that she wanted to come to California. Carlotta handled almost all the correspondence and was presumed to have blocked Oona's messages. If she did in fact do so, it probably was at O'Neill's request since he continued to leave to his wife the dirty work of making excuses to his children. Carlotta, in fact, became Oona's chief correspondent. Her letters generally began with the lofty salutation, "Dear Child." The word *child*, in fact, was peppered throughout and served as a constant reminder that even though Carlotta discussed many adult issues with her, Oona was simply that—a *child*. In one exchange, dated March 25, 1938, Carlotta started out simply enough by complimenting Oona's handwriting: "It is gratifying to see that you take pains and are neat and orderly. You are a good child." Neatness counted in Carlotta's world, a world that was drastically changing, and she wrote that Oona would live to see a new world with new ideas, morals, and customs. "Learn to be independent, child," Carlotta counseled, "then you will be *free* and personal freedom is the greatest of all joys."[7]

In September 1938 Carlotta wrote to wish Oona well in the coming school year and to inform her that her father soon would be writing to tell her of their plans for the summer, including Oona's proposed visit—but *soon* became six months later. In her letter Carlotta stated that she was not very happy with young children around; indeed, they terrified her. She and Oona's father lived very quietly in the country with little to see or do to amuse the young, she explained, but now that Oona was no longer a child and able to look after herself, she was welcome to join them. Besides, added Carlotta magnanimously, it was time for Oona to see something of her father. When at last Eugene O'Neill himself replied in March, it was to say that Oona could not be accommodated until the end of the summer because he and Carlotta had scheduled visitors, which probably was not true. He did offer to pay Oona's fare and added that she could stay for a week or ten days. In his chatty reply O'Neill complimented his daughter on the fine work she had done in school and ended by saying that it was about time the two of them got together again. "It has been too long since the last time," he wrote. Too long? According to Oona, she had not seen her father in eight years.

Understandably apprehensive, Oona was tense when she arrived at Tao House late in August. Carlotta diffused the fourteen-year-old's concerns by taking over and familiarly chattering away from the moment Oona arrived. Once more confessing that she really disliked children and that she had half-expected Oona to show up wearing lipstick and red nail polish, Carlotta expressed relief that Oona's childhood was over. Not only could the two of them be friends, but her father could enjoy her too. Oona was won over by her stepmother and that evening at dinner was even more impressed. Seated at the table and being ner-

vous in her father's presence after so long, Oona became faint.
When she turned pale, quickly and quietly Carlotta rose from
her chair and hurried the youngster upstairs to bed—a common
courtesy, to be sure, yet Oona regarded Carlotta's action as special; she did not take for granted any kindness from her father or
his wife. During Oona's stay Carlotta took Oona shopping, took
her to a local fair, and bought her presents; O'Neill himself joined
them for a trip to the zoo. In all, Oona had far more contact with
her stepmother than with her father.

Carlotta Monterey awed Oona. Flattered by the open adoration of the attractive youngster, Carlotta majestically spread her
wings and took her husband's child under them. Carlotta did not
talk down to Oona, either, and confidentially expressed her opinions. Among other things they discussed clothing, hairstyles,
makeup, and shopping. At home Aggie was too busy with her
writing for such frivolous conversation, so now Oona reveled in
the attention from her father's wife. Convinced that Carlotta was
very original and very funny, Oona never thought that her stepmother might have a hidden agenda. Over and over, Carlotta
stressed the importance of being independent (which probably
was motivated by her resentment that O'Neill had to pay alimony and child support). Encouraging her stepdaughter to
strive to be on her own was another way of saying "Earn your
own way and don't depend on your father."[8] In truth, Carlotta
Monterey was hardly a role model of independence. Several
years before she married O'Neill, Carlotta had been the mistress of James Speyer, a Wall Street financier who provided her
with an annuity of $12,000 for life. She told Eugene that her
money came from her wealthy Aunt Sophie, and in fact
O'Neill did not discover the true source of his wife's income for
many years.[9] Had he done a little investigating, he would have
discovered that Aunt Sophie had died a charity case in a California home for the aged.

Oona quickly fell into the daily routine of Tao House.

Breakfast was brought to her room, after which she spent the mornings reading, sunbathing, swimming, or shopping with Carlotta. O'Neill was working, of course, and not to be disturbed. Around 1:30 P.M. the three would have lunch on the terrace. Following the midday meal O'Neill took a nap. At 4:00 he would meet Oona at the pool, and after a swim they would have tea on the terrace. Following afternoon tea they strolled around the grounds until dinnertime. Dinner was served in the formal dining room, and evenings were spent reading and talking. O'Neill regularly listened to news of the war on the radio, often playing solitaire during the broadcasts. Occasionally he played records from his extensive collection of jazz recordings, greatly impressing his teenage daughter. This schedule, or something quite close to it, was carried out at Tao House with or without Oona being present. Having a routine really appealed to Eugene O'Neill; the stately order of his daily activities was a benefit of his marriage to Carlotta.

In the hour or so that Oona spent alone with her father in the afternoon, O'Neill might discuss the series of eleven plays on which he was working. Or he might question her about Shane, or tell her about Europe and the Orient, and almost always bemoan the problems of building Tao House. He showed his daughter theatrical posters of her grandfather which were hung in the bathhouse, and Oona especially remembered one depicting James O'Neill as Edmund Dantes crying out his immortal curtain line, "The world is mine!!" Although she and her father did not talk a lot, they were not uncomfortably silent. And, although she was unable in later years to recall, for Louis Sheaffer, any vital quotes or intimacies that O'Neill shared with her, she did feel that there was something between them—not *intimacy*, but an unspoken sympathetic understanding, an empathy which she believed was experienced by her father as well. Oona was particularly pleased that he admired her swimming style and stated that she believed he admired her in general.[10]

After her successful stay at Tao House, Oona returned home. Full of joy at having been so well received by her father and stepmother, Oona immediately regaled her mother with tales of her trip—most of which centered on Carlotta. At first Aggie listened patiently, but when Oona showed no signs of stopping Aggie called a halt. Perhaps, suggested Aggie, some of Carlotta's statements were more calculated than Oona realized. Why, for instance, would Carlotta be expecting a child to be wearing red nail polish? Aggie interpreted this remark as a direct insult to herself, the mother who would allow a daughter to indulge in such excesses. Thus a tacit competition between O'Neill's second and third wives was waged through the obvious conduits, Oona and Shane; and although their loyalty went to Agnes, both of O'Neill's children were fascinated by Carlotta and declared on more than one occasion that they liked her.

Elated by her auspicious visit, Oona proudly told schoolmates that she had been with O'Neill and that among other shared moments he had played his jazz records for her. "His favorite is Fats Waller's *Your Feet's Too Big*," she told Grace Penington. Grace remembered this as the one and only occasion on which she heard Oona mention her father's name.

Impressed by his daughter's good looks, good manners, innate sensitivity, and obvious intelligence, O'Neill wrote friends of his pleasure at seeing her again. With that out of the way, he immediately turned to his most beloved child—his work; in the process, the real child quickly faded into the background. Oona placed far more significance on their meeting than he did. Yet on some level she must have been aware that their infrequent encounters always were a result of *her* requests to be with him, not *his* desire to see her.

seven

THE GOOD-TIME GIRL

While Old House remained Oona's childhood home, her mother often took up residence elsewhere—sometimes on her own, at other times with her daughter. In the fall of 1940 Oona entered Brearley, and Aggie moved them into the Hotel Weylin on Madison Avenue. Shane, too, was in the city and occasionally stayed with his mother and sister. Already floundering, Shane was drinking and experimenting with drugs—still, he attempted to get some kind of informal education. He had shown a gift for drawing and was attending the Art Students League, where Oona joined him for a few classes. With Shane and Oona occupied at school, Agnes went about her business and her social life. In pursuit of the latter she frequently absented herself from the Hotel Weylin, especially in the evenings. According to former Brearley student Kitty Hamilton, the school administration learned of Aggie's poor home attendance record and, concerned about Oona's lack of supervision, arranged for her to spend the spring semester in the home of Kitty's parents, Dr. and Mrs. Wallace Hamilton, on East Sixty-fifth Street.[1]

An Upper East Side citadel of upper-echelon education for girls, the Brearley School was founded in 1882 by Samuel Brearley Jr., a graduate of Phillips Andover Academy and Harvard, whose desire was to establish a learning institution for girls that would function on an equal academic level with similar schools for boys. It was exactly the kind of first-rate school specified in the O'Neills' separation agreement. Oona was one of forty-four members of the class of 1942. Because no yearbook was published on account of the Second World War, the available information on her two-year stint is contained in brief notations on her registry card. Eugene O'Neill's name is listed as Parent or Guardian, but except for paying tuition he had as little to do with the education of his daughter as he did with his son. During her two years at Brearley, Oona took the standard eleventh- and twelfth-grade courses and was considered a moderate rather than outstanding student. Her interests were listed as Music and Piano, information that apparently came from a faculty member and was not self-described. Oona participated in the Dramatic Society and also was a member of the Senior Chorus. She took French and Math achievement tests and SATS and did well enough to be admitted to Vassar College.

At the end of her junior year, in the summer of 1941, Oona made her second and final visit to Tao House. No longer the ingenuous fourteen-year-old of the earlier trip, she was preoccupied with her own concerns and unwilling to listen attentively to her stepmother's lengthy reflections. Oona wanted to talk about herself and chattered away, giving Carlotta little opportunity to get in a word. A problem arose when Carlotta failed to recognize that Oona's babbling was merely a stage in the girl's development. Moreover, Carlotta O'Neill did not relish yielding center stage to anyone except, of course, her husband. She took Oona's giddy pronouncements with utter seriousness and, instead of brushing them off, chastised her stepdaughter for being frivolous. Nor did she stop with simple rebukes; she had to tell Oona how to run her life. When Oona confided that she wanted to go on the stage rather than to college, Carlotta, the former actress, swiftly remonstrated. Forget acting! she scolded, the world situation was far too grim to be thinking of anything like that. A war was imminent; how could Oona talk like such a featherbrain? In such trying times there was no place for flippancy even from a sixteen-year-old girl. No! The most useful thing that Oona could do, insisted Carlotta, was to take a nursing course. Stepdaughter and stepmother carried on their disputations until, shortly before her stepdaughter left for home, Carlotta launched into a last-ditch oration on the benefits of nursing as a career. By now Oona had had enough, and looking her stepmother straight in the eye, she took her stand. She began by complimenting Carlotta for the manner in which she dealt with the complexities of living with Oona's father and the admirable way in which she ran the household. The laudatory portion finished, Oona next declared that she herself never could do all that Carlotta was doing—any more than she could become a nurse. Oh no, Oona announced, she had a simple solution: she would ensure her future happiness by marrying a very rich man. At this point Carlotta exploded. Struggling to catch her breath, she began a lecture to end all lectures. Oona could not be talking seriously, she could not think that way. First of all, rich men hardly existed anymore and certainly would not exist in the changing world in which they lived. In a frenzy of caution Carlotta cited one of her own unhappy marriages to a wealthy man. She had had everything—"a castle in Scotland, servants, money and, still," she cried out, "I WAS MISERABLE."[2] Oona was surprised that her facetious remark had drawn such a violent reaction and later claimed she was just being sassy, not serious.

Their ability to communicate with each other having been shattered, the genial relationship between Oona O'Neill and Carlotta O'Neill ended. Surprisingly, Oona did not experience a similar rift with her father at this time, probably because she saw even less of him during her second visit than during her first. Absorbed in his work, he remained aloof from the bickering between his daughter and his wife. When Carlotta reported Oona's behavior to him, he dismissed her dire predictions for the future by telling her that Oona was just acting like a teenager. This rare example of paternal understanding most likely reflected his desire to keep the peace and not a genuine interest in Oona's thoughts or opinions. Later he would reverse his judgment completely and use the innocuous episode between his daughter and his wife as an example of Oona's calculated avarice. But that was many months away. Father and daughter parted on good terms, and once again O'Neill told friends that he found Oona a most delightful and charming young lady.

Oona continued to write to her father over the fall and winter months; as in the past, his replies were scarce. In a handwritten postcard from Tao House dated March 9, 1942, O'Neill expressed his gratitude and delight in receiving a picture from Oona, adding that he would have written his thanks sooner but had been ill. The card ends, "Much love to you, Daddy." That brief note may have been the last instance in which Eugene O'Neill found anything good to say to his daughter; eventually he would say nothing to her or about her, good or bad. Within the year—a year in which he would be misdiagnosed with Parkinson's disease (his illness was posthumously revealed to be a familial neural degenerative disease), and a year in which Oona would make headlines as New York's number one debutante—Eugene O'Neill would become irrevocably estranged from his only daughter. Her visit to Tao House in the summer of 1941 was their last in-person contact.

What was Oona like during her school years? On certain points former acquaintances agree—she was intelligent and, despite her shyness, outgoing. One girl described her as "a sunny, fun-to-be-with, good-time girl who may have had a good mind but was uninterested in anything serious." Others commented on "a barely controlled rebelliousness in her, a constant impulse to kick against the traces, that bespoke something more than a mere determination to have a good time." A couple of friends "discerned a darkness within her sunniness, a core of isolation at the heart of her sociable manner, that was related in their judgment to the tension between her and her mother."[3] Oona and Aggie's relationship had grown increasingly strained. Each tried to exercise her will, and just as Jim Delaney had jokingly predicted years before, neither wanted to knuckle under. Agnes O'Neill was a working mother long before that term was popularly recognized, and although her children were important to her and she sincerely wanted the best for them, she was drawn in different directions. Her constant absences, beginning with the enforced departure to seek her divorce, left all three children essentially on their own. In theatrical terms Aggie was a *producer* overseeing the general scene; children, however, need a *director* to attend to specific details. Absorbed in her own affairs, Aggie did not want to play the demanding and thankless role of parent to a teenage daughter. Oona was no longer a child and could not be put down peremptorily; left to her own devices, she grew accustomed to doing her own thing.

In the fall of 1941, soon after she returned to Point Pleasant from her visit to Tao House, Oona was introduced by her mother's friend, Elizabeth Murray, to an aspiring young

Oona's grandfather, James O'Neill, matinee idol and inspiration for James Tyrone in Eugene O'Neill's *Long Day's Journey into Night.* *(Harvard Theatre Collection, The Sheaffer-O'Neill Collection, Connecticut College Library)*

Oona's grandmother, Ella Quinlan O'Neill, the model for *Long Day's Journey into Night*'s haunted heroine, Mary Tyrone. *(The Sheaffer-O'Neill Collection, Connecticut College Library)*

Cecille Williams Boulton, Oona's maternal grandmother. *(The Sheaffer-O'Neill Collection, Connecticut College Library)*

Agnes Boulton pictured around the time of her meeting with Eugene O'Neill. She became his second wife and the mother of Shane and Oona. *(The Sheaffer-O'Neill Collection, Connecticut College Library)*

Playwright Eugene O'Neill with his daughter, Oona, in Bermuda. *(Photofest)*

Mrs. Fifine Clark, affectionately known as "Gaga," was a powerful presence in young Oona's life. *(The Sheaffer-O'Neill Collection, Connecticut College Library)*

Oona, dressed in gypsy costume. Her father's imminent desertion would wipe the smile from her face. *(Nikolas Muray/The Sheaffer-O'Neill Collection/Eastman House)*

A family portrait. Eugene, Agnes, Oona, and Shane O'Neill photographed at Spithead, Bermuda, March 3, 1927. *(AP/Wide World Photos)*

Eugene O'Neill and his oldest child, Oona's half brother Eugene O'Neill Jr. *(The Sheaffer-O'Neill Collection, Connecticut College Library)*

On the ferry to Westport, New York. Oona waits with her surrogate father, James J. Delaney. *(Frank Conley)*

"Old House," the Boulton family's residence
on Herbertsville Road in West Point Pleasant,
New Jersey, and Oona's childhood home.
(© 1958 Asbury Park Press,
All Rights Reserved)

Eugene O'Neill and his third wife, Carlotta Monterey,
in France, awaiting his divorce from Agnes.
(The Sheaffer-O'Neill Collection,
Connecticut College Library)

Agnes and her children,
(left to right) Barbara
Burton and Oona and
Shane O'Neill.
(UPI/Corbis-Bettmann)

Tao House, California.
A rare smile from Eugene O'Neill
as he regards his teenage daughter.
After two brief visits, Oona never
saw her father again.
(Bienecke Library, Yale University)

Relaxing in her Brearley gym suit,
Oona, cigarette in hand, pensively
bites her thumb.
*(The Sheaffer-O'Neill Collection,
Connecticut College Library)*

A muskrat fur coat draped over
her shoulders, Oona takes a stroll
in Central Park with her svelte,
stylish mother. *(The Sheaffer-
O'Neill Collection,
Connecticut College Library)*

Carol Marcus and Gloria Vanderbilt, two-thirds of the 1940s dazzling debutante triumvirate.
(*AP/Wide World Photos*)

From schoolgirl to celebrity, the Stork Club's glamour girl is proclaimed New American Debutante #1 of the 1941–42 social season. Photos like this infuriated her father.
(*UPI/Corbis-Bettmann*)

Backstage at the Maplewood Theatre in Maplewood, New Jersey, Oona poses with Georgie Tapps, one of the stars of *Pal Joey,* in which Oona had a small part.
(*UPI/Corbis-Bettmann*)

At her Hollywood apartment, Oona is questioned in connection with the paternity suit brought against her "good friend" Charlie Chaplin by Joan Barry. Within a week, the just-turned-eighteen Oona would become the fourth wife of the fifty-four-year-old Chaplin.
(*UPI/Corbis-Bettmann*)

Attended by his publicist, Harry Crocker, and his secretary, Catharine Hunter, Chaplin slips the wedding ring on Oona's finger as Justice of the Peace C. P. Moore looks on. (*Photofest*)

Charlie escorts Oona and Hollywood legend Mary Pickford to the world premiere of *Monsieur Verdoux* in New York City. (*UPI/Corbis-Bettmann*)

writer named J. D. Salinger, and they began seeing each other. Salinger told Mrs. Murray that he was "crazy about" Oona, but the course of their relationship was rocky and Salinger expressed reservations about Oona's personality. He took her out on a date in New York in December, after which he confided to Elizabeth Murray that "Little Oona's hopelessly in love with little Oona."[4] Despite the put-down, Salinger kept up with Oona in person and through the mail; obviously he was very interested in her.

About Oona O'Neill's physical appearance, everyone agreed. She was lovely. Perhaps favoring her father, the dark eyes and dark hair bespoke her O'Neill heritage; she also inherited her mother's high cheekbones and straight nose. Oona's lips were full and her toothsome smile was open and radiant. Her figure was exceptionally shapely. As early as her Warrenton days, Grace Penington remembered Oona as being "lovely in a buxom way." She recalled that Oona matured earlier than most of the girls and was enough embarrassed about it to undress in private. At Brearley, Oona was looked up to by schoolmates, particularly younger ones. "We really idolized the older girls," recalled author Anne Bernays, who caught glimpses of the vivacious Oona in the school hallways. "I remember one occasion when my mother took me for lunch at the Quo Vadis restaurant," reminisced Bernays, "and while we were eating, Oona and her mother walked in. Most of the tables were set against the walls so that you could see all the comings and goings while you dined, and I watched as the two of them were shown to a table. Agnes Boulton was gloriously beautiful, and Oona looked a lot like her except that Oona was staggeringly beautiful." Oona cultivated her attractiveness—she wore makeup and "had bottles of nail polish and lipstick galore."[5]

Not only was Oona the bright and beautiful daughter of a Nobel laureate, by her senior year she had become one of the city's most sought-after debutantes and a regular on the café society circuit. Oona's decidedly unstructured family life had helped to push her into the glitzy nightclub world, where instead of being ignored (as she was by her parents) she was fawned over and doted upon—by strangers. Oona was attracted to mature men, among them the sophisticated thirty-six-year-old satirical cartoonist Peter Arno. One classmate believed that Oona dated older men because she was searching for the "organized supervision lacking at home."[6] With her mother away so much Oona continued to play, and during her Brearley years she found a couple of ideal playmates: Carol Marcus and Gloria Vanderbilt.

Carol Marcus, a student at the Dalton School, met Oona O'Neill in dancing classes, the preferred method of imparting social graces to proper young ladies and gentlemen. The two girls hit it off immediately and would get together after school on a Park Avenue street corner and from there walk to Carol's home at Park and Fifty-fifth Street. Aggie granted her daughter blanket permission to stay at the Marcus's spacious apartment. In fact, in her 1992 autobiography, *Among the Porcupines*, Carol (who became the wife of actor Walter Matthau in August 1959) stated that Oona practically lived with her. Holed up in Carol's bedroom, the two girls indulged in the kind of philosophizing dear to the hearts of the young and channeled all their energies into exploring the universe—their own personal one, and the big one beyond Park Avenue.

From the dancing classes they went on to attend school proms, where, alleged Carol, they were wallflowers. When one looks at pictures of both girls and considers Oona's popularity with boys, it is difficult to believe this statement. Yet Carol Marcus Matthau maintains that at that time the boys passed them by. She and Oona would return home from the proms, cry their eyes out, and find solace in reading books. To better prepare themselves for the social life they were sure would be coming, they engaged in girlish diversions and danced together in front of a mirror, alternating as the male while trying out different methods of looking over a partner's shoulder in an attempt to learn how to flirt. Practice made the girls perfect; soon the boys were falling over themselves to get the girls' attention, and Oona and Carol became the belles of any ball they attended, positions they never relinquished.

In pursuit of good times the girls giggled, chatted, and shopped all over the city. They visited cosmetics counters and experimented with beauty products; they sat at drugstore fountains drinking sodas and poring over movie magazines; they gobbled up burger after burger at Hamburger Heaven and, in the course of their shopping, eating, drinking, and reading, ultimately decided that being beautiful was more important than being brilliant. Once again Oona applied her acclaimed fashion sense to herself and her friend, and for one gala Christmas dance she declared that she and Carol had to buy their dresses at Klein's, a downtown department store famous for bargains. Oona already had definite tastes; she never followed current fads but wore what she liked and what she thought looked good on her. This time she chose identical strapless, tulle dresses, one in white for Carol and the other in black for herself. Going strapless was a rather daring move at the time and was typical of Oona's independent decisions.

The girls often double-dated and spent one memorable football weekend at Brown University. Fixed up with two college boys, they took the train to Providence, checked into a designated boardinghouse, and awaited the arrival of their escorts. They waited, and waited, and waited until it became quite evident they had been stood up. Instead of feeling forlorn and defeated, they stole over to the fraternity house and peeked at the dance through a window. Their dates never showed up for any scheduled event that weekend and later the girls invented their own version of what happened. They told friends that they attended every function, were showered with attention, wowed the collegiates, and had a fabulous time. Since none of their contemporaries at Brearley or Dalton had been there, no one questioned them.[7]

Giddy, yes, but not complete flibbertigibbets, both girls were voracious readers, and Oona apparently had learned to express herself since Warrenton days. Her no-nonsense approach to most everything carried over to her reading, and she gave opinions freely on the subject of writers and writing. Chiding Carol for doing a paper on T. S. Eliot, Oona told her friend not to waste time on an anti-Semite. On another occasion Oona referred to the idolized Ernest Hemingway as the man with fake hair on his chest. Oona particularly liked Willa Cather. Later she expanded her reading to include a wide spectrum of authors from the classic to the contemporary. Awed by Oona's intelligence, Carol was equally impressed by her friend's light touch about her knowledge. That *light touch* may have been what others felt reflected a "good-time girl" attitude. Carol was one friend who sensed that Oona's sunny exterior masked a hard core of inescapable sadness, a sorrow which came out of her being a deserted child or perhaps a sorrow built into her Irish soul. Her former schoolmate Grace Penington felt that "Oona was a very nice person leading a very difficult life and she did not want to talk about it. The family situation was too troublesome so she pulled the covers up over her head."

The friendship between Oona and Carol already was flourishing when Carol met Gloria Vanderbilt at a private party on Long Island. A boarder at the Mary C. Wheeler School in Rhode Island, Gloria had an air of sadness and a tenderhearted, sweet nature which Carol Marcus found similar to Oona's. She introduced them to each other and all three girls instantly clicked. Oona's bond with Gloria had a lot to do with their remarkable resemblance; they looked enough alike to pass for sisters, and Gloria once commented that their eerie similarity was the real link between them. Photographs from that era clearly illustrate the likeness between the two debutantes, especially their identical toothy smiles (so alike that one writer jokingly suggested they shared a set of dentures). Separately Oona, Gloria, and Carol each had a distinctive aura; together they were dazzling. Leila Hadley, a contemporary, described them as "The most radiantly beautiful girls you ever saw. They all had pearly luminous skin which they powdered pale white and they had lively eyes and laughed constantly."[8]

The solidarity of the girls' charmed circle played off their erratic family lives—each of them was, or had been, either through death or desertion, fatherless. Born of an unknown father to a sixteen-year-old girl, Carol Marcus was boarded out to foster homes until her mother married a moneyed gentleman, retrieved her eight-year-old daughter from penury, and deposited her on Park Avenue. Carol never knew her biological parent yet could imagine that had he known about her, he *might* have loved her. Gloria Vanderbilt's father died when she was seventeen months old; later she became the object of a deplorable custody battle between her mother and her aunt. Gloria maintained that she remembered her father's death and always held to the belief that he had loved her. She and Carol were free to weave fantasies about their fathers, but Oona was not so fortunate—her father was neither unknown nor deceased, and the harsh reality of Eugene O'Neill's behavior toward her could not be whitewashed or dreamed away. And while Gloria thought that having any father was better than having no father at all, Carol observed that Oona *knew* her father and still was fatherless.[9]

By the time Oona finished school she was a bona fide celebrity, and a goodly portion of her fame came from her association with the Stork Club. A popular hangout for café society denizens and celebrities, the club flourished on East Fifty-third Street in New York City from the thirties to the fifties. Oona's Brearley registry card noted that she worked there. What, one might ask, was a teenager at an exclusive prep school for girls doing at an East Side boîte? That very question provoked and ultimately outraged Oona's father. Brearley administrators, too, looked askance at Oona's many appearances at the club. Headmistress Millicent MacIntosh (later, president of Barnard College) evidently wrote to Sherman Billingsley, the Stork's owner, questioning the propriety of allowing an underage schoolgirl on the premises with such frequency. The letter may have been written, but Oona continued to visit the club and the photographers continued to take her picture there.

The war escalated and the pace quickened as everyone sought to sieze the moment. In this heightened atmosphere Oona O'Neill thrived. Over fifty years later in the August 1993 issue of *Esquire* magazine, "Sixty Years of Women We Love," she was listed as Teen Heartthrob of the forties. She went from being just another pretty prep school kid to being written up in Walter Winchell's *New York Daily Mirror* column as the toast of café society. Earl Wilson devoted *his* entire column in the *New York Post* to the beautiful daughter of the great playwright, and accompanying photographs showed her escorted by men in their thirties and even forties rather than by preppies or college boys. Pictures of her working at the Stage Door Canteen were circulated, and a photograph taken at a Russian War Relief benefit at the Lafayette Hotel was syndicated nationally. One nightclub, probably the Stork, purportedly wanted to underwrite her coming-out party to the tune of thirty thousand dollars. The Stork Club, in fact, underwrote many of the expenses that brought Oona and the club into the public eye.

Her name and picture appeared in newspapers and magazines around the country, and by the spring of 1942, when she was crowned Debutante of the Year, the media was in an

Oona Blitz. At a large press conference she was given a bouquet of red roses and asked a number of questions. One reporter, who must have had his head in the sand, asked Oona what her father did for a living. "He writes," she answered with a giggle. The next query? How would her father react to her being elected Number One Debutante? "I don't know," responded Oona, "and I'm not going to ask him. He'll find out for himself." Another reporter asked for her thoughts on world affairs. Oona paused and replied that with a world war raging it would be out of place for her to sit in a nightclub and express her opinion.[10] Articles such as this came to Eugene O'Neill's attention, and the more he read the angrier he got. Preternaturally guarded about his private life, he was furious at Oona for bringing his name into play because of her shenanigans and not his art.

In her senior year, after being accepted by Vassar, Oona formally announced plans to forgo college and become an actress. Immediately the rush was on: movie studios, modeling agencies, and publicists began calling; strangers sought to become her business and personal managers; Max Reinhardt, an august name in the theater, invited her to try out for his repertory company; and one press agent guaranteed to get her into the Screen Actors Guild and from there into an upcoming MGM tropical island extravaganza. Eugene O'Neill heard about these offers and wrote to his friend Hunt Stromberg, asking the producer to use his influence to keep Oona out of films. Apparently O'Neill's request was honored, because the movie bids ceased. Nonetheless Oona kept on—she was determined to be an actress. Blocked from the silver screen, she decided to follow in the footsteps of her illustrious grandparent and go on the stage. Once again her father vehemently opposed her career choice and demanded that she complete her education. Aggie, although more cooperative, insisted that Oona finish Brearley first.

Oona did complete her senior year and receive her diploma, thus ending her formal education. Ready to launch her theatrical career, she obtained the requisite head shots, did some modeling, and posed for beauty product advertisements. She landed a bit part in a summer stock production of *Pal Joey* and on July 17, 1942, made her stage debut at the Maplewood Theatre in Maplewood, New Jersey. Among the cast members was Vivienne Segal, the star of the original Broadway show. Ms. Segal was amused at the manner in which Oona went around barefoot and called the already famous ingenue "a delightful, friendly child. She was like some wild Irish sprite. Her charm, her smile, her lovely teeth and hair made her a remarkably beautiful girl. We all loved her."[11]

Agnes was in Hollywood working on her novel *Tourist Strip* when Oona wrote to say that she wanted to enter dramatic school, specifically the Neighborhood Playhouse. A major obstacle loomed—the financing. Since Harry Weinberger handled all monetary matters between Eugene O'Neill and his former wife and children, Agnes asked the lawyer to request the tuition money. Infuriated, O'Neill would not hear of it. The detached and vague delight he heretofore had taken in the pretty girl who wrote him frequently and visited him rarely had been replaced by the same venomous hatred which he had conferred on her mother. Disgusted that Oona had turned down Vassar, O'Neill was further irked by all the notoriety, especially the articles that contained references to him. One in particular vexed him—when asked whether she was shanty or lace-curtain Irish, Oona responded, "I'm shanty Irish and proud of it!"[12] That was all O'Neill needed—provide tuition for an insolent daughter who mocked her heritage as well as her parent? Not likely.

In a letter to Harry Weinberger dated September 28, 1942, O'Neill stated that if he was not legally bound to pay Oona's tuition for the Neighborhood Playhouse, he would not do it.

Unalterably opposed to Oona's going on the stage at any time, O'Neill added with certainty that his daughter had little if any talent for acting, an assumption he based on reports about the *Pal Joey* production. "I believe," he wrote in an exceptionally mean-spirited letter, "that if she had really serious ambition, she would have the sense to know that the way to learn to act is to get a job in the theater . . . not to go to an acting school."[13] O'Neill suggested that Oona's desire to attend classes was simply another typical Boulton trick to avoid real work or study, a lazy way to continue to trade on his name, which she had already done cheaply and shamelessly. The son who had once condemned his father for taking the easy way now attributed the same motivation to his own daughter. He felt that Oona wanted to go on the stage because it was easy and his name was the key. Her reasoning was stupid, he claimed, and he predicted that using the name O'Neill and being spotlighted from the start would prove a terrible handicap to overcome; the breaks would be against her rather than in her favor. He thought the publicity she had received was particularly damning. As far as her succeeding on the stage, O'Neill was certain she would fail. "It practically takes geniuses to pull something of this order off. Oona is no genius but merely a spoiled, lazy, vain little brat who has, so far by her actions only proven that she can be a much sillier and bad-mannered fool than most girls of her age."[14] His displeasure blazed from the page. To further denigrate his daughter, O'Neill drew a rather far-fetched analogy between her and his brother, Jamie. Jamie traded on his father's name, went on the stage, and turned out to be an embittered third-rate actor; that easy start, asserted O'Neill, murdered the life he might have had. In pronouncing his brother a failure, O'Neill chose to gloss over the fact that Jamie's alcoholism had dissipated what many considered an excellent, not third-rate, talent. Furthermore, what name was Jamie to use on the stage other than his own?

Sneering at Oona's lack of pride, her father accused her of being much more Boulton than O'Neill. Oona, he continued, ought to wake up and realize that the country was at war and that it was no time for young Americans to aspire to theatrical or movie careers. If his daughter wanted training that meant something, she should train to be a Red Cross nurse (one almost can hear Carlotta urging him on) or to do any war work which might make a real woman of her. Broadway yearnings, he declared, were "apt to make her a tart," and the "dramatic school business is simply more laziness, more sly evasion, more talentless pretense, more parasitism, more prideless begging and grafting, more weak failure to face the world and the war—or, for that matter, to face oneself in any world of decent values—in short, pure Boultonism. I'll take no more of it than the law allows, thank you."[15]

The son of an actor and a man who made his living from the stage equated his daughter's theatrical aspirations with harlotry and presumably could not have evinced more displeasure had Oona announced plans to go into prostitution. Then again, O'Neill had always had a yearning for respectability, doubtless an ideal fostered by his mother, whose social status was diminished because of her marriage. Despite his own early vagabond existence, he would not tolerate the sowing of the smallest wild oat by his children. Above all else, his daughter especially had to behave properly. After nearly two decades of distance O'Neill took full notice of Oona, and rather than using this opportunity to apply his understanding of human nature (which was explored so fully in his dramatic works) to his daughter's situation, he cut her down instead. This further illustrated that when it came to family matters Eugene O'Neill was a writer first, last, and always— a man who could painstakingly construct his plays even as he destroyed his children.

Ironically, most of the playwright's acquaintances would

not have believed that the shy, courtly gentleman they knew was capable of such behavior. A few, however, were aware of it. Fellow dramatist Clifford Odets saw something very vindictive in O'Neill's behavior and thought that perhaps O'Neill could not forgive Oona because *he* had abandoned her.[16] Odets did not know that O'Neill had abused her further by stubbornly refusing to allow her to disremember him. Meanwhile, Oona, questioned by the press regarding her father's strictures against her becoming an actress, was quoted in the *New York Daily News* of October 25, 1942: " 'He's my guardian until I'm eighteen,' she says meekly, then adds with a twinkle in her big brown eyes, 'I'll be eighteen next May. A girl ought to earn her own living.' "[17]

eight

"P.S. I JUST MET CHARLIE CHAPLIN"

P*al Joey* closed in the summer of 1942, and Oona, for reasons financial or otherwise, dropped plans to attend the Neighborhood Playhouse and instead set her sights on Hollywood. The opportunity to go west came via Carol Marcus. When Gloria Vanderbilt married in December 1941, Oona had been unable to make the trip, but Carol was a bridesmaid for her friend. While in Los Angeles the seventeen-year-old schoolgirl met William Saroyan, a thirty-three-year-old author and playwright. Not long after their meeting Carol returned home and Saroyan was inducted into the army. On his way to basic training in Sacramento, he telephoned Carol in New York and announced that he wanted to marry her. To expedite matters, she was to return to California and meet his family. Carol's mother agreed but insisted that someone accompany her daughter. Despite Oona's reputation as a party girl, Mrs. Marcus considered her a steadying influence on Carol and asked her to go along. Oona gladly consented. Playing chaperone was a lark which would provide wings for Oona's main objective—pursuing an acting career. True, her immediate destination was Sacramento, not Hollywood; still, getting to California constituted half the battle. Once on the West Coast, surely she could find some reason to journey to Los Angeles. Of course, another inducement beckoned—the opportunity to see her father. Although Oona had not written to him in many months, she spoke to Carol of a possible reunion.

The trip across the country proved both exhilarating and dismaying—exhilarating because the train was filled with young servicemen and Oona and Carol partied all the way to the coast; dismaying because the boys were on their way to an uncertain fate overseas. Oona did take time out to mail a letter to her father from Omaha, Nebraska, and requested to see him. She included the name of the hotel where she would be staying and expressed the hope that O'Neill would contact her there. Once they arrived, Saroyan met the girls at the Sacramento station and drove them to the Senator Hotel. En route, miffed at the way the soldiers had crowded around Carol and Oona, Saroyan sarcastically commented that the girls must have had quite a time for themselves. Oona replied simply and quietly that they had had an awful time; how could they enjoy themselves when they knew that those young men were on their way to a war from which they might not return? Oona did not approve of her friend's choice; she did not like William Saroyan's manner, and her first impression later was confirmed. Saroyan equated marriage with having children, and to prove that she was fertile he wanted Carol to get pregnant before their wedding. Calling this the most ridiculous and insulting request she had ever heard, Oona told Carol that if she were that crazy about Saroyan, she should just have an affair and steer clear of marriage.

Oona may not have liked William Saroyan, but she played Cupid of a sort during the early days of the courtship between

him and Carol Marcus. Saroyan wrote many letters to his fi-
ancée, and convinced that her feeble written attempts would
put him off, Carol felt inadequate to the task of responding.
She confided her fears to Oona, who straightaway concocted a
plan. Jerry, one of Oona's many ardent beaus, wrote brilliant
letters; why not lift pithy passages from his notes and incor-
porate them into Carol's letters to Bill Saroyan? Carol liked the
idea and proceeded to take from Jerry and send to Bill. Thanks
to Oona O'Neill, William Saroyan received letters from Carol
Marcus with additional dialogue by the young J. D. Salinger.
Years later, when the incident was recounted in biographies of
Eugene O'Neill, Oona, aware of Salinger's reclusive nature,
was concerned lest her former boyfriend think that she had
had anything to do with using his name.[1] More sensitive than
most, Oona's own reserved nature made her especially sympathetic to other people's desire for privacy.

Since mailing her letter from Omaha, Oona had heard
nothing from O'Neill. Again and again she spoke of telephon-
ing Tao House, but convinced that Carlotta would pick up the
phone, she kept stalling. Finally, in Carol's presence, Oona did
call. The connection was made and Oona signaled that as anticipated, the voice at the other end of the wire belonged to her
stepmother. Oona said hello, explained that she was in Sacramento, and asked to see her father if it was convenient. Carlotta told her to hold the phone. According to Carol, Carlotta
returned to the phone in far less time than it would have taken
to have a conversation with anyone and told Oona that she
was sorry but her father preferred not to see her. Moreover, he
saw no point in Oona's calling and requested that she not telephone again. Oona politely thanked her stepmother and put
down the receiver. She had been dismissed.

Several days later, still unwilling to give up, Oona drove to
Tao House with Carol. Barred at the door by Carlotta, Oona
went back to the hotel and wrote another letter to her father.

In response to this plea O'Neill mailed a reply—not of a conciliatory nature but one intended, he declared, to knock her ears down. His letter actually had been written in answer to her correspondence from the train; however, since she had not included her California address, he had been unable to mail it. First, he questioned her writing to him en route rather than letting him know long enough in advance so that he might have informed her whether he *wanted* to see her. Next, he went on to chastise her for joyriding around the country in a time of national austerity—and at a rich friend's expense, no less. "All I know of what you have become since you blossomed into the night club racket is derived from newspaper clippings of your interviews . . . all the publicity you have had is the wrong kind, unless your ambition is to be a second-rate movie actress of the floozie variety—the sort who have their pictures in the papers for a couple of years and then sink back into the obscurity of their naturally silly, talentless lives."[2] Accusing her of simply riding on his name, O'Neill further reproached Oona for not writing him previously to tell him what was going on in her life, to take advantage of his experience and to ask his opinion. He could have warned her against every stupid blunder she had made, he announced grandly. The father who barely could get a letter off now suggested that he would have guided his daughter through career choices. "You don't want to see me," he continued; "your conduct proves that. So let's cut out the kidding. And I don't want to see the kind of daughter you have become in this past year. . . . Here's hoping you change as you grow out of the callow stage. I had hoped there was the making of a fine intelligent woman in you, who would remain fine in whatever she did. I still hope so. If I am wrong, goodbye. If I am right, you will sometime see the point in this letter and be grateful—in which case, au revoir."[3]

Eugene O'Neill once more employed the push-pull technique that characterized his relationship with his daughter—

"Go away but maybe you can come back, if you do what I want. I'm here for you but I'm not here for you." All the mixed messages added up to one fact: he had no wish whatsoever to see her then, and possibly ever again. Stunned by his invective, Oona gave up and, along with Carol, traveled by train down the coast to Los Angeles. Soon after their arrival Carol left for New York and the erstwhile chaperone was on her own—well, not exactly, because Aggie was in Los Angeles. Owing to wartime housing restrictions, she was living in a trailer park while working on a screenplay.

In letters to Carol, Oona mentioned meeting a lot of men, most of whom wanted to take her out. "They want to sleep with me. It makes me nervous," she wrote.[4] Nervous or not, Oona was in demand. Her reputation as New York's number one debutante had preceded her, and the members of the Hollywood press were as intrigued as their colleagues back east. With no screen appearances to her credit, Oona O'Neill was labeled a starlet—that much-maligned term once defined by Ben Hecht as any young woman in Hollywood under the age of twenty not actively employed in a brothel. Oona was different; she was the well-bred daughter of a Nobel laureate, which made her good copy. Pictured with various eligible men, Oona once more became a staple subject in newspaper and magazine stories. One of her escorts was the film colony's youngest resident genius, twenty-six-year-old Orson Welles. The charismatic Welles escorted Oona to a nightclub on their first date and volunteered to read her palm. He took her upturned hand in his, gazed at it intently, then raised his head and, looking deeply into her eyes, declared that he saw a love line which led directly to another, older man. The Boy Genius further proclaimed that he knew who this man was. In the very near future, predicted Orson Welles, Oona O'Neill would meet and marry Charlie Chaplin. Was Welles's forecast a bona fide prophecy or a damn good guess? According to British drama critic Kenneth Tynan, Welles did make the prediction. Welles himself referred to it later in a televised interview with David Frost, and when she was asked to verify the story, Oona Chaplin answered that while she did not recall the incident she supposed it could have happened. In any event, she did not want to stand in the way of a good story.[5]

Besides acquiring a stable of suitors, Oona acquired an agent, Minna Wallis. Minna, sister of producer Hal Wallis, started out as an acting coach and after tiring of the tedious efforts to train the often unspeakable in how to speak, changed careers. By the time Oona arrived in Hollywood, the former coach was at the top of her new profession. They were introduced at a Hollywood party. Whether Minna was bowled over by the young woman's looks, demeanor, and talent, or simply by her illustrious name, or by any combination of assets, is not clear. One thing is certain; Minna Wallis must have been fairly confident that she could sell Oona O'Neill. Minna arranged for a screen test with director Eugen Frenke, who was engaged in preliminary work on *The Girl from Leningrad*, a vehicle for his wife, Anna Sten. Less than a minute and a half in length, the screen test is the only record of the young Oona O'Neill on film.

Opinions of the test vary. Chaplin biographer David Robinson felt that her brief moment indicated that Oona would have been a striking screen personality. In his opinion "her radiant and fragile beauty coupled with a personality, at once diffident and eager, yielded a vivid presence."[6] Others who viewed the film were not as enthusiastic. In the screen test, despite a kerchief covering her luxurious dark hair (employed no doubt to give her a Slavic air) Oona's beauty shines forth. The babushka notwithstanding, she does not look like a peasant girl from Leningrad. If anything she resembles a starry-eyed colleen from Dublin. Although Oona has little to say, her cultivated and preppy voice resounds with the accents of Park Avenue, not the Kremlin. Eugen Frenke can be heard in the background exhorting her in heavily accented directives to do such things as turn her head and look up. In these swift recorded seconds Oona's discomfort is palpable; she is obviously self-conscious. To help overcome her anxieties, the director and at least two others speak out and try to loosen her up. "Now, come to ze front and just wait. Now, say somesink," prompts Frenke from behind the camera. "I don't know what to say," answers Oona, furrowing her brow. "Give me something," she pleads, then declares with embarrassment, "I'm sorry, OOO, I'm sorry," to which Frenke responds, "Don't be so sorry, dear." In the background a woman, (perhaps Miss Sten) begins singing in accented English, "The bells are rrrink-ink for me and my gal" and a crestfallen expression appears on Oona's face. She drops her head and sighs, "Oh gee." End of test.

When one looks at this strip of film today, disregarding its original purpose and judging it simply as a record of the young woman herself, Oona's innate sweetness, charm, and gentle diffidence shine through and provide a living document of her special appeal. As a potential actress, however, aside from her comeliness and her effulgent smile, Oona O'Neill projects little more than a youthful glow and an intense vulnerability. She had the looks, certainly, and a lovely demeanor, but whether she would have matured into a bona fide screen artist is strictly speculation.

Soon after the Frenke test, Minna Wallis came up with what she considered an ideal role for her new client and quickly set things in motion. Through her brother Hal, Minna knew Charlie Chaplin on a personal as well as professional basis. She believed that Chaplin was then at work on a film version of Paul Vincent Carroll's play, *Shadow and Substance*. The Carroll drama, a study of the conflict in faith between Bridget, an innocent young Irish servant girl, and the Reverend Canon Skerritt, a scholarly priest, had opened at the Abbey

Theatre in Dublin in 1937 and on Broadway in 1938. On Broadway, Bridget was played by the ethereal Julie Haydon. Unaware that Chaplin actually had taken a hiatus from the Carroll drama and was currently working on the screenplay for *Monsieur Verdoux*, a black comedy about a serial wife murderer, Minna telephoned one morning and urged the filmmaker to see her new discovery, a girl whom she believed would be perfect as the saintly Bridget. At that moment Chaplin was having trouble with *Verdoux* and took the agent's message as a sign that he should reconsider *Shadow and Substance*. Minna mentioned that her client was the daughter of Eugene O'Neill, a revelation which did not entirely thrill Charlie Chaplin. He had never met the playwright and later declared that from the solemnity of O'Neill's plays, he had a rather sepia impression of what the daughter would be like. Squelching his negative reaction, Chaplin asked a vital question, "Can she act?" Minna told him that Oona had done some work in summer stock and further suggested that he do a film test of her to find out. Or, if he did not want to commit himself before meeting Oona, she would invite him to dinner at her house and make sure that her client also was present. Chaplin selected the latter approach and on the appointed night went to the Wallis home. Two decades later he wrote about that evening in his autobiography:

> I arrived early and on entering the sitting room discovered a young lady seated alone by the fire. While waiting for Miss Wallis, I introduced myself, saying I presumed she was Miss O'Neill. She smiled. Contrary to my preconceived impression, I became aware of a luminous beauty with a sequestered charm and a gentleness that was most appealing.[7]

Thus did Charlie Chaplin describe Oona O'Neill at their first encounter. What she thought remains a mystery, although she was impressed enough to add an exclamatory postscript to her next letter to Carol Marcus: *"P.S. I just met Charlie Chaplin!"*

The dinner party at Minna Wallis's consisted of the agent herself, Chaplin, Oona, and Chaplin's good friend, Tim Durant. In general they bypassed business talk, but Charlie did discuss the character of Bridget, mentioning that she was very young. Eager to promote her protégé, Minna proudly announced that Oona was barely seventeen. At this disclosure Chaplin later said that his heart sank. In his opinion Bridget, though young, was complex enough to require the interpretation of an older and more experienced actress—Julie Haydon was twenty-eight years old when she portrayed Bridget on the stage—barely seventeen did not fit the bill. Chaplin professed that before the good nights were said, he had reluctantly put aside the possibility of Oona ever playing the role.

That was not the end of it, however.

As a result of his search for a screen heroine, Charlie Chaplin found his real-life heroine. As for Oona, until that evening her existence had been dominated, in absentia, by her father; now she would move under the protective shelter provided by her soon-to-be husband.

nine

THE LITTLE TRAMP

Charles Spencer Chaplin was born in London on April 16, 1889, into a childhood marked by desolation, separation, and poverty. His parents, Charles and Hannah Chaplin, were music hall performers. Though the former was a popular entertainer, drinking eventually brought down his career as it did his family life. Charlie was about two years old when his mother moved out, taking him and his older half brother, Sydney, along with her. For a while Hannah Chaplin eked out a living by performing in the music halls and, during this time, via entertainer Leo Dryden, produced two more sons (one of whom, Wheeler, later worked for Charlie in Hollywood). Charlie's early life was a constant struggle, and to the end of his days he railed against the merciless England of his childhood as a damnably cruel place. Perhaps the grimmest circumstance of his childhood was the mental condition of his adored mother. A diagnosed schizophrenic, Hannah Chaplin's erratic behavior terrified even as it grieved her son, and the specter of her madness plagued him all his life.

Entering the music hall world at the age of nine, Charlie rose through the ranks and became a member of Fred Karno's popular theatrical troupe. In the fall of 1910 the Karno entourage came to the United States and successfully toured for a year. A second tour was arranged in the fall of 1912, and this time Chaplin elected to stay in America. After signing a contract with the Keystone Film Company, Charlie began his full-time movie career in January 1914. Over the next few years he worked at various film corporations including Keystone, Essanay, and Mutual before creating his own eponymous company. Throughout his early years of film stardom, as Charlie Chaplin honed to perfection his screen image of The Little Tramp, he worked painstakingly on his *off-screen* persona as well. The distinguished white-haired, blue-eyed patrician whom Oona O'Neill met was a far cry from the bumptious comic who had made his name many years before she was born. In 1915 a visiting Englishman spent time with the young Charlie and, although thrilled to be socializing with the already famous comic, was put off by the actor's crude behavior. He reported that it was "a shock to notice the coarseness of Chaplin's table manners, his brusqueness with waiters, his cocky assumption that he was the smartest moviemaker in town."[1] Over the years Charlie succeeded in smoothing his Lambeth edges and evolved into the polished gentleman Oona O'Neill beheld. Beloved as he was on the screen, the baggy-pants comedian had a dissolute real-life reputation as a Casanova specializing in young women. Whatever his reasons were—and speculations on that point abound—there is no question that Charlie Chaplin's tastes ran to *very young* women.

His first wife, Mildred Harris, was eighteen years old when they met; Chaplin was twenty-nine. Chaplin spotted Mildred, an aspiring actress, at a beach party at the home of Samuel Goldwyn. A year later—after Mildred told Charlie she was expecting a child, they were married. That pregnancy was a lie. Subsequently Mildred did become pregnant and gave birth to a boy, whom they named Norman. Sadly, the infant was malformed and died within days. The marriage itself died not long after.

Chaplin's second wife, Lillita McMurray, met the comedian when she was six years old and her future husband was twenty-five. At their next encounter she was all of twelve, and Chaplin gave the pretty youngster a small part as an angel in his film *The Kid*. Four years later he signed her to a contract and changed her name to the more theatrically viable Lita Grey. Lita got pregnant, and threatened by the teenager's uncle who was also a lawyer, Chaplin agreed to marry her. Accompanied by Lita's mother, Charlie joined his pregnant protégé across the border to Mexico, where their relationship received the blessing of clergy. The bride was sixteen; the groom, thirty-five. Subsequently Chaplin, along with Lita and her mother, settled into a new Beverly Hills mansion on Summit Drive. Two years and two sons later, Mr. and Mrs. Charlie Chaplin officially separated—their divorce proceedings provided the paradigm of sensationalism which Eugene O'Neill's lawyer had brought to the playwright's attention during O'Neill's altercations with Agnes Boulton. Many headlines later, the Chaplins' divorce was granted with Charlie paying out the largest settlement yet recorded, a combined alimony and child support of $825,000—$125,000 more than he paid the lawyers. (Allegedly, this marriage was the inspiration for Nabokov's *Lolita*.)

The third time around the marital ring Chaplin, at age forty-three, came up with a variation on his familiar theme. True, a generation separated him and his inamorata, but twenty-one-year-old Paulette Goddard, née Marion Goddard

Levy, was not in the same minor leagues as her predecessors. The bright, vivacious Paulette already had been married and divorced when she met Charlie. She and Chaplin were rumored to have wed in 1936 in the harbor of Canton, China. Although the legality of their marriage never was entirely confirmed, Paulette Goddard was granted a divorce in 1942.

At age fifty-three Charlie Chaplin, veteran of numerous affairs and thrice-divorced, was old enough and seasoned enough, one might think, to err on the side of caution; yet he proved unable to resist and soon fell for Joan Barry, a starlet who, in this case, appeared to fit Ben Hecht's definition. Born Mary Louise Gribble in 1920, she took the surname of her stepfather, John Berry, and eventually became known as Joan Berry. After finishing high school Joan Berry came to Hollywood and, while pursuing an acting career, she became a paid companion to wealthy gentlemen—including J. Paul Getty. Introduced to Berry by his friend Tim Durant, Chaplin immediately found himself attracted to the buxom redhead; Durant was not impressed and likened her to a respectable Brooklyn stenographer. In his autobiography Chaplin described the aspiring actress as "a big handsome woman of twenty-two, well built, with upper regional domes immensely expansive." Chaplin's quaint assessment of Joan Berry's attributes are telling. Hopelessly old-fashioned in certain ways, Chaplin's prose disguised his carnal cravings and soon he became intimately involved with the young lady. Apparently, though, she was not without talent. Chaplin signed her to a contract and arranged for her to study at Max Reinhardt's acting school. The studio changed her name to "Barry," and Charlie planned to test her for the role of Bridget in *Shadow and Substance*. He believed that he had found a new star, both on and off the screen. Later Charlie claimed not to have been aware of Barry's history of mental instability, a condition aggravated by her alcoholism.

Joan Barry became a drunken liability and, among other violent acts, drove her car over Chaplin's lawn, threw mud at the windows of his home, and, brandishing a pistol, threatened to kill him. Their relationship was far too volatile for Chaplin's, and he tried to break it off. However, she would not let him get away with his usual "love-them-and-leave-them" policy; after becoming pregnant a third time (the first two had ended in abortions) she initiated a paternity suit against him. Chaplin, already under investigation by the U.S. government for alleged communist sympathies, was now further overwhelmed by the adverse publicity emanating from the Barry case. In the midst of this nightmare—bedeviled by Miss Barry, badgered by the press, and beleaguered by the government— Charlie Chaplin found Oona O'Neill, the source of his greatest happiness and the wellspring of his future.

Who contacted whom after Oona's and Charlie's initial meeting is a matter of conjecture. According to David Robinson,[2] Oona showed up unannounced at the Chaplin Studio several days after the Wallis dinner party and asked to see him. General manager Alf Reeves and cameraman Rollie Totheroh, long-standing members of Chaplin's film company, were used to young ladies coming around looking for the boss, and attempted to divert her. Reeves and Totheroh were extremely wary of admitting any girls through the gates at this time because of the legal situation with Joan Barry. If Oona did make the first move, it probably had a lot to do with Chaplin's reluctance about becoming involved with yet another very young woman. Under ordinary circumstances the screen's revered comedian never would have let someone as deliciously nubile as Oona O'Neill slip by. Meanwhile, Minna Wallis, eager to get her client before the cameras, again telephoned Chaplin—this time to ask what he intended to do about Miss O'Neill, adding that she had to know because another studio,

Fox, was very interested. Chaplin was roused to action and straightaway put Oona under contract. Once she signed, he elected to give her acting lessons. They had to spend much time together as teacher and student, and Oona soon was a regular at the Chaplin home on Summit Drive. There she became great pals with Charlie's sons by Lita Grey, Charles Chaplin Jr. and Sydney, who spent weekends with their father. Oona and Charlie Jr. were exactly the same age; Sydney was a year younger. Neither boy knew that Oona was related to the great playwright Eugene O'Neill, nor did they know of her acting aspirations. Chaplin Jr. believed that his father had met Oona at Minna Wallis's by mere coincidence, not because Minna was trying to land her client a role. Oona was different from the Hollywood lovelies who usually surrounded Chaplin, and her almost elfin quality combined with her naturalness, easy sense of humor, and lack of ostentation endeared her to his sons. "Oona O'Neill! Her name sounds like a spring breeze—as ethereal, as lovely as the girl herself," wrote Charlie Jr. Calling her attractive in an offbeat way, he described admiringly Oona's "slender, long-stemmed figure, the way she wore her straight black hair, and the brooding look in her dark eyes that could so quickly sparkle with an inward humor. She was shy and yet there was a calm about her, a native sweetness that drew Syd and me to her."[3]

Like their father, the brothers Chaplin went for Oona in a big way and in pursuit of her attention engaged in a friendly unspoken rivalry. They compared notes and agreed that each wanted to date her. Syd, however, saw that it would not happen. "We might as well lay off," he told his big brother; "Oona has eyes for Dad."[4] The boys enjoyed teasing Oona, and she reacted with the bashful good humor of a child. Yet according to Charlie Jr., just when she seemed most naive she would catch them off guard by making appropriate comments illustrating her intelligence and depth. Despite their closeness to her in age, the brothers ruefully recognized that in many ways Oona was much more mature. Their obvious regard for and interest in Oona are all the more remarkable when one considers that she became their second stepmother and that they were very devoted to the first, Paulette Goddard. Further, they had a strong allegiance to their birth mother, Lita Grey. Charlie was enchanted by Oona, although at first he would say no more than "Oh yes, she's a lovely girl." He did not need to say any more; when he spoke her name an expression came over his face that made it clear to his sons that he was as fascinated by Oona as she was by him.

On her visits to the Chaplin home, Oona often was accompanied by her mother. Aggie and Charlie had known each other for many years, and while no hard evidence exists, a rumor circulated that the two of them had had a brief affair in the past.[5] It was not altogether out of the realm of possibility. Aggie, as has been pointed out, was no saint, and when it came to sexual conquests, Charlie once bragged that he had slept with 2,000 women by the time he was fifty years old.[6] Sharing a lover with her mother certainly would add another Oedipal fillip to Oona O'Neill's story. But, *if* anything did occur between Charlie Chaplin and Agnes Boulton, it was well in the past when he met her daughter.

Once Chaplin got over the fear of being pilloried for lusting after yet another teenager, the pupil-teacher relationship quickly escalated into romance. Oona embodied just about everything Chaplin wanted in a woman; moreover, her delightful sense of humor, her steady and evenhanded way of looking at things, her shy charm, her tolerance, her beauty, her intelligence, her open adoration of him—all these qualities were contained in an irresistible seventeen-year-old girl.

And what of Oona? What was in this for her? Exactly what she was looking for. A father, a lover, a provider and protector who wanted her beside him, always. Photographs taken during this period show her looking at Chaplin with sheer worship. How the forsaken daughter must have thrilled at having this genius, this King of Comedy, look at her with love. Soon he was escorting her to restaurants and nightclubs, and gossip columnists were forecasting an upcoming fourth marriage for The Little Tramp.

Despite his overwhelming attraction to Oona, Chaplin remained understandably concerned. For one thing, the age disparity spanned a monumental thirty-six years, and more ominous than the age gap, Charlie was embroiled in the Barry paternity suit. Having to play out a love affair with someone young enough to be his granddaughter while dealing with the court case made him very nervous. He had misgivings about becoming involved. Oona did not. She was, Chaplin said, "resolute, as though she had come upon a truth."[7] Information regarding their courtship, although scant, does suggest that Oona was determined. Nothing could dissuade her from being with Chaplin, and soon enough an opportunity to move in with him presented itself.

As a youngster Oona had been subject to sore throats. Around this time she became quite ill with an upper respiratory infection and a hacking cough. Convinced that Oona required immediate and special care, Charlie informed Aggie that he was going to bring her daughter to his home, put her to bed, and call the doctor—a rather daring move in light of the Joan Barry situation. Busy with her own schedule, Aggie was quite content to have someone else take over. Charlie brought Oona to Summit Drive and announced to his servants that the young lady had tuberculosis. Extremely sick at first, Oona recovered and after regaining her health stayed on in the Paulette Goddard bedroom. Joan Barry showed up at Summit Drive one evening and in her account of events went up to Paulette's room, where (Version A) she found Chaplin, fully clothed, seated at the end of the bed on which lay a naked woman, or

(Version B) she found women's clothing in the room and ran down to the pool to accuse Chaplin. Barry later described the scene between her and Chaplin to the FBI. "Whose clothes are up there? Oona O'Neill's? Is she living here?" demanded Barry. Chaplin said, "No." "She is living here," Barry rejoined, and Chaplin answered, "It's your unsubstantiated word against mine."[8] However questionable Joan Barry's word might have been, the fact that Oona was living with Chaplin was not a well-kept secret. Indeed, Hollywood was abuzz with stories ranging from the ridiculous to the nasty. According to one tidy bit of scuttlebutt, Oona had an abortion performed on the day of her marriage. If so, she was in remarkably good shape for the ceremony.

On May 14, 1943, Oona O'Neill turned eighteen years old. Chaplin, now convinced that this special person "was not subject to the caprices of that age,"[9] decided that they belonged together and informed the press of their engagement. One New York newspaper ran a full-length picture of the bride-to-be wearing her Brearley gym suit. The photograph infuriated school administrators and delighted the student body. Eugene O'Neill read about the engagement and immediately accused his former wife of masterminding the affair. Aggie denied having any part in it and asserted that she had cautioned against the match, only to be stonewalled. "If I don't marry Charlie; if you don't give consent," Oona had argued, "I'll never marry anyone. This is going to be the love of my life."[10] Faced with Oona's overpowering certitude, Agnes yielded—at least that was the story she told the press. According to a neighbor in Point Pleasant, Aggie was tickled pink. "Oona's marrying Charlie Chaplin and he has millions," she boasted. Agnes's consent notwithstanding, Oona held a peculiar notion that her father might withhold permission, which may have been wishful thinking on her part. Whether or not Eugene O'Neill would have provided an obstacle, out of malice if not concern, the Barry case *did* pose an immediate problem. To keep Oona clear of the nasty situation, Tim Durant advised Charlie to send her back east until the paternity question was settled. Oona dismissed the suggestion, stating that she belonged at Charlie's side. Despite all the nay-saying, Oona and Charlie went ahead with their wedding arrangements—with one slight alteration. They made secret plans to elope.

Shortly after their engagement was announced, Charlie and Oona were introduced to Harold Clurman, the renowned American theater critic and director. Clurman recalled that encounter in a 1979 interview for Columbia University's Oral History Research Project: ". . . when I first met them, they were not married; they were going to be married. She was just about nineteen [*sic*] at that time, and she was one of the most beautiful women I have ever seen—a very distinguished beauty. Of course O'Neill, as you know very well, was a handsome man; and she had almost all of his features. She was extraordinarily beautiful. And I remember sitting with them in the El Morocco. We were having dinner. And I looked at her arms—beautiful arms—and I said, 'Your arms are like soft marble.' He [Chaplin] was absolutely delighted with that. He thought the phrase was as nice as the compliment."[11]

Early in June, to avoid the Barry process servers and the press, Charlie slipped out of Summit Drive and took up residence at the West Los Angeles home of Eugen Frenke and Anna Sten. Oona covertly visited Charlie there and occasionally spent the night. The Frenkes' loyalty was impressive. They provided shelter and in the process of feeding Charlie, and often Oona, used up their own ration stamps—a real sacrifice in those days of wartime shortages. On the evening of June 15, Oona went to speak to the Frenkes at their home and told them that she would be marrying Chaplin the next day. She thanked them for everything and solemnly promised that as soon as she was married she would replace all their ration coupons. According to Frenke, Oona forgot her promise and though he forgave her, his wife did not. Anna Sten wanted those coupons back.

One of the few dissenting views of Charlie and Oona's union was expressed by Georgia Hale, Chaplin's *The Gold Rush* costar and erstwhile lover. Hale asserted that Charlie's decision to marry had more to do with his desire to ameliorate the Joan Barry situation rather than any overwhelming need to wed Oona. According to Hale, Chaplin wanted to present himself as a solid citizen, and what better way than to settle down with an adoring young wife? Georgia Hale further alleged that on the very eve of his wedding Charlie came to her house, stayed until three in the morning, and begged her to leave the country with him! She said that she refused because she believed it would have been too damaging for him in his situation.[12]

The Chaplins' wedding arrangements were overseen by Charlie's friend and publicist, Harry Crocker. A columnist for the Hearst press, Crocker convinced Charlie to give Hearst the exclusive story, a natural for the newspaper chain's syndicated *doyenta*, Louella Parsons. Far better to have Parsons break the news than her arch-rival, the columnist Hedda Hopper, an ardent anti-communist who hated Charlie and had been instrumental in getting Joan Barry to go after him. On the morning of June 16, 1943, Crocker and Catharine Hunter, Chaplin's press representative, accompanied Oona and her husband-to-be to Carpinteria, a seaside town noted for its avocado groves, just south of Santa Barbara. (Later it was reported that the Office of Price Administration wanted to know where Chaplin got the gas to drive up the coast.)

The plan called for Charlie and Oona to register in Santa Barbara. At 8 A.M., thirty minutes before the normal opening time, Oona entered the Town Hall while Chaplin remained outside. A nuptial veteran, Charlie knew that a button hidden under the clerk's desk could be used to alert the media if a celebrity appeared. Thus, Oona was delegated to fill out the preliminary forms. She gave the particulars, including her name and age, and when she had finished the clerk looked up, smiled, and asked, "Now where's the young man?" Chaplin entered the room, whereupon the clerk blanched. "Well, this is a surprise!" he exclaimed as his hand slipped below the desk, seeking the concealed button. The clerk attempted to drag out the procedure, but Chaplin urged him on and he and Oona managed to get their license and depart seconds ahead of the press. According to Chaplin it was a race for life as they drove madly through Santa Barbara, slipping in and out of side streets to elude their pursuers. Within the hour, with Crocker acting as best man and Mrs. Hunter as matron of honor, Oona and Charlie were joined together as husband and wife at the home of a Carpinteria justice of the peace, Linton P. Moore. At the time of their marriage Oona O'Neill was one month past her eighteenth birthday and Charlie Chaplin was two months past his fifty-third. Reached at her home in Point Pleasant, New Jersey, the bride's mother said she was very happy about the marriage and only the fact that she had to be in New York prevented her from attending the ceremony. The bride's father refused to comment.

Oona's marriage took place during the time that Eugene O'Neill was completing revisions on *A Touch of the Poet*. The only surviving complete work from a planned eleven-play cycle, *A Touch of the Poet* explores the relationship between the protagonist, an Irish-American tavern keeper named Con Melody, and his spirited daughter, Sara. The year is 1828, the setting is New England, and the characters Con and Sara convey unmistakable echoes of Eugene O'Neill and his daughter. However, since they were the creatures of the playwright's imagination, he could exercise complete control of their destinies—even granting them quasi-sympathetic discourses. His feelings about his real daughter's marriage were expressed in a letter to his friend Agnes Brennan, written three days after the wedding:

> You, of course, have read of the latest antics of my daughter, Oona, and I am sure you share my opinion of them. The young lady and I severed relations some time ago—because of many things. When she was here with us—two years ago—she appeared to be developing into an intelligent, charming girl. But in New York with her mother to advise her, she suddenly changed into a silly, cheap publicity grabber. That Stork Club glamour girl racket—a phony advertising-the-Club-affair—went to her head. She couldn't see that all they wanted was to use her news value as my daughter, and didn't give a damn about her. That has been her line ever since—using "O'Neill's daughter" to get any kind of display no matter how vulgar and stupid—and finally ending up in this typical Hollywood scandal and marriage with a man as old as I am (probably older, for what actor gives out his real age). Of course, he's rich and that is the answer, or one of the answers. I need not tell you, I know, that you are never going to hear of our entertaining Mr. and Mrs. Chaplin, or of their entertaining us. Enough is enough![13]

O'Neill attempted to work things out for Con and Sara in his play, but he was unwilling to do the same for himself and Oona. Never at any point did he temper his displeasure at his daughter's actions with a modicum of parental understanding; he simply grabbed onto her marriage, combined it with the leftover gossip from her café society days and fashioned the whole into a puritanical truth about her character that worked to his advantage. Finding it far easier to steer the blame toward Agnes, which he did, and to write off Oona, which he also did, Eugene O'Neill never again saw or spoke to his only daughter, nor did he ever refer to his son-in-law. Correspondingly, although Charlie Chaplin once confided to his friend, actor/director Norman Lloyd, that he thought Oona's father was a "rather boring writer," he rarely mentioned the playwright.

Long before his fourth and final marriage, Charlie Chaplin said in an interview, "I want a wife who is restful, but who knows that an artist lives more passionately, more deeply, with more seeking for life and truth and beauty than any man in the world—and who can respond to that."[14] Young as she was, Oona O'Neill fit the bill perfectly. After nearly two generations of erratic erotic relationships, Charlie Chaplin found his heartsease. And after nearly two decades of neglect in some form or other, Oona O'Neill found her haven. No matter how many times she repudiated the implication that Chaplin was a father replacement, whether consciously or unconsciously, Oona had sought a person whose fame and influence matched and possibly exceeded that of Eugene Gladstone O'Neill. She found him, and in so doing put herself in the unique position of being daughter to one genius and wife to another.

PART

TWO

ten

"I AM SO HAPPY"

FORMER LOCAL GIRLS [*sic*]WEDS CHARLIE CHAPLIN

Radio and newspapers reported the news of the marriage of Miss Ona O'Neil [*sic*], 18-year-old daughter of Playwright Eugene and Agnes Boulton O'Neil, to Charlie Chaplin, Wednesday morning. The marriage, according to reports, was performed Tuesday. Mrs. Chaplin, who is the fourth wife of the screen comedian, formerly resided in Point Pleasant Borough and attended local schools. She was recently voted the Glamor Girl of 1943.

In announcing Oona's marriage, the *Point Pleasant Leader* misspelled the bride's first and last names and the headline typo suggested that Chaplin wed not one but a bevy of local maidens. Other reports of the marriage were less ingenuous. *LIFE* magazine published a full-page photograph of the groom slipping the ring on the bride's finger, while in another picture the camera caught the two of them leaving the town hall hand-in-hand. Chaplin, wearing a double-breasted gray suit, looks down and beneath his gray homburg grins from ear to ear. Oona, her long hair framing her face, stares right at the camera and smiles openly and happily. The hem of her simple V-neck dress is knee-length, and her gorgeous legs are very much in evidence. Although Oona looks older and Charlie appears sprightly, if the circumstances were not known the picture could be assumed to be that of father and daughter.

Oona O'Neill was presumed to have married for money and power and was cast, by some observers, in the unflattering role of a gold digger who had found her sugar daddy. Drawing on reports that Charlie had been treated with monkey glands, Jerry Salinger, Oona's former beau, wrote her a scathing, scatological letter describing in disgusting detail his version of the Chaplins' wedding night, which pictured Chaplin leaping around the bedroom waving his prostate.[1] The letter was offensive, but the writer's ire might have had more to do with Oona's spurning of him as a suitor than anything else. Even Oona's strongest critics—and save for her father there were relatively few of those—could not fit her into the role of a money-mad madcap for long. After all, she had had a number of well-to-do admirers. "The charming Miss O'Neill," noted a contemporary article, "could make her debut in society and marry one of the wealthy young blades who have been fascinated by her demure self-possession, her large brown eyes, her beautiful complexion and her lovely curves."[2] Oona basked in the attention but had her eye on something else; consciously or subconsciously she wanted a mate who was a contender in an arena dominated by Eugene O'Neill, and just any wealthy young blade did not make the grade.

Although Oona herself pooh-poohed the idea that she was looking for a father substitute, undeniable signs indicated that the theory hovered in the psychological background. Aware of the way many people stared with puzzlement, first at her and then at her husband as though trying to figure out whether they were happy together or just putting up a good front, Oona always maintained that she never thought about Charlie's age except at "the annual shock" of his birthday. No matter how others viewed them, Oona stated that her security and stability came not from Charlie's wealth but from the very difference in their ages. "Only young women who have married mature men will know what I mean," she concluded.[3] Oona both denied and cited the generation gap, and if it is true as reported that she called her husband "Pops,"[4] the Oedipus/ Electra case cannot be rested. Charlie Chaplin's reasons for marrying Oona seemed clear. She was beautiful, intelligent, and *young*. Years later Chaplin told Lita Grey that one of his reasons might have surprised the public. All his life, he told his former wife, he had been searching for *identity*. If he ever found it, he solemnly declared, it would be because of Oona.[5]

Following the wedding Chaplin rented a house in Santa Barbara, and for the next eight weeks, miraculously, the couple's whereabouts remained a secret. During those two months husband and wife enjoyed a tranquil existence. They sat without speaking for hours, took long walks in the evening, and in the process the pattern of their marriage, one of mutual veneration and awesome affinity, was set. Occasionally overwhelmed by the feeling that the acrimony and the hate of a whole nation were upon him and convinced that his film career was finished, Chaplin would become depressed. At those trying times Oona lifted his spirits as she would do for the rest of his life. Among other comforting acts she read aloud to him from George DuMaurier's *Trilby*. Both of them were amused by the orotund prose of the novel in which Trilby, a young girl, comes under the influence of the forceful Svengali, a hypnotist who dominates her life by forcing her into a singing career, which he controls. Were they conscious of any parallels to their own lives in DuMaurier's far-fetched story of the commanding male and the docile female? Apparently not. Anyway, Oona already had decided that being Mrs. Charles Chaplin was all she wanted. The screen test for *The Girl from Leningrad* was the beginning and end of her film career, and "without a regret" she gave up acting. Charlie said that if she had chosen to pursue a vocation he would not have interfered; yet he was pleased at Oona's decision and proudly declared that at long last he had a wife and not a career girl. Was it a sacrifice? Probably not. Oona's interest in acting may have had more to do with impressing her father than with a driving ambition to perform. Her choice centered on a discipline in which O'Neill excelled; furthermore, he had left her mother (and her) for an *actress*.

Like Carlotta Monterey, Oona allied herself with an ultra-industrious man who craved domestic serenity. Indeed, in her married life she would play a somewhat comparable role with Charlie to the one Carlotta took with O'Neill. In a study of the relationship between Oona and her father, Boston psychiatrist Lora Heims Tessman theorized that Oona *preserved* the very father who left her by marrying and catering to another tormented genius whose history of separation anxiety from his mother and whose compellingly sad eyes had uncanny echoes of O'Neill.[6] Father and husband demanded quietude at home, but an important difference between O'Neill and Chaplin made life with the latter a more bearable experience. Ella O'Neill was aloof; Hannah Chaplin was loving. Bleak as his childhood may have been, Charlie at least had had a mother who doted on him.[7] Unable to console and comfort her father, Oona married Charlie and assumed the role she had yearned for all her young life—helpmate to the great man. Her emotions and needs were unchanged; they simply were transferred to a willing replacement figure.

*   *   *

The honeymoon ended; Charlie and Oona left Santa Barbara and settled in at Summit Drive. While he returned to the business of making movies, she took up her position as Mrs. Charlie Chaplin, a role already well defined but, until Oona, not well filled. Part Eden, part Gomorrah, and totally fascinating, Oona Chaplin's new home, Hollywood, was the amusement capital of the world. In that palm-treed paradise movie stars lived splendidly, splashing in private pools, smacking tennis balls on private courts, wining, dining, and dancing in exclusive nightclubs, and then, arising with the dawn, performing their magic behind walled studios. Like ancient Egypt, Hollywood had its Old, Middle, and New Kingdoms. The Old (Silent) yielded to the Middle (Talkies) in the early thirties, and the New (Technological) Kingdom arose in the early fifties when filmmakers tried to best the demon television by going bigger and deeper via CinemaScope, Cinerama, and 3-D. Oona O'Neill arrived in town at the peak of the Middle Kingdom and had married the most illustrious citizen of the Old Kingdom. The Second World War created a distinctive Hollywood bloc composed of European refugees who had fled from the advancing Nazis and found their way to Southern California. Distinguished émigrés, such as Thomas Mann, Lion Feuchtwanger, Otto Fenichel, Arnold Schoenberg, and Hanns Eisler, were exactly the kinds of persons with whom the erstwhile Little Tramp liked to associate. Soon Charlie Chaplin's house at 1085 Summit Drive became a gathering place for intellectuals and artists.

In the early twenties, at the urging of his friends Mary Pickford and Douglas Fairbanks Sr., Chaplin had purchased six acres of land on a slope overlooking the town of Beverly Hills just above Harold Lloyd's estate and just below the Fairbanks' showcase, Pickfair. Gardeners turned the barren property, formerly the stomping grounds of rabbits and coyotes, into a forest of hemlock, cedar, spruce, fir, and pine. At the top of the hill was built a seemingly impregnable tile-roofed yellow fortress combining modern Spanish and Basque architecture outside and dashes of Oriental within. In this baronial mansion Chaplin had lived and entertained like royalty for twenty years. Now, joined by his fourth consort, he would continue that reign for another decade.

Three of Chaplin's four wives—Lita Grey, Paulette Goddard, and Oona O'Neill—inhabited the house. Besides Charlie himself, all three had something in common—undependable fathers. Paulette and Oona had particularly troubled relationships with their fathers. Joseph Levy had deserted his daughter, Paulette, and subsequently she, like Oona, preferred the company of older men. "When you have been abandoned by your father," commented Celestine Wallis, a close friend of the actress, "it is a very great thing to have men desire you, to prove to yourself that it wasn't your fault."[8] In this respect Oona O'Neill's and Paulette Goddard's case histories definitely meshed.

The story is told of a woman seated between William Gladstone and Benjamin Disraeli at a dinner party in nineteen-century London. Asked the next day what she thought of the prime ministers, the woman replied that Mr. Gladstone had discoursed dazzlingly on a variety of subjects, "convincing me," she told her interrogator, "that he must be the most brilliant conversationalist in the world." And what of Disraeli? "Oh," smiled the lady, "Mr. Disraeli spent most of the time questioning me, and by the end of the evening had me believing that I was the most brilliant conversationalist in the world." While definitely of the Gladstone school, Charlie Chaplin had a dash of the Disraeli and took great pleasure in playing Pygmalion to his roster of espoused Galateas. Paulette Goddard, in fact, credited him with molding her intellect. "Charlie was a great talker. He loved an audience and would hold forth on every subject in the world. We used to play 'pass the evening,' doing little three-minute speeches. He trained me so I was able to speak for three minutes on any subject. But not four. Not one minute longer. Any subject. He just threw it at me. It is a lovely game. And that's the way I learned everything I know."[9]

Chaplin dominated everything and everyone around him, and most people believed that included his fourth wife. Others disagreed. "Charlie wanted the best for Oona," explained Norman Lloyd. "He truly believed that *he* knew what was best. Oona went along with it, but willingly, and that's not domination." Carol Matthau regarded the relationship with Chaplin as a necessity for Oona but felt that a certain part of her friend had to remain dormant because Charlie had to be number one. Howsoever friends interpreted their union, Oona recognized and happily acceded to her husband's sovereignty. Why not? His loving authoritarianism must have provided a welcome antidote to her father's utter neglect.

A confirmed workaholic, Chaplin went about his tasks in a manner his eldest son described as a "ruthless sacrifice of all other interests, family included, to an inexorable rush of creativity which peaked and then crashed," leaving Chaplin drained and his family disaffected. That overwhelming, inwardly directed concentration was especially hard on his wives. It made their lives difficult and lonely, for, as Charlie Jr. noted, "with a genius in the house you can't expect an atmosphere of sustained normalcy."[10] Left to their own devices, Mildred Harris and Lita Grey proved too young and inexperienced to cope and grew bored with being hearth-bound. "I couldn't live with a genius," Mildred explained to the press. And, although Paulette Goddard was able and willing to enjoy the pleasures of sitting at home reading and musing, she, too, liked to kick up her heels. Unlike her predecessors, the fourth Mrs. Chaplin wanted to concentrate solely on her husband.

Oona O'Neill, her character already tempered by the vicissitudes of life with a great man, was uniquely equipped for her marriage—even his former wives had good things to say about her. In Paulette Goddard's opinion Oona profoundly understood Chaplin, and that understanding would make a whole new life for the man whom Goddard continued to refer to as enchanting, captivating, fascinating, and sweet.[11] Oona's independence may have been nipped in the bud, but in its place came a searing togetherness that anchored her. Furthermore, if she was a *prisoner*, 1085 Summit Drive was no Chateau d'If, and the warden was an adoring and indulgent husband, not a jailer. Imagine the fun of being young, beautiful, smart, beloved, in love, famous, and rich—a heady place for an eighteen-year-old. For a long time Oona wallowed in the sheer joy of being Mrs. Charles Spencer Chaplin.

"I am so happy now—Charlie is a wonderful man," Oona declared in a chatty letter to Jim Delaney dated August 17, 1943. Her absolute delight at being Mrs. Chaplin is immediately evident. "What do you think of the name at the top of the page!" she wrote, calling attention to her personalized stationery. In the correspondence Oona went on to explain that she and Charlie did not go out much, perhaps to a movie or to the Hollywood Bowl for a concert, but basically they stayed at home. She also confided that she had given up her movie career even though things were starting to break for her. She had lost interest in acting and planned to pick up where she left off in her education by taking courses at UCLA. The past year had been a waste of time, the eighteen-year-old solemnly declared, but not really a waste because she had met Charlie. He was working day and night on the script for *Monsieur Verdoux* and, Oona proudly announced, was so completely caught up that he would not eat or sleep if *she* did not force him to.

Oona was besotted with her husband. In his presence, reported Charles Jr., a rapt expression would come into her eyes. "She would sit quietly, hanging on his every word. Most women are charmed by Dad, but in Oona's case it was different. She worshipped him, drinking in every word he spoke, whether it was about his latest script, the weather or some bit of philosophy. She seldom spoke, but every now and then she would come up with one of those penetrating remarks that impressed even our father with her insight."[12] Charlie Chaplin provided intellectual and emotional tonic for Oona. He had the power to interest and stimulate her mind, and perhaps most important, he could make her laugh—and that shared pleasure cannot be underestimated. Oona loved to laugh and with Charlie inspiring her she did so, often and heartily. He actively tried to make her happy, and his aim to please played directly into her exuberant sense of fun and her craving for attention. Chaplin's talent to amuse permeated their relationship; he never tired of entertaining his young bride, nor did she ever seem to tire of his antics. He screened his old movies for her, and one always must bear in mind that howsoever Charlie Chaplin comes across off screen, on screen he was sublime. Oona viewed most of his films for the first time and then watched them again and again, reacting with the same uninhibited glee at each showing.

Charlie's efforts were not limited to screening film clips, either. On one occasion he took Oona to a jewelry shop in Beverly Hills, and while waiting for her vanity case to be repaired they looked at some bracelets. Oona particularly admired a diamond and ruby piece but thought the price too high, so another tray was brought out. Advising the jeweler that he would think about the bracelet, Charlie led Oona out of the store. They got into the car, and as Oona slid in behind the wheel, Charlie cried, "Hurry up. Drive on quickly!" The car took off and Charlie reached into his pocket and slowly brought forth the bracelet that Oona had admired. He told her that he had taken it while she was looking at other jewelry. She turned pale, said, "Oh, you shouldn't have done it!" and pulled the car over to the curb. "Let's think it over," she told him. Unable to keep a straight face, Charlie burst into laughter and told her that while she was distracted he had taken the jeweler aside and bought the bracelet. "And you," he said, "thinking I'd stole it, were willing to be an accessory to the crime." "Well, I didn't want to see you get into any more trouble," she answered.[13]

At his first meeting with the new Mrs. Chaplin, Alistair Cooke was struck by Oona's beauty and charm, and—noting that she wore a plain sweater, a plaid skirt, and white *bobby socks*—her youth. The disparity in the Chaplins' ages also was remarked upon by Oona's contemporaries. Irving Berlin's daughter, Mary Ellin Barrett, two years behind Oona at Brearley, recalled a party at Samuel Goldwyn's house attended by Charlie Chaplin and his girl-bride. "With his wavy gray hair, Chaplin seemed even older than my black-haired father (they were both fifty-seven); an old man married to a girl more or less my age. I did not see that he was a sexy, dangerous fellow. I was shocked, and even more so when, during the after-dinner movie, the two of them held hands and snuggled."[14] The age difference, so noticeable in their physical appearance, seemed less conspicuous in the ways in which Oona dealt with Charlie. Oona long had exhibited a maturity beyond her years; one Brearley friend defined her schoolmate as being someone who was born "knowing the ways of the world. When she's with a man of sixty, you'd think he was twenty-five and she was sixty, she manages things so well." Oona's noteworthy composure was remarked upon by the actress/writer Salka Viertel, who found the young Mrs. Chaplin as beautiful and poised as a Goya princess.[15]

Like the fabled Beauty who lived in the Beast's castle where all needs and desires were met by invisible servants, the youthful bride found herself free from any demands. Unseen hands were in control, leaving her with nothing to do; consequently she lived like a guest in her own home—hardly surprising when one considers that Charlie himself lived there in much the same manner. The Chaplin Film Corporation owned 1085 Summit Drive, and everything related to its administration was handled through the studio. (One ripple in the smooth operation of Summit Drive occurred shortly before Oona moved in. Chaplin had been attended by a superb staff of Japanese servants upon whom he relied totally. When the war in the Pacific began, the staff was sent to relocation camps for the duration. Various new employees were hired to fill in, and not all of them were loyal. Some leaked stories to the press about Charlie's sexual escapades—when the unmarried Oona lived at 1085, one maid reputedly threatened to tell the newspapers unless Charlie paid her off. This story gave rise to yet another tale suggesting that Charlie opted to marry Oona simply to get the blackmailer off his back.) Alf Reeves, general manager of the Chaplin Film Corporation, also acted as managing director of the Chaplin household, and disbursements for Summit Drive emanated from Reeves's office via his secretary. She, in turn, took a stern proprietary interest in the care and maintenance of Mr. Chaplin's residence, even questioning the charges for an excessive number of telephone calls to a certain Santa Monica number. The calls were made to Carol Marcus Saroyan, with whom Oona talked for hours on end; she needed to talk to someone, because other than being with her husband when he was available, she had much time on her hands.

In an effort to protect the sanctity of his fourth marriage and to provide Oona with some kind of companionship in his absence, Charlie asked his cousin, Betty Chaplin Tetrick, to act as a sort of big sister for his new wife. Married to Ted Tetrick, a Hollywood costumier and producer who worked with Charlie, the vivacious Betty, ten years Oona's senior, was lively and youthful in her outlook and, most important, someone whom

Charlie could trust. Oona and Betty clicked. Oona called her cousin "Betty Boop," which evolved into "Boopsy," and together they gadded about the city. Although Oona could be out with her all day, Betty felt that Charlie kept his wife on a ball and chain, although a gilded one. In time Oona tried to remove some of the shackles.

She had entered into marriage with little in the way of personal possessions—everything in the house belonged to Charlie; the bedroom she occupied, decorated by the third Mrs. Chaplin, still was referred to as Paulette Goddard's suite. In a move to establish her presence, Oona had bookcases installed in her bedroom and filled them to overflowing. Simply having her books around inspired her and made her feel better. After the first small step was taken, Oona went further. "Boopsy, I want to take charge," she announced to Betty Tetrick one day; "I don't want the studio running my life. I want to pay the bills. This isn't going to be a hotel anymore; this is going to be our home." Oona's declaration of independence at 1085 did not please the interested parties at the Chaplin Film Corporation; they were used to calling the shots. Reeves's secretary was particularly miffed when Oona asked to see the household bills and only reluctantly allowed the young bride to view them.

Oona quietly asserted herself in different minor ways, and her triumphs continued to be behind-the-scenes, small-scale domestic coups of the bookcase kind. For example, Chaplin always had worn button-top shoes (probably because they were a sign of elegance when he was a child) and no one, not even Paulette Goddard who tried for years, could get him to change his hopelessly old-fashioned footwear. Oona, too, found them quaint, and soon after he began seeing her Chaplin's button-tops vanished. He updated his personal appearance for her and, eventually, even modernized his castle. The heavy old furniture was scuttled and his sacrosanct Teutonic bedroom was lightened up. Most surprising, he parted with the pipe organ which had been installed in the cathedral-like vestibule when the house was built. Like the swimming pool, pipe organs became a status symbol among silent film stars and were a popular addition to many majestic Hollywood homes. The King of Comedy, however, was one of the few stars able to play the king of instruments and so loved his musical white elephant that it came as a great shock when Oona convinced him to have it taken away. According to Charlie, he agreed to this and other wishes because, for the first time in his life, he was secure in a woman's love. "If only I had known Oona or a girl like her long ago," he told Norman Lloyd, "I would never have had any problems with women." But he did have his problems.[16]

On October 2, 1943, Joan Barry gave birth to a daughter whom she named Carol Ann. About one month later Oona Chaplin became pregnant, and during her pregnancy, Charlie was brought to trial. Blood tests proved that Chaplin was not the father of the Barry child, and on April 4, 1944, he was found not guilty of violating the Mann Act, a 1910 statute prohibiting the transportation of women across state lines for immoral purposes. Oona heard the news over the radio and, overcome with relief, swooned. That evening she and Charlie celebrated his victory with a quiet dinner together. After dinner Oona made a couple of stiff gin and tonics, and the two of them sat together by the fire. Normally Chaplin was not a drinker; he knew what alcohol had done to his father and stayed clear, but he was not a teetotaler, and this was a special occasion. Unfortunately their tribulations were not over. Within eight months Charlie would be brought to court again. The first trial had cleared him only of violating the Mann Act; despite the blood tests, he had yet to face the paternity charges. Meanwhile, to avoid all the publicity and furor, he decided to get out of town.

At the end of May, Chaplin took Oona back east for a well-deserved rest. He rented an isolated cottage in Nyack, New York, where he intended to stay for at least six months, long enough for Oona to have the baby on the East Coast. But away from his studio and his associates, Chaplin could not concentrate on his work and in little over a month took Oona back to Los Angeles. Four weeks later, on August 1, 1944, their first child, Geraldine, was born. Chaplin, jubilant at fathering a daughter, also commented that his joy was diminished somewhat by the ongoing Barry trial and that he was further saddened because Oona's little girl had to start life under the cloud of scandal.

The second Barry trial opened in December 1944; the jury failed to agree and a retrial was ordered, which opened in April 1945. Since blood tests were not admissible as evidence in California state courts at this time, the verdict went in favor of the plaintiff. Named as father of a little girl whose blood type did not match his own, the comedian was ordered to pay child support for Carol Ann until she reached legal age. Chaplin unsuccessfully petitioned for a retrial. After years of bitter contesting, the Barry case, an obvious miscarriage of justice, was closed.

eleven

A MARRIAGE WELL IN HAND

During Oona's first years of marriage, the pall that the Barry affair created paled in comparison to the far more ominous and consequential cloud of the Second World War. A tireless worker for peace, Charlie Chaplin made speeches and contributed money to that cause even as his sons went into the armed services. Shipped overseas with the 89th Infantry Division, Charlie Jr., save for one direct personal letter, heard from his father through Oona. Charlie Chaplin rarely if ever wrote to any of his children. However, no comparisons should be made to Eugene O'Neill. O'Neill was an inveterate correspondent and, excluding his children, wrote to many people; Chaplin, as a rule, did not write letters but occasionally dictated them.

Discharged in February 1946, the junior Chaplin returned to Hollywood where he found his eighteen-month-old half sister, Geraldine, scampering around the house, his stepmother

Oona near term in her second pregnancy, and his father, looking exactly the same, working on the script of *Monsieur Verdoux*. A month later, on March 7, 1946, Oona gave birth to a son, Michael. Photographs of this time show her looking more like an older sister or baby-sitter, playing on the lawn with the first two of what ultimately would be eight children. The unusually large number is even more remarkable when one considers that Chaplin began this family at the age of fifty-four.

Oona's many pregnancies generated much speculation. Who wanted all those children? Did Charlie want to prove his virility and keep his wife "down on the farm," or did Oona either want to make up for her own aborted family life or perhaps compensate for having married someone many years her senior? Most friends felt that the passion for a large family came from Oona and that Charlie, who was known to have an abhorrence of contraceptives, went along. (A 1998 interview with the youngest Chaplin offspring, Chris, quoted Oona as saying that "she wouldn't be happy until she'd had seven children. She loved children and enjoyed being the matriarchal lynchpin of a large family. But I suspect I was an accident.")[1] At any rate, Oona obviously was thrilled at churning out children, and Charlie remained pleased. In a 1959 interview, still one shy of the final count, Chaplin declared that he never got impatient having them around and that far from disturbing him in his work, their youthful merriment was an asset. He and Oona found them amusing and enjoyed their company; however, they could be "very irritating, too." At this point Chaplin waggled his finger at the interviewer and added, "But get this, our happiness is not governed by the children. We would be just as happy—just Oona and I."[2]

During the decade that Oona spent in Hollywood her time was wrapped up in her husband, in her children and in presiding over the household. In the competitive film community

Oona's youthful loveliness endeared her to women as well as men; at one dinner party Greta Garbo said to Charlie, "I think your wife is beautiful, Charlie Chaplin." Her beauty notwithstanding, Oona also demonstrated an ability to make people feel welcome and relaxed in her presence—and, more crucial, in the presence of her illustrious husband. In the past Chaplin's friends had gathered at 1085 Summit Drive on Sunday afternoons for quiet English teas, but by the time Oona came into his life Charlie's passion for the game of tennis had accelerated and the staid tea ceremonies were superseded by lively tennis parties. Chaplin grew increasingly sociable, and intimates believed that Oona, not tennis, was the source of this new gregariousness. Sunday Open House became one of Hollywood's hottest tickets, and an invitation to join the Chaplins was analogous to receiving a royal summons in England. Summit Drive bulged with literati and glitterati from Noel Coward and Thomas Mann to Evelyn Waugh and Albert Einstein. (Told about the weekend gatherings, Paulette Goddard dryly commented that she could not believe Charlie was spending money on food for strangers, even if they were talented.) No matter how famous the guest list, when Charlie entered the scene everyone rushed to his side. People hung on his every word, and no one listened more intently or more eagerly than Oona.

Given the often quixotic nature of the guest list, Oona had many opportunities to demonstrate her skills as a hostess. On one occasion Shelley Winters drove over in the company of the Welsh poet Dylan Thomas. The inebriated Thomas managed to commandeer the car from the actress and steered it onto the Chaplin tennis court, right into the net. Unfazed, he got out and, followed by the mortified Ms. Winters, staggered up the path to the house. "Oona O'Neill Chaplin stood at the front door, very pregnant and very amused," Winters recalled years later. "She could see how upset I was, but she still greeted Dylan warmly and kissed me, saying, 'Don't worry. No damage.' "[3] With a minimum of fuss Oona arranged for someone to back the car out into the street and fix the net as she steered the drunken poet into an armchair and fortified him with a cup of black coffee—thereby saving the day for the embarrassed young actress, not to mention the tipsy Welshman.

Oona's tact was combined with a fierce loyalty: she stood by her friends. For example, she had great regard for Bill Tilden; the former tennis champion was down and out on his luck in Beverly Hills and a constant at the Chaplin household. Charlie invited the fallen sports idol to teach on the Chaplin tennis court and paid him to give Oona lessons. When Jim Delaney had tried to teach the game to Oona back in Point Pleasant, he had used Bill Tilden's lesson book. Oona gleefully wrote Delaney to say that she was being taught by the man himself! Nor, she added, was the impatient Tilden as good a teacher as Jim.[4] Not long after Oona Chaplin's lessons began, Bill Tilden was jailed for molesting a boy, and while most of the Hollywood community quickly disassociated themselves, the Chaplins came to his aid. Kathy Parrish, a friend and fellow tennis enthusiast who had introduced the Chaplins to Tilden, believed that Oona actually urged Charlie to help. Afraid to appear at the prison himself, Charlie sent Oona to see the former tennis star. She did her best, but Tilden wanted to handle things his way—the wrong way, as it turned out. He never extricated himself from his ignominious doings, and in 1953 the onetime golden boy of tennis died alone and impoverished in a cheap motel off Olympic Boulevard.

Kathy and her husband, actor-director Robert Parrish, were frequent guests at the Chaplins and very involved in the Summit Drive tennis tournaments. Oona liked tennis but did not have Charlie's absolute ardor for the game; he had enough enthusiasm for both of them. During the finals of a ladies' singles match Oona played against Talli Wyler, wife of film director William Wyler, in a game that went on and on. Charlie watched from the balcony and rooted passionately for Oona, so passionately that he put on a show, leaping with joy when Oona made a good shot, and then dropping to the floor in a faint when she missed. Charlie, the spectator, cavorted so vividly that everyone watched him instead of the two women struggling in the hot sun.[5] Chaplin never shied away from taking center stage, not even from his beloved wife. Then again, Oona willingly yielded the spotlight. Whether it was a tennis match or an intellectual discussion, she remained far more comfortable basking in her husband's glory than promoting anything of her own.

The English author Christopher Isherwood met Charlie during the filming of *The Great Dictator* and, at first, was quite taken with the comedian and found Charlie's ability to laugh at his own jokes endearing. Isherwood thought that Charlie retained all the gaiety and snap of a cheeky, cocky East End boy—he was not simply being funny for a living, but really enjoyed himself and constantly wooed everyone with his antics. Later the writer became disenchanted, and writing of a dinner with the Chaplins in December 1944, Isherwood lamented that Charlie had become an opinionated, elderly club-bore Englishman. "He talked about the war, bullfighting, politics, and everything he said was silly—until he began to act it out: his gestures are so much more intelligent than his conversation. He was very funny describing his new Bluebeard picture, and taking off his jacket to show us how to make passes at a bull. His wife Oona, who looks about sixteen, scarcely spoke, but I had the impression that she has the marriage well in hand. 'Eat your soup,' she told Charlie in the midst of one of his performances."[6]

Christopher Isherwood could afford to change his opinion of Charlie, but Oona Chaplin could not. Her husband's greatness had to remain fixed. Anyway, Isherwood probably bore a bit of a grudge. In a well-circulated story he reportedly passed out on a sofa in the Chaplins' living room and urinated all over himself and the furniture. Oona took charge, got fresh clothing for the sodden writer, had the couch washed down, and never mentioned the incident, which nevertheless immediately hit the rumor mill. Isherwood denied the event and wrote in his diary, "I shall never believe I did this, because I've never done such a thing before or since." In a later entry in his diary, along with another put-down of Charlie, he got off a shot at Oona by writing that she and Charlie were offended when Dylan Thomas told someone "to go and fuck [his] bloody eyebrows." "This greatly displeased the Chaplins," wrote Isherwood, "especially Oona who is prudish." That adjective does not fit the Oona Chaplin described by most friends; shy, reserved, quiet, yes, but prudish seems to be a singular interpretation on the part of Christopher Isherwood.

During the Hollywood years the people with whom Oona socialized were her husband's peers or near contemporaries and almost always years older than she. Invariably the youngest of the group, Oona maintained a steady composure and did not seem to get ruffled. The aura of calmness surrounding her provided a welcome counterbalance to Charlie's volatility. Many times she mediated when her husband's relationships hit snags, seeing to it that problems, instead of festering, were quickly resolved. Chaplin recognized and prized his wife's sensitivity and stability. She's so sensible, he told friends, and that sensibility stood her in good stead, for as noted by his previous wives and his children, living with Charlie Chaplin was not all sunshine. Like her father, Oona's husband was subject to frequent spells of moodiness during which he became unusually quiet and withdrawn. These moods could be brought about by almost anything, even a newspaper article; but basically the clouds descended when he felt deserted by the creative muse, a misery he likened to being "bound hand and foot in some dark dungeon of the mind."[7] One Chaplin biographer took *moody* up a few notches and suggested that Charlie suffered from bipolar, or manic, depression.[8] Morose and temperamental, Charlie's angers were quick and intense, yet no matter what afflictions and/or dispositions overtook him, his love for Oona remained steadfast.

Befitting his genius status, Charlie's mood swings were expected and accepted by family, friends, and associates; less acknowledged were Oona's desperate moments. Her placid conduct was consistent, yet as far back as her early teens her inability to discuss upsetting subjects, the darkness that could come over her, had been noticed. Friends found Oona's flashes of despondency unnerving. "You never knew whether it was something someone had said, or something she was carrying around with her, but a kind of cloud would descend and it would get very somber and Irish and you had to wait for it to pass," Norman Lloyd's wife, Peggy, observed years later in an interview. Oona never could shake off the Irish in her, but under the sheltering wing of her husband the dark side remained in check. And if Oona's melancholy had its roots in her heritage, so too did her passion.

Surprisingly, considering her youth and beauty and her husband's obvious dedication, Oona became upset when Charlie noticed anyone else. At one party he spoke for a long time to another woman, and Oona confessed her apprehension to Peggy Lloyd. "Maybe when I'm fifty-five and Charlie's ninety, I won't be jealous anymore," confided Oona. "But, you know what?" she added softly, "I think I still will be."

Despite the grandeur of her new life, the vast estate, the servants, the cars, and the money, Oona did not lose her down-to-earth quality, one that her husband, for all his posturing, seemed to share. She loved beautiful clothes and jewelry and Charlie showered her with gifts, yet Oona could be very casual about her dress and her possessions. She would throw on one of Charlie's sweaters or jackets and go to a Beverly Hills ice cream parlor with Betty Tetrick. "People would stare and whisper, Why that's Charlie Chaplin's wife. What on earth is she wearing?" remembered Betty. On one occasion Charlie presented Oona with a strand of magnificent pearls, and thinking them too long Oona nonchalantly hiked up the necklace with a safety pin and went out for the evening. As far as her wardrobe was concerned, the bobby sox ensembles were fazed out as Oona's clothes-horse tendencies went from a mild trot to a full gallop. Right after they were married Charlie bought her a mink coat, which so excited her she practically wore it to bed. Charlie liked the coat too, and according to Oona would slip it on and walk around in it.[9] Oona dressed simply, if expensively, was not a slave to style, and remained as comfortable in a peasant blouse, a dirndl skirt, and sandals as she was in couturier outfits.

In Hollywood the prevailing method of child rearing followed the British example. You were supposed to love your dogs and horses, but children were another story. You had a child and then appeared at a party a week or two later and never mentioned it. Oona did not go along with the preferred method. Nannies were employed, of course, yet Oona loved having her children around and talked about them a great deal. One time, during an impromptu visit from the Lloyds, Oona chatted for a while and then suddenly stood up and said, teary-eyed, "I'm so sorry, I just can't stay here anymore. You'll have to excuse me. The baby has a fever and I must go upstairs and be with her." Nor was this an isolated incident, acquaintances and friends witnessed many such moments when Oona would leave parties in order to fuss over her brood.

Charlie, too, loved the children, but in his own way— which was distant and had a definite Victorian bent. As with his peer relationships, Oona often had to intercede to offset Charlie's strictness with the children, and he *was* strict. One time he and Norman Lloyd were in the library when young Michael came into the room dragging his sweater behind him. Charlie lost his temper and began shouting. "You pick that up!" he cried. "People had to work hard to earn money to buy that sweater, and you drag it on the floor!" He was severe; Oona was protective. She wanted her children to have a better start emotionally than either she or Charlie had experienced. Her protectiveness, however, was generally of a passive nature; she did not plead her children's causes directly, nor did she need to in many instances. Norman Lloyd felt that her very presence made a difference. "Charlie never would do anything to hurt Oona, and, since railing against the children *would* have hurt her, he usually mellowed his rage." When he did not, however, Oona was unable to stand up to him. In certain ways, she was as much his oldest daughter as she was his wife.

Temperamental outbursts aside, life with Charlie Chaplin was not all shouting and disciplining by any means; in the early years the family shared many happy times. Chaplin owned a few cars, a formal Rolls Royce, and two Fords—with special engines—one for him and one for Oona. At Christmas he would get out his Ford and Oona and the children, along with Peggy and Norman Lloyd and their two children, would pile in for a holiday drive and motor around Hollywood taking in all the sights. Charlie made up a game in which the children had to ooh and aah every time they passed Christmas lights, and the car rocked with their delighted cries. The contrast between the way Charlie acted with his youngsters and his older boys was very evident to his longtime friends, and even Charlie himself admitted that he had been a neglectful father to Charlie Jr. and Sydney. According to the Lloyd's, it was not just Charlie; Lita Grey Chaplin was uncomfortable in the role of mother and really did not know what to do with her children whereas Oona Chaplin, they agreed, did.

Meanwhile, Oona's own less-than-attentive mother continued to make guest appearances in her daughter's life. During the late forties and early fifties Aggie was on the Hollywood scene. At first, Chaplin seemed quite taken with his mother-in-law. When her novel, *The Road Is Before Us* (originally entitled *Tourist Strip*) was published in 1944, he threw a party for her. Aggie's book caused a bit of a stir. The *New Yorker* review called her a "talent worth following" and found that most of the main characters emerged "with startling clarity in a series of pictures done not only with skill but with compassionate understanding." The *New York Times* review noted that *The Road Is Before Us* left "a definite hope that Miss Boulton will keep her feet on the very promising road that lies before her."[10]

In many ways a beneficiary of Oona's good fortune, Aggie was not looking to attach herself to her son-in-law's coattails. She did meet people through him, among them Betty and Ted Tetrick, with whom she became quite friendly. Aggie started weekly literary sessions at which friends gathered together and were called upon to read aloud, often from their own works. The Tetricks were part of this assemblage, and before long Ted and Aggie were working together on a screenplay. Ted Tetrick remembered Aggie as a pretty, powerful woman, a little on the wild side, with a sparkle in her eye. Betty saw her as shy and very quiet, just like Oona. She also observed that the shyness and quietness evaporated when Agnes Boulton drank. With a cocktail or two under her belt, Aggie became outgoing and flirtatious, especially with young men. The Tetricks did not agree on the extent of Aggie's alcoholism; Ted talked about her excessive drinking, whereas Betty tried to play it down.

While Agnes occupied her time with writing and socializing, Oona immersed herself in being Mrs. Charles Spencer

Chaplin and had so many children she always knew what to do. Her daughter procreated and Aggie battled on, organizing her reading groups, working on books and screenplays, and keeping company with a variety of gentlemen. Appreciative of what Chaplin had done for Oona, Aggie also found him too domineering and in time began voicing her opinion. Oona did not want to hear it. Her daughter's closed-mindedness on the subject, coupled with Charlie's avowed preference for having Oona to himself, resulted in a tapering off of Aggie's active presence in the Chaplin household. She became an occasional and, generally speaking, welcome guest.

In 1947, following a nasty divorce case in which she was named as correspondent, Agnes Boulton married for the third time. The object of her affection was Morris "Mac" Kaufman, a screenwriter who wore a black eye patch and was ten years Aggie's junior. Some friends looked askance at the union, but Aggie loved the gruff, one-eyed writer, called him "Mackie," collaborated with him on screenplays, and under his tutelage learned to drive a car. Most significant, she loved him well enough to give up her alimony, something she would not do for any of her other lovers, including Jim Delaney. Money was not the pressing need that it had been in the past when she had to provide for her children; now she just had to look out for herself, and, occasionally, Shane. Meanwhile Oona, a woman of means, delighted in giving her mother expensive gifts. Perhaps she felt that by pampering Aggie she could make up for the lean times when they had been dependent on the closefisted O'Neill. Agnes enjoyed receiving her daughter's bounty yet remained relatively indifferent to material things; Aggie prized her independence and, as she proved again and again, liked to go her own way.

Life at Summit Drive had fallen into the orderly pattern Charlie Chaplin favored, with Oona's presence adding a degree of love and security he heretofore had not known. Close as they were, they maintained separate sleeping quarters with a double bed in Charlie's room and twin beds in Oona's. While both quarters remained sacrosanct, Oona was less stringent and practiced a comparatively open door policy for the little ones. Whenever the newest baby made the move from Oona's room to the nursery, the older children would fight for the privilege of sleeping with their mother, and whichever child stayed with her was assured that for that brief time he or she would be treated as though he or she were the only one. Oona literally basked in having babies and became wistful whenever the crib was taken out of her bedroom, only to joyfully welcome back the bassinet upon its inevitable return. "She absolutely mesmerized herself to become pregnant," recalled Betty Tetrick, "and Charlie adored her in that state. He loved the serenity of it."

The children came along regularly: on March 28, 1949, a second daughter, Josephine, was born; and then, on May 19, 1951, the last of the American-born Chaplins, Victoria, arrived. Birthing a baby is one thing, but caring for a child is quite another, and much as she loved becoming a mother, Oona's involvement with the nitty-gritty of child raising had to play second fiddle to meeting the demands of her husband. The children's everyday needs were tended to by nannies, and time spent with their parents, especially their father, was measured. Two, four, six, eight—no matter how many children they had, Oona had to appreciate Charlie above all else. She did find excellent nannies, though, especially a no-nonsense yet sympathetic Scotswoman named Edith MacKenzie, affectionately known as "Kay-Kay," who became a permanent fixture of the Chaplin household.

Shortly after her marriage, Oona had written to her father, she said, "out of a sense of duty to explain her actions."[11] Although Oona later referred to the letter as a silly thing that probably never got beyond Carlotta, she must have held at least a hope of reconciliation. O'Neill never responded. Despite the constant slights, something in Oona would not allow her to give up. At one point she asked Waldo Frank, an editor and friend of O'Neill, to intercede for her with her father. "Frank wrote to O'Neill on the basis of their old friendship and received a curt reply from Carlotta, precluding any other attempts on Oona's behalf."[12] She did not mention her father's name and yet held on to the letters he had written, including the last, that furious blast of parental outrage that turned out to be good-bye.

Biding her time until after Michael's birth in 1946, she wrote a brief note and mailed it, along with pictures of the children, to the ailing playwright. No response. In 1951 Oona received a phone call from Dudley Nichols, a close friend of her father, Nichols told her that Carlotta and O'Neill had separated and that her father was hospitalized in New York City. Eugene O'Neill's third marriage was marked by periods of mental and physical cruelty and included a number of separations as well as a stay or two in mental institutes for both parties. He placed Herculean demands on Carlotta, relying on her for everything from running his household to typing and retyping his manuscripts, and on a few occasions Carlotta walked out. During these breaks some of the playwright's friends, who believed that Carlotta had estranged him from them, attempted to get him permanently away from her. (Carlotta disdained many of his old buddies and was biased, in particular, toward those who were Jewish, like editor Saxe Commins.) Dudley Nichols urged Oona to seize the opportunity to fly to O'Neill's side, reconcile, and save him from returning to his wife. Eight months pregnant at the time, Oona told Nichols that she could not fly, but she did send a letter, along with photographs of the children, to Saxe Commins and asked him to deliver them to her father. Commins brought the envelope to the hospital and handed it to O'Neill. The playwright took the packet and, without a word, slipped it, unopened, under his pillow. He could not accept anything *from* her any more than he was able to accept *her.*

Despite her father's repeated rebuffs, Oona thrived in Hollywood. Back east, however, her brother Shane's struggle continued unabated, his despondency and hopelessness darkly mirroring the upbeat quality of his sister's life as Mrs. Charles Chaplin. Oona often spoke of Shane to friends, usually to bemoan the fact that he was not working and was living on a park bench somewhere. She conversed rather matter-of-factly about him, yet the underlying emotion remained evident, she cared very deeply. As a child Shane did not talk much, had no guile, and was easily taken advantage of. While Oona prized his sweetness, she realized that his very nature worked against him; he trusted others and inevitably was disappointed. Too, his ingenuousness was thought to be a direct result of his not being overly bright. In truth he had a good mind, but one that was paralyzed from self-doubt and drugs. Shane smoked marijuana (sticks of tea, as they were called in those days), a habit which expanded to include cocaine and heroin. He was a mess, but a sweet, loving mess, and not a few young women were attracted to him. In 1944, after a brief stint in the merchant marine, he married Cathy Givens, a girl from a good home who had fled to Greenwich Village where she supported herself by working as a department store salesgirl. In November 1945, Shane became the father of a son, Eugene O'Neill III. The baby succumbed to crib death barely three months after he was born—and a scant month before Oona Chaplin gave birth to Michael. Everyone was distraught about the tragedy, including Eugene O'Neill.

Shane had kept up with his father, and although he rarely

saw him, unlike his sister, he remained on speaking terms. At first O'Neill cast no blame for what he considered to be the symbolically significant death of his namesake. Carlotta, on the other hand, immediately condemned Shane and Cathy as immature and shiftless Bohemians with no right to have children. Devastated by his loss, Shane called Aggie in Los Angeles. Comforting her son from afar, Aggie arranged for him and Cathy to go to Bermuda for a change of scene. Once there, Shane and Cathy ran out of money and, in desperation, began selling off the contents of Spithead. O'Neill learned what had happened and, angered by his son's action, cooled toward Shane. In fact, he never saw or spoke to him again. It had taken him many years, but ultimately Eugene O'Neill successfully excised both his children by Agnes Boulton.

twelve

IN THE LIMELIGHT

n 1944 Charlie's son Sydney appeared in a production of Elmer Rice's *The Adding Machine* presented by Hollywood's newly established Circle Theatre. Oona and Charlie attended. Impressed with the performance, they became regular patrons of the Circle Theatre and struck up a friendship with the company's founder, Jerry Epstein. At Epstein's request, Chaplin started coaching and directing the players and, before long, was conducting rehearsals on a regular basis. According to Epstein, Charlie could not accept the fact that, unlike movies, a stage performance must be frozen at some point. Consequently he conducted marathon rehearsal sessions that lasted into the wee hours of the morning. They might never have stopped, commented Epstein, had not Oona telephoned her husband. "Charlie! Those poor kids need their sleep!" she would admonish, whereupon Chaplin would turn to the ensemble and say, "The old lady's on the phone, and she wants me home."[1] The calls did not always work, and Oona sometimes showed up in person to drag him off. At home the Chaplins frequently entertained members of the Circle Theatre, especially Jerry Epstein, who soon became an integral part of the family.

Summit Drive had a full staff of ten, but owing to Charlie's quirks some positions were in a constant state of flux. Cooks, for instance, came and went regularly because if the master of the house did not like the way food was prepared, he tended to spit it out. Few chefs could stand up to such pointed criticism and left of their own volition. Household positions were vacated and filled, but the Chaplins did not do the honors since neither one felt comfortable firing employees. When crises arose the Chaplin Film Corporation was contacted and someone from the company did the firing and hiring. Both Chaplins loved gossip and wanted to hear about everything that was going on in their household, downstairs and upstairs. Their pipeline into the domestic staff's doings was Kay-Kay MacKenzie, who cheerfully carried tales. Oona repeated the stories to her friends, and one particular tale absolutely delighted her. She and Charlie had remained in the bedroom for a long, long time one morning, and Kay-Kay overheard the maids speculating as to why the Chaplins had not appeared. "Oh, you know those two," chuckled one, "they're at it again!"[2]

Out of the bedroom, Oona proceeded to become an exceptionally good cook and regularly took over on the chef's night out. She learned how to prepare the homespun dishes that Charlie had been raised on, and he downed the meals with gusto.

Although life at home was sweet, events had been chipping away at Charlie Chaplin's position as a beloved icon. In the aftermath of the Barry case, and with a volatile postwar political situation geared to anticommunist sentiments surrounding him, Chaplin went from idol to social outcast. Everyone was seeing "Red," and no more so than in the case of the comic king of the screen. During the war years Charlie, like other concerned celebrities, had lent his name and support to various causes and, also like many of his well-intentioned colleagues, had failed to make a thorough check of these organizations. If an organization was against Hitler and his minions and for the poor and downtrodden, that was enough. However, it turned out that many of the associations had leftist leanings.

No one, not even the beloved Little Tramp, was immune to the witch hunts instigated by the House Un-American Activities Committee (HUAC) of the U.S. Senate. Slowly and surely Chaplin began to be ostracized by the very people who heretofore had sought his company eagerly. No matter what happened, Oona remained steadfast in her adoration. From their earliest days together she absorbed much from Charlie's teachings; certainly her liberal political views agreed with his—both were enthusiastic supporters of Henry Wallace's presidential campaign, and both embraced many humanitarian causes. Chaplin was generous with his time and his energies, yet though he gave unstintingly of himself physically, doling out cold cash was another matter; his monumental frugality got in the way. Charlie always had a reputation for being a skinflint, and story after story was told of his tightfistedness. Paulette Goddard called him sweet and staunchly defended his morals, yet even she unhesitatingly referred to him as stingy. Lita Grey termed his attitude toward spending money *bewildering* in its inconsistency.[3] Charlie gave money toward the cause of peace, but his main contribution was in personal appearances at rallies and fund-raisers. He traveled quite a bit on these missions, especially to New York, and though Oona did not welcome the brief separations she knew they were necessary. Before the end of the decade, though, his New York social life came to a standstill. No longer invited for weekends in grand country manors, he had no choice but to take refuge in his hotel room when his speaking engagements were over.

In early April 1947, Oona and Charlie, accompanied by Mary Pickford, flew east to attend the premiere of *Monsieur Verdoux* in New York. It was a dismal evening. Charlie's adverse publicity, both political (thanks to HUAC) and personal (thanks to Joan Barry) had taken its toll. Certain members of the audience were determined to demonstrate their resentment and began hissing when the film began. Upset by the reaction, Charlie exited and waited in the lobby while Oona and Mary sat it out. Oona managed to get through that portion of the evening, but the subsequent supper party proved too much of an ordeal and she left early. The next day Chaplin faced the members of the press at the Gotham Hotel. They pounced on him. Following the conference Charlie and Oona went up to the hotel suite of a gentleman named George Wallach to hear a transcript of the proceedings. Charlie sat cross-legged on a high-back upholstered chair, and Oona sat on the bed as they listened to the tape. During the playback Charlie kept turning to Oona asking, "How was that?" or "Did you think that was all right?" Charlie's queries were so insistent, remembered George Wallach, that Oona was kept busy calming him down and reassuring him that he had done well.[4] Disheartened by the New York reception, Charlie quickly recovered upon returning home where the familiar surroundings and the soothing presence of Oona and the children worked their magic.

The attacks on *Monsieur Verdoux* set a new standard for judging Chaplin's work; now they were subject to the behavior of their creator. The burden was heavy, yet he managed to deal with the criticism. The secret, according to Charlie, was the unqualified success and happiness of his marriage.

Oona did not suffer public humiliation in the way that her husband did, but she too took her lumps. At the time of the

Verdoux opening she and Charlie were in a New York restaurant when Oona noticed George Jean Nathan seated across the way; she had dated the drama critic during her debutante days. After dinner, as she started out of the restaurant, Oona stopped in front of Nathan's table, and with a big smile on her face extended her hand. He cut her dead.[5] On another occasion, the Lloyds and the Chaplins attended a New Year's Eve party together, and Charlie's presence caused an immediate stir. The atmosphere proved more hostile than hospitable—some people were afraid just to be seen talking to him. The two couples did not stay long. Oona went to the powder room while Charlie, Norman, and Peggy waited for her at the front door. Presently she joined them, and turning to Norman Lloyd, matter-of-factly asked him if he had a handkerchief she could use. "Of course," he replied, reaching into his pocket. Oona took the hanky and began to brush the front of her dress with such composure that the others had no idea what she was removing. Later she told them that she had been presented to a guest. Upon hearing that she was "Mrs. Charlie Chaplin," he spat on her. Helpless to protect Oona from such unwarranted affronts, Charlie was appalled and sickened. Fittingly, his next movie plumbed the depths of his feelings for his young wife.

In the late forties Chaplin started work on a film tentatively called *Footlights*. He spent three years on the scenario, the longest for any of his scripts, and it was during those years that the social euphoria surrounding the Chaplins dissipated. It was no longer considered a privilege to be a guest at their home, and the little tennis house and green lawn where Charlie once had held court were just about deserted on Sunday afternoons; people were terrified to be seen there lest they, too, become suspected communist sympathizers. "It must not be supposed that my father's fight for his convictions was made without sacrifice," wrote Charlie Jr., who called his father the loneliest man in Hollywood.[6] Calvero, the protagonist in *Footlights*, now entitled *Limelight*, also was a lonely man. A has-been music hall performer, Calvero saves Terry, a young dancer, from committing suicide and in the process of building her up recovers his own self-assurance.

Chaplin's voluminous notes indicate that while much of the material was based on characters from his own life, his father and mother in particular, there can be no doubt that the soul of the film owes its inspiration to the bittersweetness of his own relationship with his young wife. Fully expecting to predecease her, Charlie realized that his passing would be very hard on Oona and tried to work something into his film that might help. Calvero's speeches to Terry clearly reflect Charlie's sentiments toward his real wife. In the movie Calvero, acting as a kind of fairy godfather, rescues the ailing girl, heals her through loving care, and then conveniently dies, allowing her to take her place in the world. Unlike other damaged heroines in his films, Terry was allowed to mature into a strong, independent woman. In the opinion of the actress who ultimately created the role, the character of Terry benefited from Oona's example of loving devotion and quiet strength; Oona was responsible for erasing the image of broken womanhood that Hannah Chaplin's suffering had imprinted on Charlie's artistic conscience.

Perhaps because Terry was the personification of Oona, finding an actress to play the female lead proved to be a major hurdle. On one search mission they went to New York City along with actress and acting coach Constance Collier. The three of them saw a performance of *As You Like It* starring Katharine Hepburn. Collier took Oona and Charlie backstage and introduced them to the star and Hepburn's mother, an outspoken advocate of birth control. Gesturing toward Oona, Collier proudly proclaimed, "Isn't it wonderful? This young girl is the mother of three children!" "Nothing wonderful about that," Mrs. Hepburn quickly replied. "The wonderful thing would be not having them."[7] (One only can imagine what Mother Hepburn might have said upon hearing the final count.) Although Charlie thought that Cloris Leachman, a member of the *As You Like It* cast, might be a good bet for Terry, the script was not ready so nothing came of it.

The Chaplins returned to California and a bit later Charlie flew to New York again, this time to test a nineteen-year-old English actress, Claire Bloom. He took Bloom and her mother out to dinner, and both women noticed that other diners kept looking his way, expressing opinions ranging from adulation to loathing. Chaplin paid no attention and instead told Bloom and her mother about Oona. Lauding his wife's loyalty and devotion to him, he explained that were she not expecting their fourth child, she would have come with him. In Oona, he told the Blooms, he had found a woman with whom he was completely happy. Charlie returned to California, and shortly thereafter Oona gave birth to Victoria. While mother and child were in St. John's Hospital, Charlie moved out of the house and 1085 Summit Drive received its final renovations—the grand front hall was divided, and a new floor was added to accommodate the growing family and assorted nannies.

Chaplin continued to procrastinate about casting Terry until, at last, he selected Claire Bloom. In September 1951 she flew to California to be his leading lady and, subsequently, Oona's close friend. The two young women looked remarkably alike. Bloom related that the pronounced physical resemblance was strong enough to confuse people into congratulating Claire on her husband and Oona on her performance. Claire Bloom, in fact, remained convinced that Chaplin was interested in her *because* of that resemblance. (Indeed, Oona stood in for the young actress in a scene reshot after Bloom returned to London.) Of their initial encounter at Summit Drive, Bloom wrote, "Oona Chaplin appeared to greet

me—appeared dramatically enough to satisfy even my expec-
tations—at the top of the stairs, wearing a green velvet gown
that offset her dark Irish coloring."[8] That evening the young
actress, unaccustomed to formal dining, watched her hostess
closely and followed Oona's lead, especially when it came to
the finger bowl. "Though I didn't make the mistake of lifting
it to my mouth, I had no idea what it might be there for and
waited until I saw Oona put it to one side."[9] This action
marked the beginning of a long course of Oona-watching on
the part of Claire Bloom.

Rehearsals began for *Limelight* and they were, as usual, intense. Melissa Hayden of the New York City Ballet was engaged to do the actual dancing for the ballerina heroine.
Hayden was svelte, and since Charlie wanted a perfect physical match between his dramatic and dancing Terrys, he ordered
Claire Bloom to attend exercise classes with his wife. Rehearsals went on for about two months and Oona, sometimes
accompanied by her three older children, would arrive every
day around noon. "You could see that Chaplin adored her," recalled Melissa Hayden, "and she glowed in that adoration
without a trace of self-consciousness." Despite the chaos surrounding him on the outside, Chaplin was elated during the
shooting of this film, an exhilaration heightened by the constant presence of his wife. Oona would sit at the side of the set
doing handiwork, and the minute a scene ended Charlie would
dart over to her side. One member of the *Limelight* crew previously had worked on *Modern Times* and remembered watching
Charlie in action with Paulette Goddard. "He was very gruff
with her, very critical. But, he was just the opposite with
Oona—totally solicitous and making sure she was okay. Of
course, Paulette was an actress in the film, but even so he was
awfully hard on her. He spoke so harshly I was convinced that
they weren't married. No man would talk to a *wife* in such a
manner."[10] Oona brought Charlie's lunch to the set, a carton

of cottage cheese and pineapple, or hard-boiled eggs, and the two of them would go into his small portable dressing room and dine together. Occasionally Chaplin would alter the routine and take his wife and his leading lady to the Farmers Market for a bite to eat. When it came to indulging his own tastes, like Eugene O'Neill, Charlie Chaplin was willing to spend money and proceeded to astound Claire Bloom by purchasing a *sliver* of pâté for the unbelievable price of eighteen dollars. Oona laughingly declared that Claire's standard of living changed from that day on—and who would know better than Oona, whose own lifestyle had been dramatically altered by Chaplin.

Shooting on *Limelight* ended and Charlie, assisted by Jerry Epstein, began the editing. During the noon break they would drop by the Farmers Market for lunch, where Oona often joined them. Jerry Epstein noticed a significant change in the way the famous couple was identified. Seated alone, Charlie was not recognized; only when Oona appeared would people put two and two together. Had she not been there, Epstein was certain that Chaplin would have gone unnoticed, just another sweet-faced, white-haired old gentleman taking his midday meal.

Working on *Limelight* was an exciting time for Charlie Chaplin the creative artist. He firmly believed that this film would be his greatest, and he was equally certain that it would be his last. Chaplin proved to be wrong on both counts. *Limelight* was neither his greatest nor his last movie, just his Hollywood swan song.

thirteen

IN THE BACKGROUND

According to the House Un-American Activities Committee, the amusement capital of the world was overrun with communists in the early fifties. To combat them the Screen Actors Guild, headed by Ronald Reagan, drew up a loyalty oath; even before that, in 1948 and 1949 respectively, the University of California and the City of Los Angeles had imposed a similar oath for all employers. In the entertainment industry the names of suspected sympathizers were circulated via the much feared blacklist, a reprehensible roster of the guilty, the not guilty, and the guilty by association. Although Charlie Chaplin's name stood out prominently, unlike others on the list he had the resources to withstand the brunt of the onslaught. In Chaplin's case, his leftist leanings seem to have been of less importance to the U.S. government than his sexual proclivities. Overlooking Chaplin's full and happy life with Oona, the authorities exhumed the comedian's past sins of the flesh—his

Lolita-esque liaisons, the Barry paternity suit—connected them to his present politics, and presented the package to the people. Ever avowing that he was a *comedian* and not a *communist*, Chaplin believed that he engendered the antagonism of the country by being a nonconformist and refusing to kowtow to the ruling powers. Good reasons to be sure, but others existed.

Charlie never became a citizen of his adopted country because, in his words, he was a citizen of the world. A substantial portion of the populace found this explanation wanting, especially since the self-proclaimed world citizen had made a lot of money in the land whose citizenship he spurned. In their eyes Charlie Chaplin was a paying guest who had outlasted his welcome. Tired of his leftist philosophy and his wanton, albeit quiescent, sexuality, these Americans tacitly supported the comedian's comeuppance. If in receiving his just deserts the punishment happened to spill over onto his innocent wife, well, that was unavoidable. Like that of most women of her generation, Oona Chaplin's fate was tied to that of her husband, and while the government did not go after her directly, whatever happened to Charlie happened to Oona. He was under constant harassment, but whether her husband was being ostracized by the public or investigated by the authorities, Oona never seemed to get flustered. Friends reported that when panic seized many of them, Oona remained calm, maintaining her poise during situations that ranged from the grossly insulting, such as the spitting incident, to those of a more threatening nature.

Peggy and Norman Lloyd frequently joined the Chaplins on board Charlie's boat, the *Panacea*, and part of the sailing ritual was the morning swim. During a cruise off the coast of Catalina Island, the two couples splashed about for the morning dip and then all but Oona returned to the boat. She continued to swim while the others stood on deck watching her.

"Oona was a brilliant swimmer," recalled Peggy Lloyd, "and we were all admiring her skill when suddenly a speedboat appeared out of nowhere and began to buzz around and zero in on her. Everyone knew who owned the *Panacea*, and since sentiment was very anti-Charlie at that time we were pretty sure the man in the speedboat was trying to scare Oona to get at him. Anyway, the boat kept getting closer and closer and we stood there on the deck, paralyzed. Fortunately Oona wasn't. She swam over to the side and we pulled her up just as that maniac made a final swoosh and zoomed off." Chaplin grabbed his wife, held her in his arms, and rocking her back and forth, cried over and over, "My God, if anything happened to you. That's all I would have needed, that's all I would have needed." Even Oona appeared uncharacteristically disconcerted, remembered Peggy Lloyd decades later, but only momentarily, and soon was comforting Charlie. "Oh, come on, it's going to be all right. I'm fine," she told her shaken husband.

Chaplin remained concerned, and as antipathy toward him intensified he sought a way to alleviate the situation. He needed an excuse to get himself and Oona and the children away from the heat, and the completion of *Limelight* provided it. Announcing that the world premiere of his movie would be held in the city of his birth, Chaplin made plans to take his family abroad for the big event. The comedian had not been in London since the premiere of *City Lights* in February 1931 and often expressed the desire to return. Oona never had been abroad, and Charlie wanted to show her his native land almost as much as he wanted to get away from his persecutors. The premiere was set for October 1952, and in the spring of that year Chaplin applied for a re-entry permit.

Thrilled at the prospect of a first visit overseas, Oona made the necessary preparations at home while Charlie went about putting his business affairs in order. Her task proved easier than his. The Internal Revenue Service discovered a discrepancy in Charlie's tax returns and would not issue a re-entry permit unless he put up a $2,000,000 cover during his absence. Chaplin argued for an immediate hearing, got it, and made a settlement. He re-applied for the permit and, receiving no response, notified Washington that he was going whether or not the permit came. The Immigration Department then arranged to interrogate him at his home. During the interview Chaplin repeatedly told a three-man delegation that he had never been a communist nor had he ever joined any leftist organizations. The questions then took a nonpolitical turn and Chaplin was asked if he ever had committed adultery. The comedian replied that, to his knowledge, he had never fornicated with another man's wife (the key words appear to have been *to his knowledge*). Days later, at the request of the Immigration Department, Charlie, accompanied by his lawyer, went to the Office of Immigration. The gentleman in charge politely informed Charlie that he was being granted a re-entry permit good for six months; if he stayed away any longer, he would have to apply for an extension. The Immigration Officer signed the permit, wished Chaplin a bon voyage, and urged him to hurry back home. Despite the upbeat tone Charlie felt uneasy; he had to protect his family, himself, and his fortune (not necessarily in that order) and, realizing that he could not handle everything alone, turned to his wife. Quickly, arrangements were made for Oona to sign papers giving her access to the safe-deposit boxes where most of Chaplin's fortune resided. *Most*, yet perhaps not *all*. Years before, Charlie told Norman Lloyd that he had buried a million dollars in the ground so that whatever financial disasters might befall him, he would always be able to get his hands on that dirt-encrusted security blanket.

The time came for the Chaplins to depart for the East Coast, and while Oona took care of last-minute details with the staff at Summit Drive, Charlie, overcome by feelings of anxiety, waited outside. Putting aside his gloomy reflections, he re-entered the house and joined Oona in bidding farewell to the servants and then exited. She remained behind for a last look and later informed her husband that once he went through the door, the cook and the maid dissolved in tears. Oona was deeply touched by their devotion, but if she shared her husband's premonition of impending misfortune, she did not mention it to him.

After a relaxing train ride across the continent and a brief stay in Chicago, the Chaplins settled in at the Sherry-Netherland Hotel anticipating a week of sightseeing and general fun before boarding the ocean liner *Queen Elizabeth*. Oona called their friend Lillian Ross and, explaining that she would be unable to join them because she had blisters on both heels from a four-hour trek imposed by her husband during the Chicago stopover, asked the author to go walking with Charlie. Ms. Ross appeared in the hotel suite the next morning and found Charlie raring to go and Oona rubbing her feet. Looking at his wife with unabashed affection and admiration, he called her a bloody Victorian. She was, he told Ms. Ross, the only woman he knew who carried smelling salts.[1]

A few days shy of the sailing, Charlie received a phone call from his lawyer advising him that a former employee had brought suit against United Artists, Chaplin's studio. The distinct possibility that he would be served with a summons could not be ignored, and to avoid the process server Chaplin was told to remain in his room. For the rest of their New York sojourn Oona and the nannies took the children sightseeing while Charlie stayed put in the hotel, venturing out only for a luncheon with editors from *Time* and *LIFE* magazines.

On Wednesday, September 17, 1952, a small group of travelers boarded the *Queen Elizabeth* docked in the Cunard Line's pier on West Forty-ninth Street. The band, which included Oona, her children—Geraldine, 8; Michael, 6; Josephine, 3; Victoria, 16 months—and the children's nurses were quickly shown to their staterooms, where, hours earlier, Charlie Chaplin had been installed. Chaplin continued to remain below as the children, along with their mother and nannies, went up on deck to participate in the departure. During the ceremonial leave-taking, musicians played as passengers at the ship's rails waved good-bye to cheering relatives and friends standing along the dock. One of those well-wishers was Charlie Chaplin's loyal supporter, the American writer and critic James Agee. Apprised by Oona of Agee's presence, Chaplin caught sight of his friend through the porthole. Pushing his hat through the opening, he waved it back and forth in a desperate effort to catch the writer's attention. Much as he wanted to acknowledge Agee, Chaplin was afraid to appear above deck until the actual departure. Soon, with Chaplin's fedora feebly flapping at her side, the *Queen Elizabeth* shuddered away from shore, floated smoothly down the Hudson River toward the great lady of the harbor, and then put out to sea.

The second day out the Chaplins were at lunch with pianist Artur Rubinstein and his wife and entertainer Adolph Green, when Harry Crocker, Charlie's publicist, who was traveling with the Chaplins, received a telegram. Advised that the sender awaited an answer, Crocker called Charlie to his cabin and revealed the cable's contents. Chaplin was being barred from the United States and would not be allowed to re-enter the country unless he answered charges of moral and political turpitude before an Immigration Department Board of Inquiry. Charlie professed shock, yet he could not have been completely surprised—certainly he had shown some inkling of disaster by setting Oona up as cosigner for his papers. Shocked or not, everything Chaplin owned was in the United States, and if he wanted to save his empire he could ill afford to ignore the telegram. Inwardly fuming, he decided to issue a statement announcing that he would return home to answer any and all charges.

The *Queen Elizabeth* made its first stop at Cherbourg, and Chaplin held a press conference in the ship's dining room. The *Queen* next moved to the south of England, where, setting aside his problems with the U.S. government, Chaplin turned to other issues. One of his chief concerns was how Oona would respond to his native land, particularly since he had been praising it for years. The ship docked in Southampton and the Chaplin party disembarked and boarded the boat train. As the train pulled out of the station and moved through the city, Oona gazed at the rows of regimented brick buildings flashing by and, turning to her husband, flatly commented that all the houses looked alike. She did not seem impressed by what she saw, and Charlie was disappointed at her reaction. The train arrived at London's Waterloo Station, where they were met by a large and cheering crowd of loyal fans—or so Chaplin wrote in his autobiography. Others remembered that the welcoming group at Waterloo was not that large and thought it reflected a lack of interest in the comedian. In the opinion of many, the British hoi polloi really did not consider Chaplin to be one of them anymore—he had been away too long and had made his success in another country. True or not, Charlie Chaplin certainly did not draw anything like the vast throngs which had mobbed him on earlier visits.

During his press interviews Oona stood to the side until reporters, charmed by her reserved and lovely presence, urged her to step forward. Asked what Charlie was like as a husband, Oona answered, "Charlie is a half-and-half personality. One half is difficult—the other easy. But I find we manage very happily. He is an attentive husband and wonderful father." To questions about herself, Oona responded, "I'm happy to stay in the background and help where I'm needed. Perhaps that is why I am the only one of his four wives he took to London, and I am very proud."[2] Although Chaplin had said that he expected to return to the United States, Oona remarked that it would come as no shock to her if he decided to stay in England.

The Chaplins were driven by limousine to the Savoy Hotel on the Strand and installed in a fifth floor suite overlooking the Thames. As they stood in front of the window gazing at the river, Charlie glanced at his wife and saw that her face was "tense with excitement, making her look younger than her twenty-seven years." Younger, and yet Chaplin was moved to see, for the first time, "one or two silver threads playing about her dark hair." Following a long silence Oona said quietly, "I like London."[3]

After settling into the Savoy suite the Chaplins' social life went into high gear, especially when compared to the recent dearth of convivial activity in America. They went to parties and to the theater, and with Oona at his side Charlie took long walks around the city, especially in his old neighborhood, Kennington. In the afternoons, while the children were out with their nannies, Oona and Charlie would have tea at Fortnum and Mason's. She came to know London as well as Charlie did himself and grew to love the city. One afternoon, with Charlie otherwise occupied, Oona invited Claire Bloom for tea. The British actress found her friend extraordinarily calm about what had happened. Oona told her that Charlie was steaming mad and expressed uncertainty about his ever returning to the United States, even if he were granted permission by the government. While candidly admitting that she was unsure how the American public would respond to *Limelight* now that Charlie had been banished, Oona, in an obvious attempt to make the movie's leading lady feel good, described how well received the film had been at a prerelease showing in Hollywood. Before the visit ended, Oona confided that she would be returning alone to Los Angeles. "Oona dreaded the journey and all that went with closing down a house she'd loved and looked after for eight years," wrote Claire Bloom, "but there was no one to do it but herself and she was ready to leave immediately if that was Charlie's decision."[4]

The Chaplins' social life continued at top speed. They were shown the town and invited into the homes of London's most illustrious denizens. The masses may have been slightly indifferent to Charlie, but the British social set lionized him and was positively enchanted by his lovely, demure, and dignified wife. The *Limelight* premiere, a charity benefit attended by Princess Margaret, took place on October 23, 1952, at the Odeon in Leicester Square. A few days later, at a royal command performance, Charlie and Oona were presented to the Queen. Following *Limelight*'s London debut the Chaplins traveled to Paris and Rome for those cities' respective premieres, and in each location they were feted by dignitaries and notables. Charlie was made a Chevalier of France's Legion of Honor, but the American ambassador, in a pointed snub, did not attend the Paris opening. America reviled Charlie Chaplin even as other nations acclaimed him. Boycotted by many theaters in the States, *Limelight* still managed to gross more money than any of Chaplin's previous movies, and as always the bottom line remained of paramount importance to the King of Comedy. On the subject of money, sooner rather than later Charlie Chaplin had to get his holdings out of the United States; and as his wife had intimated to Claire Bloom, only one person was capable of retrieving the fortune. The *New York Times* reported on November 17, 1952:

MRS. CHAPLIN COMING TO U.S.

SHANNON—Ireland, Nov 17 (Reuters) Mrs. Charles Chaplin

daughter of Eugene O'Neill arrived at Shannon Airport

tonight from London on her way by air to Hollywood, Calif.,

where she said she would attend a meeting of a film company

of which she is an executive. She said she would return in ten days to London, where her husband and their children are staying. The family will not return to the United States until next spring, she said.

Under the guise of attending an executive meeting, Oona, never anything but a figurehead at the studio, flew to Los Angeles to handle the disheartening tasks of dismissing the staff, closing the house, and dealing with bankers and lawyers. At the bank the clerk looked long and hard at her signature and instead of escorting her into the vault, went to get the manager. Fearing that she would not be granted entry, Oona was relieved when at last her signature was honored and the deposit box surrendered. She emptied the contents and returned to the house on Summit Drive. Everything was the same, yet so very different without Charlie and the children. During Oona's brief stay Betty Tetrick came over to keep her company. "Oona was a light sleeper," Tetrick recalled in May 1994, "and was up practically all night. I brought hot milk to her room late one evening and found her sitting there surrounded by securities and bank notes and money."

In a few short days Oona had closed up the house, arranged for the furniture to be shipped abroad, and transferred funds to overseas accounts. Also, she had gone to the vaults in Chaplin's studio to retrieve his films. She took only the completed ones and abandoned the odd bits and pieces, including the Mutual films, which Charlie did not own. The leftover reels remained stashed in the middle of the deserted studio for many months until Raymond Rohauer, a movie enthusiast dedicated to preserving film, heard about the cache, hired a truck, drove to the studio, climbed over the wall, opened the gate, backed the truck in, piled all the films into the vehicle, and drove off. Thanks to him, priceless footage was saved— much of which was used in making the Kevin Brownlow and

David Gill documentary film *The Unknown Chaplin.* Allegedly Oona O'Neill's screen test was among the celluloid leftovers rescued by Raymond Rohauer, and because of him, her brief screen scene was copied and made available to collectors.[5]

With Oona's mission accomplished, she made ready to leave. Weighed down by the thought that she might never return, she gave way to her emotions and often found herself crying. Her tears quickly dried when she learned that the FBI had come calling on two occasions to quiz Henry, the Chaplin's Swiss butler. Questions had been asked about Charlie's character, and inquiries had been made about household activities—were there, for instance, any wild parties with nude girls? Henry answered that his employer lived a quiet family life, which was not what the FBI wanted to hear. According to the butler, the agents then began to badger him, questioning *his* nationality and forcing him to produce *his* passport. As Oona listened to the butler's account, her feelings toward her home and her homeland froze.

On a rainy California morning Betty Tetrick accompanied Oona to the airport and walked onto the tarmac with her. "Tears were streaming down my face as I stood there under an umbrella," remembered Betty. "Oona looked so incredibly young and vulnerable, that sweet little face with her hair all pulled back in a bun. 'Oh thank you, Betty, for everything,' she said. 'I'll see you very soon. You'll be coming to see me.' " The cousins embraced and kissed good-bye; Oona turned, walked up the boarding stairs, and without a backward glance disappeared into the plane.

Arriving in New York City, Oona arranged to meet Jerry Epstein, whom she had seen briefly on the way out to the West Coast. She and Epstein went to dinner at Manny Wolf's Steak House, where she was recognized by a diner who began making insulting remarks; among other slurs, he called Oona a "Commie Red." Epstein was outraged, but Oona laughed.[6]

The next day, November 27, 1952, the *New York Times* printed a brief blurb:

MRS. CHAPLIN OFF FOR LONDON.
Mrs. Charles Chaplin, wife of the comedian, left from the New York International Airport, Idlewild, Queens, yesterday to rejoin her husband in London. She was here a week on business for Mr. Chaplin's film company.

Over the years Oona Chaplin remained closemouthed about her trip back to the United States, and not until 1967, when she returned to America to visit her ailing mother, did she open up. She spoke quite candidly to George Beecroft Jr., a young neighbor from Point Pleasant, New Jersey, and he never forgot one intriguing detail. Oona told him that in following Charlie's instructions she had gathered up the funds, turned everything into thousand-dollar bills, and had the money sewn into the lining of her mink coat. With the fur draped nonchalantly over her arm, she boarded her transatlantic flight and flew back to England. At Oona's arrival in Vevey, the contents of the coat lining were removed and deposited in a Swiss bank account. While the veracity of this particular story, like so many tales about the Chaplins, could be questioned, there is no doubt that Oona was a key figure in saving her husband's assets and that had she not been up to the task, the bulk of the Chaplin fortune might have been lost. The ten days Oona spent in America pulling the Chaplin assets together proved to be the longest span she ever would be separated from her husband; she never again left his side for any appreciable amount of time.

With his money safely put away, Charlie Chaplin proclaimed himself a political martyr and declared that he never would return to America. In Charlie's version, the expulsion had come about because the U.S. government wanted to persecute him for being a communist, yet according to more than one recent biography of The Little Tramp (Joyce Milton's *Tramp*; Kenneth S. Lynn's *Charlie Chaplin and His Times*), the government probably was more upset with his morality than with his political leanings and likely would have allowed him to return if only he had agreed to be interviewed. Nevertheless Charlie Chaplin chose this opportunity to close the American chapter of his life, and in so doing he also ended Oona's days in her native land.

With their fortune rescued, the Chaplins now faced their most pressing problem: Where would they live? Both had been very comfortable in Los Angeles. Charlie had built his kingdom there—the warm climate agreed with him, and although Oona always retained her East Coast sensibility, she too had adjusted well to California's easy lifestyle. Like Charlie, Oona had found a real home in Hollywood, but now there was no turning back. Although they both loved London, neither found the climate suitable. There was another important factor as well: because of the reciprocal relationship between Great Britain and the United States, access to Charlie's currency could have been blocked—an even greater deterrent than the issue of weather. On both counts, London was out. Various locations on the Continent were discussed, and when one friend suggested Switzerland it seemed a good bet—the currency was fluid and the climate was tolerable.

The Chaplin entourage left the Savoy for the Beau Rivage Hotel in Lausanne, and during the next few months Charlie Chaplin diligently searched for a permanent residence. He did most of the looking because Oona was pregnant again. On edge and understandably restive because of their homeless state, Oona balked at the idea of bringing the new baby back to a hotel and pressed her husband to find a home quickly. Charlie did try but was hampered somewhat by his own feelings. Convinced that whatever he bought would be the last house he ever would purchase, he told Oona that he was being fussy because he wanted to enjoy living in his home before he died in it. At last he found something appropriate, yet even then he remained indecisive. Exasperated with hotel living and determined not to give birth to a homeless child, Oona put her foot down and told Charlie this was the house she wanted.

On January 5, 1953, Oona and Charlie Chaplin moved into the Manoir de Ban, a fifteen-room estate on nearly forty acres of land in the mountain village of Corsier above the lakeshore town of Vevey. A large drawing room on the ground floor opened onto a colonnaded terrace, and at either end of the drawing room double doors led into a library and dining room, respectively. On the second floor, reached by an oval-shaped stone staircase, were the master bedrooms and guest suites. The third floor was given over to the children and their nannies. A wine cellar was built in the basement along with a climate-controlled vault in which Charlie stored his films. In another large cellar room archives, scripts, cutting books, records, and the glass negatives of still photographs were stored. The panoramic view from the Manoir took in sweeping lawns, gardens, and orchards and, in the distance, the breathtaking vista of Lake Leman and the Alps. As Charlie Chaplin predicted, this Alpine villa would be his home for the rest of his life.

On August 23, 1953, Oona gave birth to her fifth child, Eugene. She sent an announcement of the birth of his namesake to her father. He did not respond. Five months later, and some nine months after Charlie surrendered his re-entry permit, Oona O'Neill Chaplin renounced her American citizenship and adopted British nationality. She did not have to; *her* loyalties and morals were not under fire, but ashamed and angry at the manner in which her husband had been treated, she opted to join him in exile. Long estranged from her father by *his* choice, Oona, by her choice, now severed the ties to her fatherland.

fourteen

EXILES

A picture-postcard village, Vevey comes to life in the summer months as tourists pour into the Hôtel des Trois Couronnes, the Hôtel du Lac, and other luxury lakeside lodgings. Once the bustle of the sunny months ends, Vevey slips back into its predominantly sleepy mode, but just before the winter hibernation, in a last burst of autumnal liveliness, the town plays host to Switzerland's National Circus. In October 1953 Oona and Charlie, accompanied by the children, attended their first performance of the Knie Circus, and that occasion marked the onset of a Chaplin family tradition, one that Oona herself described three decades later:

> Every October, for the last thirty years, an excitement has
> grown in our household as traditional as autumn itself: the
> Knie Circus is coming to town, coming to Vevey. It always has
> been, as it still is, a magic time, beginning with the animals'

arrival, camels and elephants walking calmly through the streets as if it were an old story to them, as indeed it must be, though never to us, waiting happily on the sidewalk. What is an old story, however, is the friendship between our two families. The first time my husband saw the circus, he was overcome by the excellence and the charm and the enterprise of it; it was unique, and it's remained unique. Every year the rumor starts from Geneva—it's better than ever this year—and every year, if possible, it's true. Our children have grown up together, and we have an affection and admiration for the Knie brothers, fathers and sons, that is a pleasure that endures through time and change.[1]

The summer tourist hubbub and the Knie Circus notwithstanding, Vevey was a long, restrained way from cosmopolitan Los Angeles.

Twelve servants, including a butler, cook, chauffeur, and assorted maids and gardeners, were hired to look after the house and grounds of the Manoir de Ban. The domestic staff, Italians for the most part, were very animated—always arguing and fighting over something or other just for laughs, according to Michael Chaplin, who also noted that his shy and gentle mother usually stayed out of their way.[2] Mabel Rose "Pinnie" Pinnegar was hired to assist Kay-Kay MacKenzie with nursery chores—no easy task considering that following Eugene's birth Oona would produce three more Chaplins: Jane, in May 1957; Annette, in December 1959; and finally, in July 1962, Christopher. Oona herself once commented, "I love going to the hospital to have a baby. It gives me a chance to re-read *War and Peace*—in peace!"[3]

When she left the United States, Oona told friends that they would be together again soon, but in all probability they would have to travel to see her—and they did. A never-ending parade of visitors, including Carol and Walter Matthau, Gloria

Vanderbilt, and Betty and Ted Tetrick, descended on the Chaplins' Swiss home. Oftentimes when things got too crowded, guests were put up at the Trois Couronnes and chauffeured to and from the estate. Not only did family and friends visit Vevey, but world figures also began to wend their high-profile ways to Charlie's summit in Switzerland. Indeed, photographs of the Chaplins entertaining celebrities ranging from Pablo Picasso to Jawaharlal Nehru, from Pablo Casals to Chou En-lai, were flashed around the globe. At the age of twenty-eight Oona Chaplin had become chatelaine of yet another mansion, where in the years to come she refined her talents as a hostess.

It took a bit of work to blend into the environment, and starting with the language all the transplanted Chaplins experienced discomfort in adjusting to their new lives in the old world. Geraldine and Michael were sent to a village school in Corsier, and following some early difficulty the youngsters soon were babbling easily in French, much to the annoyance of their nannies and their parents. The language remained a continuing barrier for Oona and Charlie; her grasp of French was rudimentary and his was even less so, although his cousin Betty swears that even if he did not speak French he understood it well enough. The Chaplin children became completely bilingual, so much so that one daughter was overheard bragging to her sister, "My French is frencher than yours!"[4] Despite their fluency they spoke English in the presence of their parents. Eugene, Annette, Jane, and Christopher, all born in Switzerland, spoke French as their first language; and even the last American-born Chaplin, Victoria, once admitted that she felt slightly uncomfortable reading and writing English.[5]

The family reacted in varying degrees to the change from warm, sunny Southern California to warm, sunny, cold, snowy Switzerland. The shift was particularly hard on six-year-old Michael, who later termed his new homeland "a drag from the first touchdown."[6] During the Chaplins' early stay in London, Michael had asked his mother again and again when they were going home. "I want to go back to California" became his rallying cry, and his fussing continued after they moved to Vevey. On one occasion Charlie was conferring with a business associate when Michael burst into the room singing "God Bless America, Land that I love!" at the top of his lungs. "Oona, get that boy out of here!"[7] cried the irate Chaplin. Gradually the Chaplin children adapted, and after a while only Geraldine and Michael retained sun-drenched memories of the Hollywood lifestyle. James P. O'Donnell, a writer for the *Saturday Evening Post*, reported that Oona and Charlie, who dressed casually and favored American-style cuisine—charcoal-grilled steaks and corn on the cob—remained as Californian as two avocados.[8] A swimming pool and tennis court were installed, and the Manoir itself was filled with furniture that had been removed from Summit Drive. Charlie supervised everything. His second home, like his first, reflected his likes and dislikes. Locals referred to the staid old estate's decor as *Beverly Hills baroque*.

Somnolent rather than scintillating, life in Switzerland proceeded at a far slower pace than life in America. Nevertheless Switzerland became the Chaplins' permanent home, and in Vevey just as in Los Angeles, everything in the household ran like clockwork. The children would join their parents for lunch on the verandah and at the end of the meal would be whisked away by the nannies. Shortly before six they were served the evening meal in their own dining room, taken downstairs for a brief cocktail-hour visit with their parents, and then sent off to bed, a routine that continued until the youngsters grew old enough to join their parents in the adult dining room. Oona and Charlie dined at 6:45 P.M. sharp and retired to their rooms at around nine, at which time the doors to the Manoir were bolted. On the first night of what would be many stays with the Chaplins, Jerry Epstein, unused to such early hours, climbed out of his bedroom window and walked into town in search of activity. There was none; Vevey was locked up as tightly as the Manoir.[9] Although television eventually alleviated the nocturnal situation, in the beginning early to bed was the only game in town.

Separated by an ocean, and buoyed by a successful marriage and a growing family, Oona Chaplin still tried to make contact with Eugene O'Neill. Direct communication with her father had ceased with her marriage, and although Oona said that she felt no obligation toward him, had no profound feelings about him, and felt no guilt, she kept the lines open by continuing to mail him birth announcements—none of which were acknowledged.

Through the years of their estrangement, a number of people endeavored to effect a reconciliation between father and daughter. In the late forties Sherlee Weingarten left a position at the Theatre Guild to work with Eugene O'Neill and grew very close to him and Carlotta, becoming, she said, "like a daughter" to them. The closer she got to O'Neill, the more she found herself wondering about his real daughter. She knew that the playwright was not well disposed toward his second wife and his Boulton children; Sherlee Weingarten was present, in 1947, when O'Neill learned that Agnes had married Mac Kaufman, and witnessed how joyously the playwright received the news that his alimony payments were over. With Agnes Boulton no longer a financial threat, Sherlee tried to bridge the gap between the alienated father and daughter. Pointing out that the Stork Club embarrassment had happened a long time ago, she suggested that he make up with Oona. He answered that they had been separated for so long that a reconciliation could accomplish nothing at this late date. Recalled Sherlee Weingarten, now Mrs. Robert Lantz, "He was gentle and nice, but he said no." And no it remained until Eugene

Gladstone O'Neill's death on November 27, 1953, three months after the birth of his namesake, Eugene Chaplin.

"Born in a hotel room and Goddamn it, died in a hotel room!"[10] were Eugene O'Neill's alleged last words. As the self-proclaimed epitaph implied, the end of his life was as doleful as the beginning. In and out of hospitals, his final months were spent in a suite at the Shelton Hotel in Boston, where Carlotta, herself in poor health, looked after him. Upon learning of her father's death, supposedly through the media, Oona experienced a sorrow which she attributed less to the death itself than to the fact that with his demise all possibilities of a rapprochement had ended. Saxe Commins wrote to her and, recounting his own deep sadness at being cut out of O'Neill's life, lay the blame directly on Carlotta. Calling O'Neill the "gentlest and noblest man" he had ever known, Commins went on to say that it was "very, very important that I tell you how deeply I've felt the enforced alienation by a will not your father's. You have probably felt it yourself, as I have reason to know."[11] Whatever extenuating circumstance Commins might have been referring to, it seems clear that Oona's estrangement from her father was instigated by O'Neill, not by her stepmother. Carlotta may have thrown fuel on the fire, but O'Neill struck the flame.

Just as her friends Gloria Vanderbilt and Carol Marcus long ago had spun fantasies about their absent fathers, once her father was gone Oona began to find excuses for his dreadful behavior and consoled herself with the notion that even if he had wanted to make peace with her, he could not budge from his untenable position because circumstances had been too much for him.[12] Her touching willingness to turn the other cheek came to an abrupt end at the reading of her father's will. Not only did he exclude his daughter and son, but, in an act of vengeance as fierce and terrible as any exacted by the characters in his plays, he further stipulated that their issue, now or hereafter born, be similarly excluded. Oona viewed this scornful act as a vicious message from the grave saying "Don't think I relented for a moment, because I didn't!"[13] Any fantasies she might have held about his true feelings faded in the dark light of that lasting testament to his unremitting fury. Unlike his sister, Shane O'Neill was neither upset nor surprised to learn that he was excluded. O'Neill once told Shane that he did not think he would have much to leave anyone but that he had provided for Oona and Shane by leaving them Spithead. They did inherit the property, and Oona turned her share over to Shane.[14]

Following O'Neill's death Dr. Harry Kozol, a Boston psychiatrist, attempted to reach Oona. He had treated the playwright and was certain that she would want to hear what he had to say, particularly about O'Neill's actual feelings concerning her. Resenting the implication that she would be eager to find out anything regarding the man who had remained aloof for twelve years, and then, through his will, had extended the disassociation beyond death, Oona put off any formal meeting. Dr. Kozol persisted until Oona, sensing that the physician himself needed some kind of closure, agreed to see him. According to her, the psychiatrist's momentous revelations actually were rather meager. Apparently her father had looked at some clippings and photographs of the Chaplin family and did not object to her name being mentioned.[15] Oona politely accepted the information but classified it as nothing very much; a case of too little, too late. Her need to be loved and to love had been placed squarely on her husband, and that closeness to Charlie continued to be the most potent curative to O'Neill's brutal affronts.

Since their exile Oona and Charlie had become, if possible, even more joined at the hip; rarely were they apart, and then usually for a matter of hours rather than days. Carol Matthau wrote of one Chaplin visit to Paris when she, Oona, and their old friend Truman Capote got together for lunch. (Holly Go-

lightly, the heroine of Capote's *Breakfast at Tiffany's*, supposedly was a composite of Carol, Oona, and Gloria.) Not surprisingly, considering the cast of characters, it was a spirited
reunion and the luncheon might have gone on and on except
that Oona happened to glance at her watch.

"Oh my God," she cried, "I've got to run. Charlie will be
back at the hotel now."

"How can you live like this?" challenged Capote, "Don't
you have any time for yourself?"

Carol Matthau answered for her friend. "Truman, don't
you realize that every woman in the world wants a man to
need her like that!"[16]

Charlie needed Oona, but he also desperately needed to be
working. After leaving the States it had taken him many
months to come up with a new project, and while searching
for the right vehicle he hired an Englishwoman, Rachel Ford,
as his secretary. An extremely capable person, Ms. Ford's duties gradually expanded; ultimately she would take charge of
all Chaplin's business affairs. Having hired a secretary, and
then a pair of stenographers, Charlie began tossing around
ideas for screenplays. An early inspiration to try another
Verdoux-like character was nixed immediately by Oona, who
deemed the downbeat persona of a wife-killer a poor choice for
revival. Charlie also toyed with the idea of bringing back an
appropriately aged Little Tramp but scotched that scheme himself. He at last came up with a viable satirical concept based on
his observations of certain aspects of life in Switzerland, aspects Oona also had noted.

Soon after their arrival in Vevey, the Chaplins discovered
that they were living in a virtual paradise of exiles. An astonishing number of their neighbors were banished royalty; in
fact, the former King and Queen of Italy, the former Queens of
Spain and Albania, and the former Kings of Bulgaria and Yu-

goslavia all lived within a fifty-mile radius of each other and Oona and Charlie. Far away from their countries and their former lives, the regal expatriates nevertheless entertained, and were entertained, royally. Oona found their lavish parties strangely mad and declared that attending those gatherings was like going through the looking glass. Court protocol, including bowing, curtseying, and deferring in general, was strictly adhered to, and these rituals produced many odd incidents. For example, one of the banished Queens, a nonsmoker, had to pretend to light up a cigarette so that others could smoke in her presence. In another zany instance the former Queen of Spain, a passionate bridge enthusiast, took every social opportunity to sit down to a rubber. Card games, however, took place very late in the evening, and since no one could leave parties before the royal personage, the Spanish Queen would make a conspicuous exit at a reasonable hour, then turn around and slip into a back room where, long after other guests had gone, she played bridge to her heart's content.[17]

These quaint occurrences amused Oona and inspired Charlie; using the material played out before him, he devised a plot focusing on a deposed monarch living in New York. Oona recognized the potential in this idea. Encouraged by her enthusiasm and assisted by the ubiquitous Jerry Epstein, Charlie began work on a screenplay. The two men would start early in the morning and work until the lunch break; at this point Oona would join them. Following the meal Charlie and Jerry would enact for her the most recently fashioned sequences. According to Epstein, that was the most fun of all: "She was our sounding board and best audience. I always looked forward to lunch: when Oona was around there was so much gaiety and laughter, and a feeling of well-being and serenity."[18]

Serenity, a much prized state in Charlie Chaplin's charged presence, became even more desirable whenever enforced idleness turned the high-strung comedian into a demon. Isobel

Deluz, one of the stenographers hired to work on the film project, had strong words to say about her employer. Calling him an "aggressive little genius," she allowed that while he could be delightful when actually working, most of the time he was a brooding, neurotic terror. Within a year she left his employ, claiming to have been "beaten down by his tantrums—his first-rate clowning, his second-rate manners and his sixth-rate philosophy."[19] Since Ms. Deluz's description of Charlie Chaplin as a *monstre sacre* was seconded by many others (including, to some degree, those who loved him), getting him back to making films took a great deal of pressure off his staff and his family. He began preliminary work on his first post-Hollywood movie, now entitled *A King in New York*, and as his creative juices flowed a mood of cheerful ebullience warmed the Manoir.

Early in 1956 Oona accompanied Charlie on a trip to London, where preproduction work on *A King in New York* began. Once the actual filming got under way at the Shepperton Studios, Chaplin moved Oona and the children from their accustomed riverfront suite at the Savoy to the Great Forsters Hotel in Egham, Surrey, an immense Elizabethan manor built for Anne Boleyn by Henry VIII. Great Forsters proved to be a somber as well as stately setting—Hammer Studios often used the property as a background for the popular *Dracula*, *Frankenstein*, and *Wolfman* horror films. Rattling around the cavernous premises, the Swiss family Chaplin came in contact with other guests only in the communal room that housed the hotel's sole television set. There, along with the gathered assemblage, Oona, Charlie, and the children sat and watched whatever show the majority chose to view. According to Jerry Epstein, it looked as though the Chaplins had booked themselves into an old-fashioned seaside boardinghouse.

When the shooting started at Shepperton, Oona took up her customary place at the side of the set and busied herself with embroidery, as she had done before and would continue to do whenever her husband made a film. Accustomed to working in his own studio where everyone looked to him and where he reigned supreme, Charlie was uncomfortable in the cold, unfamiliar surroundings of a studio filled with strangers; consequently Oona's serene presence meant even more to him. Young Michael Chaplin had a role in the movie, and Oona could glance up from her sewing to see her son as well as her husband in action. Filming finished in July, and since the tax situation allowed them just six months in England, the Chaplins went on to Paris where Charlie worked on the rough cut. One afternoon Oona, Charlie, and Jerry Epstein stopped for lunch at a sidewalk restaurant in the Bois de Boulogne. Taking their places, they casually looked around and saw that they had been seated next to Paulette Goddard and Erich Maria Remarque. Oona and Charlie rose, went over to say hello to the third Mrs. Chaplin and her soon-to-be husband, and, after exchanging a few pleasantries, returned to their table. Jerry Epstein was impressed by the remarkable civility on both sides.[20]

The film editing on *A King in New York* ended, and Epstein left for New York while Chaplin turned to the musical score. Per usual, Oona kept up correspondences for her husband and before long wrote Epstein to tell him that Charlie had composed some beautiful songs that she was eager for Epstein to hear. In fact, since the movie soon would be opening in England, could Jerry please come over and help? Charlie, of course, was behind the request; *he* wanted Epstein but, typically, had Oona do the asking. Jerry, busy with his own work, did not answer right away. Put off by his erstwhile assistant's lack of response, Charlie next had Oona send a telegram *demanding* Epstein's return. Unable to withstand Chaplin's persistence, Jerry put aside his business, took off for Vevey, and arrived on the scene only to discover that as a kind of punishment for his delayed appearance Charlie had decided that he had no need of Epstein's participation. Oona did her best to smooth over the situation, but lacking a reason to stay, Jerry flew back to the States within twenty-four hours. As his treatment of Jerry Epstein proved, no one, not even his closest friends, were immune to Charlie's quixotic turns. Oona seemed to be the only person to escape his tantrums. Whenever he got on his high horse, she usually could bring him back to earth with a simple "Oh come on, Charlie, don't get carried away." This time, however, he resisted any appeals to his better nature. Eventually Charlie Chaplin and Jerry Epstein's friendship was reinstated, thanks in large part to Oona's gentle, insistent coaxing.

A King in New York opened in London on September 12, 1957, to mixed reviews. J. B. Priestley thought Charlie had again "turned film clowning into social satire and criticism without losing his astonishing ability to make us laugh."[21] Other reviewers were not as impressed. The *New Yorker* called it "maybe the worst film ever made by a celebrated film artist";[22] Oona, formerly an avid reader of the weekly literary magazine, promptly canceled her subscription. Critically, *A King in New York* fell far short of Charlie's hopes; hurt and dejected, he retreated to Vevey. But Oona would not let him stay despondent for long. She consoled him and at the same time urged him toward the next project. As a young man Chaplin's ideas had overflowed; now he had to pinch them out, and often they were rehashes of old material. Unable to come up with a new film idea, Charlie turned away from the actual making of movies and started a two-pronged project: first, to release three of his old silents under the title *The Chaplin Revue*, and second, to take notes for an autobiography.

Work on the film compilation once more brought the Chaplins to London and their fifth-floor suite at the Savoy. While trips to the British capital had became standard operating procedure, their journeys did not end there. Thanks to

Charlie, Oona had evolved from a relative stay-at-home to a world traveler. In her infancy she was transported up and down the East Coast of the United States while her father sought the proper ambiance in which to work; during her childhood she moved between Old House in Point Pleasant and Spithead in Bermuda; and during her teens she traveled across the country to California. Once she married, Los Angeles became a base from which she rarely roamed. Life in Vevey, far more confining than in Beverly Hills, created a need to get around, and with the exception of the United States, the Chaplins journeyed to all parts of the world. They made regular visits to the British Isles—including Ireland, where Oona felt right at home—and Western Europe; took jaunts in the Caribbean; made excursions in the Orient; and went on safaris in Africa. Underlying their extensive travels was the sobering fact that the freedom to move about arose out of the lengthening periods of enforced idleness brought on by Charlie's advancing years.

During the re-editing and re-assembling of *A Dog's Life*, *Shoulder Arms*, and *The Pilgrim*, Oona, her sewing in hand, sat beside Charlie as he worked. Occasionally she became outspoken when Chaplin announced his intention to discard some scene or other. According to Charlie she would beg him to leave in *everything*. In judging her husband professionally Oona could not separate the wheat from the chaff; willingly suspending her astute critical sense, she managed to find the seed of genius in anything Charlie did. She had to, for in the unacknowledged competition between father and husband, Charlie had to be the great(er) man in her life.

fifteen

A MUSE TOO LATE

In the early years of his exile, Chaplin was sustained by what he termed the agreeable atmosphere in his home, an ambiance created by the presence of Oona and the children, with the emphasis on the former. He and Oona, said Chaplin, only needed each other. "I love my wife and she loves me. That is why we are so happy. She is my inspiration and she is a good critic. She has a natural talent and her criticism is constructive. To get her reactions to anything I do, I let her see my day's output of work. She never discusses anything or proffers an opinion unless I ask her. Sometimes I disagree with her opinion, only to find a week later that she was right."[1] While he characterized his wife as a very busy woman, according to Charlie, Oona felt that she had no talents except as a wife and mother, a view she herself acknowledged. Clearly he liked it that way. Although he admired and adored her, had Oona shown any inclination to develop a natural talent it is doubtful that he would have encouraged her; he did not want her doing anything that took her away from him. Chaplin labored at his autobiography, and Oona provided the necessary ears. He read sections aloud to her and to Jerry Epstein, and they were unanimous in their praise. Not everyone was swept away, however. On a visit to Vevey, Truman Capote bluntly told Charlie that he did not like the title, the redundant declaration *My Autobiography*. Chaplin took umbrage, snapping back, "What's so good about *Breakfast at Tiffany's*? That's the silliest title I ever heard!"[2]

My Autobiography was published in September 1964, and that year the Chaplins' customary Christmas card picture of the family showed Charlie and Oona along with Josephine, Victoria, Eugene, Jane, Annette, and little Christopher grouped around a sofa, each holding an open copy of Charlie's book and pretending to read. Two-year-old Christopher, seated on the couch next to his mother, is absorbed in a foreign edition, *CHAPLIN: MIT LIV.*

Around this time Francis Wyndham, a staff writer on the Sunday *Times* of London, came to interview Charlie for the *Times' Sunday Magazine*. On this first of several visits Wyndham stayed at the Manoir, a place which he found slightly soulless—at least on the first floor; he likened the downstairs reception room to a Grand Hotel with a rich, more or less null decor and also noted that the Chaplins rarely were in those rooms. Wyndham saw Charlie as an active septuagenarian whose agility and vitality were most impressive—"an old man still full of beans with a manner that was confidential, demonstrative and almost coquettish." Still, observed Wyndham, the possibility of impatience, a sudden sternness, always loomed. He saw arrogance in Charlie's nature, yet there seemed not a trace of self-satisfaction. "For two days he [Chaplin] entertained me with reminiscences, imitations and jokes, to which his wife Oona reacted as if she were hearing them for the first time. I assumed this to be an expression of her loyalty, tact and love—but I later realized that she really was hearing them for the first time." Struck by Oona's devotion to her husband and her ability to listen to him with a supportive naiveté, Wyndham was beguiled by her intellect as well as her niceness. "She was tactful and unassuming and radiated a sort of grace. She obviously was intelligent but kept it very hidden. She was a sensitive person and knew what was going on, yet she did things in a very un-flamboyant way which was all the more impressive. You know how some couples are sometimes competitive with each other, or even those couples where one tries to keep up? Oona didn't do that at all. She was the least competitive woman. And, you could laugh with her."[3] In Wyndham's opinion Charlie's restless, exuberant, stimulating personality had found its perfect counterpart in Oona's quiet selflessness and subtle intelligence. He viewed their marriage as ideally happy and also commented that getting to know them made a deep impression on him.

To promote the Chaplin autobiography, Max Reinhardt, Charlie's publisher, arranged for a book tour in Scandinavia. Daughters Josephine and Victoria accompanied their parents on the trip and were mightily impressed by the receptions given to their father. One evening in Oslo the Chaplins stood on their hotel balcony as hundreds of people bearing torches marched past. Pleased, Charlie said boastfully, "You didn't know your father was such an important guy, did you?"[4] Following the publication flurry Charlie and Oona took the children to Jamaica, where, as they relaxed on the beach at Ocho Rios, Charlie began mulling over new projects. More than anything he wanted to return to moviemaking, and more than anything else Oona wanted him to do just that. Urged on by his wife, he rummaged around in his grab bag of leftover ideas and came up with a screenplay he had written thirty years earlier for Paulette Goddard. Jerry Epstein was summoned via a letter from Oona, and soon the perennial assistant joined the Chaplins on the beach and soaked up the sun even as he helped Charlie get under way. Resurrected and modernized to a thirties/screwball comedy level, *Stowaway*, the former Goddard vehicle, emerged as *A Countess from Hong Kong*.

Oona and Charlie returned to Switzerland while Jerry Epstein went to New York to cut some deals for the new picture. Once his negotiations were successful, he rejoined the Chaplins in London. Before long *A Countess from Hong Kong* was taking shape; Sophia Loren was chosen to play the female lead, and efforts turned to finding the right male star. Marlon Brando's name was suggested; he flew over, met with the Chaplins, and without even looking at the script agreed to appear in the film just for the privilege of working with Charlie. As much as he and Sophia Loren wanted to work with the great master, negotiations went on for a bit while the two stars haggled over billing. That matter was settled, but Jerry Epstein also had concerns about his screen credit. Charlie told him he had to share the title of Associate Producer with another man, someone who, according to Epstein, had done nothing except introduce Charlie to Sophia Loren. With his ego bruised, Epstein requested full credit. Although Chaplin would not agree, he did promise to think it over and then took off with Oona for a brief visit to Vevey. On their return Charlie announced that Jerry would get sole screen credit. What had convinced Chaplin? Once again, Jerry Epstein felt Oona's hand.

Filming on *A Countess from Hong Kong* did not get off to an auspicious start. Victoria Chaplin, age fourteen, came to London and one evening was shown the town by Epstein. He lost track of time and did not return her to the Savoy until twelve o'clock. Charlie hit the roof. How could a grown man keep a child of fourteen out until midnight, he raged (*this*, from a man who had made a career of keeping teenagers out too late, and for purposes less benevolent than Jerry Epstein's). Charlie declared himself outraged, announced that he was canceling the picture, and locked himself in his hotel suite. What actually set Chaplin off is not quite clear; he was known to be nervous about the picture and might have been using Epstein's minor infraction as a convenient excuse. Besieged with calls from Brando and Loren, among others, Epstein had to put everyone off as he tried to communicate with the disgruntled director. Chaplin would not answer his calls, and the alarmed associate producer was stymied. At last Oona phoned Epstein on the sly; she could do nothing right now, she reported, adding that Jerry would have to wait and hope for the best. Four days later she called to say that Charlie would see him. The two men met and reconciled, and once again Jerry Epstein credited the rapprochement to Oona's behind-the-scenes intervention.[5]

Just as friends in Los Angeles had marveled at her discreet handling of her often-cantankerous husband, visitors to Vevey admired her subtle handling of many potentially distressing situations. The actress Joan Collins, romantically involved with Sydney Chaplin in the sixties, was brought to the Manoir to meet his father and stepmother. Ms. Collins found Chaplin "both autocratic and charming at the same time, with a strong streak of irascibility. He ruled his brood of children with a patriarchal iron rod," noted the actress, adding that "his beautiful, patient wife Oona—thirty-five years his junior—catered to him with an almost geisha-like deference."[6] In Collins's opinion Charlie was a sobersides whose seriousness bordered on the pompous, and Oona supplied the only palliative to his grave and donnish nature. One evening Collins angered the comedian by telling him that when she was a schoolgirl during the war she and her friends made up jokes and sang silly songs about Adolf Hitler and dismissed him as a clown. Charlie bristled and would not allow her to continue. He brought out a recently published book of photographs from Auschwitz and made

Joan Collins look at them. The grim scenes were too much for the young woman; she covered her eyes and could look no more. "I don't believe this could have happened," she said, thoroughly shaken. Chaplin began lecturing on the importance of everyone understanding that Hitler was a monster, not a joke. He was right, but he was awfully hard on the actress. Collins became extremely distressed, and when Sydney asked his father to lay off, he was told to shut up. Oona tried to break up the situation by clapping her hands lightly and announcing that dinner was served. Still, Chaplin would not be diverted and insisted that Collins look at more photographs until the bewildered actress began to cry. Only when Oona said, "That's *enough*, Charlie," in what Joan Collins described as "her calm she-who-must-be-obeyed voice," did Chaplin relent. Joan Collins swore that she could never watch Charlie's movies from then on without feeling apprehensive.[7]

Filming on *A Countess from Hong Kong* commenced, and Oona took her accustomed place on the set and assumed her equally accustomed role as guardian of Charlie's peace of mind (ergo, guardian of everyone else's peace of mind as well). Epstein called her the rock behind the production. Whenever Charlie finished a take he would look to her for approval, and she would nod encouragement. Oona watched the rushes in the evening and took special delight in Margaret Rutherford's scenes. The eccentric English comedienne had a cameo role in the film, and no matter how many times Oona viewed Ms. Rutherford's antics, she laughed uproariously. Filming ended, and while the rushes were prepared for Charlie to edit, Chaplin took Oona for a week's holiday at a friend's villa in Porto Ercole. Refreshed, they returned to London and Charlie set to work, first on the editing and then on the scoring. At age seventy-five Chaplin was full of enthusiasm and thrilled to be doing what he loved—creating. Oona was thrilled as well to see her energized husband happily occupied.

On the afternoon of October 11, 1966, Charlie and Jerry Epstein were walking outside of Pinewood Studios when Charlie stepped into a pothole, fell to the ground, and broke his ankle. Rushed to Slough Hospital, Charlie, not wishing to worry Oona, would not let Jerry call her. A cast was put on the leg and Charlie was released from the hospital. He and Jerry returned to the Savoy, where they found a horde of shouting photographers waiting outside and a distraught Oona inside. Besieged by calls from the press, she had become frantic at not hearing from Charlie and was, according to Epstein, semi-hysterical. "Why didn't you phone me?" she cried when the two men reached the Chaplin suite. Epstein felt that the accident actually had a worse effect on Oona than it did on Charlie. Her unbridled panic proved to Jerry Epstein that Charlie was Oona's life—wholly and completely.[8]

Pictures of Charlie Chaplin seated in a wheelchair with his left leg enveloped by the white plaster cast were flashed around the world, and for nearly two months he had to drag himself on crutches to the studio. When the cast was removed in late November, Epstein maintained that Charlie resumed work at his former pace. Perhaps he did, but Chaplin had received the first intimation of his fallibility—he was an immortal only on the screen. As a result of the accident, his mobility was greatly reduced and he had to give up playing tennis. Also at this time there were indications that he may have begun to experience a series of slight strokes.[9]

During the making of A Countess from Hong Kong, in the opinion of at least one onlooker, Oona was slightly jealous of the leading lady. Sophia Loren was "perhaps too Italian with Charlie," claimed Patrice Chaplin, at that time Michael Chaplin's wife.[10] Others felt that the actress and Oona actually were "very chummy"; both were married to men who were considerably older, which created a bond between them. When Charlie looked to Oona for approval after each take, Loren found it touching. Anyway, Oona had no need to worry; not only was Charlie completely infatuated with his wife, but he had become increasingly reliant on her. Old friend Norman Lloyd arrived in London to watch the shooting of *A Countess* and was struck by the change in Charlie as a filmmaker. "At one point a scene ended and an assistant director cried out 'Cut,' " recalled Lloyd in a 1995 conversation. "Now, that was something that only Charlie would have done in the old days; no one else would have dared to issue commands. The minute that A.D. said cut, Charlie threw this look at Oona on the sidelines, a look that said, 'How was it? Was it good or not so good?' Oona smiled back. Well, when I caught that interchange, I knew that career-wise, things were not good for Charlie."

Lloyd saw a growing dependency on Oona, and Marlon Brando saw something else, which he wrote about in his autobiography. Calling Charlie fearsomely cruel and probably the most sadistic man he had ever met, Brando was particularly incensed at the humiliating way Chaplin treated his actor son, Sydney, who played Brando's friend. Brando wrote that Charlie berated Sydney over and over and that every word he said was laden with biting sarcasm. "Oona O'Neill, Charlie's wife, was always there but never defended her stepson. It was painful to watch, especially after Sydney told me that Chaplin treated all his children this way."[11] Chaplin, indeed, could be harsh with his children, and when he went into his classic Victorian father rages, Oona usually slipped into her classic Victorian mother role. Oona never would challenge her husband in public. (She could not stop her husband's tirades against her children or her stepchildren, but she could, and did, help in other ways—for instance, over the years she advanced Sydney Chaplin money for various business projects.) As sternly as Brando judged Chaplin, he still considered the tyrannical director possibly the "greatest genius" that the medium had ever produced.

The press screening for *A Countess from Hong Kong* was held on the morning of January 5, 1967, at the Empire Theatre. David Lean's epic *Dr. Zhivago* was playing at the Empire, and because the special lens that movie required had not been removed for the showing of the Chaplin film, *A Countess from Hong Kong* suffered sputters, jerks, and stops to the very end. Following the preview Epstein and Chaplin walked back to the Savoy and saw the *Evening News* placard emblazoned with the bold headline, CHAPLIN'S NEW FILM—A DISASTER.[12] Oona had not attended the preview and knowing nothing, greeted her husband and friend excitedly, and with a big smile lighting her face asked how things had gone. Crushed at the news of its reception, she quickly recovered and began to bolster Chaplin.

That evening Oona, Charlie, Jerry, and six of the Chaplin children attended the premiere, which seemed to go well; the audience reacted appropriately and had a good time. The next day the reviews appeared and joy was quickly dispelled. *A Countess from Hong Kong* was savaged; critics even cited the technical side as very bad, so bad that the film kept breaking down. The breakdowns actually had to do with the projector, but technical glitches aside, the movie was judged to be hopelessly old-fashioned. Oona believed that the critics were delighted that Chaplin had a flop and was convinced that the film had not had a fighting chance to be reviewed fairly. The Paris premiere proved more successful. The French were receptive, and not a few critics admonished their English counterparts for being unnecessarily brutal. The New York premiere on March 15 occurred on the night of a blizzard, and in reviewing the film the American critics followed the English rather than the French. Bosley Crowther of the *New York Times* even questioned whether Chaplin should have tried to make another film at his advanced age. In his *Movie and Video Guide*

Leonard Maltin, a compassionate American film critic of the present day, called *A Countess from Hong Kong* badly shot, badly timed, and badly scored.

Tragically, this muddled movie was the very last film made by one of the few real geniuses of the screen, arguably *the* genius. While unmistakable touches of that genius can be found in all of Charlie Chaplin's films, none of his later works are in the same league as his earlier efforts. Directing does not seem to be an old man's art. In the history of movies, with the possible exception of Luis Buñuel, John Huston, and Akira Kurosawa, no directors have managed to produce in their dotage anything equaling the products of their prime. And so it was with Charlie Chaplin. Oona O'Neill, his greatest love, had arrived too late to be his greatest muse.

sixteen

"CHARLIE FIRST!"

At the time of his exile, Charlie Chaplin had reached an age when losing almost everything that he loved—home, workplace, friends—easily might have crushed him. Oona made the transition from California to Switzerland bearable; she comforted and cared for him, lifted his spirits, and in due time successfully turned the home away from what had been Charlie's home, into his home. In Los Angeles she had learned how to run an orderly household, or to supervise the running of one. Once tapped, her organizational skills proved excellent. Of course, it did not hurt to have a skilled staff. At the Manoir, a downstairs room was converted into an office from which Oona handled the household affairs. In the beginning she kept an eye on things in general—going over the books, paying the staff, and setting up a filing system that she taught to Rachel Ford and Ms. Ford's eventual successor, Pamela Paumier. Oona functioned as a working chatelaine until Charlie's deteriorating condition demanded her total attention; at that point she turned over all matters to Ms. Ford and Ms. Paumier.

Always subject to the demands of her husband and her children, Oona also needed her own space. As in the past, she and Charlie kept separate bedroom suites and both of them continued to retreat regularly to those individual sanctuaries. No less than her husband, Oona coveted her privacy. The sound of her door closing meant to stay clear—I'm reading, writing, napping, thinking, or, in the later years, drinking. "When Oona went into her quarters, she was very much the queen," said Betty Tetrick. "She would not answer the door and you didn't go barging in, EVER." While Oona may have guarded her time alone, the rules occasionally were relaxed— at least in the first two decades of her marriage. Agnes Boulton remembered that in Vevey as in Hollywood, Oona often took one of the children into her room with her and the two of them then would remain incommunicado for a while.

Life at the Manoir was secluded, and for Oona everything turned inward toward her husband and her children. She kept in touch with the outside world through old friends such as Betty Tetrick, Carol Matthau, Truman Capote, and Ella and Donald Ogden Stewart. Stewart, a distinguished screenwriter, and Ella, a well-known political writer, had been close to the Chaplins back in the Hollywood days. Like Charlie, the Stewarts were blacklisted and had moved to London in the late forties. Over the years the two couples maintained their friendship and exchanged visits at each other's homes; but not just visits were exchanged. During one London jaunt Oona went into the bathroom at the Stewarts' and found towels monogrammed *O.C.* hanging on the rack. When she mentioned this to her hostess, Ella Stewart admitted having taken the towels from the Manoir, adding matter-of-factly, "Oh, you've got plenty."[1] "You always were made welcome at the Manoir," said Betty Tetrick in one of her later reminiscences, "but you had to stay out of Charlie's and Oona's way. Everyone got together for lunch and dinner, but you had breakfast in your room or in the children's breakfast room or in the kitchen or wherever, but never where Oona and Charlie were breakfasting—that was their dominion and except for an occasional visit by one of the children, they were not to be disturbed. Well, you could sort of come in on a Sunday, but you had to be invited."

When the children were old enough, they were sent to nearby boarding schools, reportedly at Charlie's insistence. While they did bring chums home for weekends and holidays, basically the Chaplins relied on the Chaplins for company—as evidenced by the glut of photographs and home movies all showing the family at play. Without question, Charlie took pleasure in his children. One only has to look at the pictures of him standing at the head of the ever-growing line of progeny to see that he delighted in playing cock-of-the-walk, especially to such a handsome brood. The children were attractive, sometimes breathtakingly so, and lively and entertaining. "When they were little ones, they were such fun," remembered Betty Tetrick, the unofficial Chaplin chronicler, "the most divine little creatures imaginable. You knew they were full of the dickens, but they were so polite. Kay-Kay would bring them downstairs while we had our drinks in the living room and then they'd come into the dining room. Each one was special in some way and all together, they were totally adorable."

Charlie Chaplin, too, thought his children adorable, but his main role in life was as artist; after that, husband; and, following that, father. Like most women of her era, Oona's role was twofold: wife first, then mother with no career to interfere. As a wife she was an unqualified champion. As a mother she received mixed reviews from her children, but of course they probably expected more of her than they did of their father. He was a working genius; she was a mother.

In a 1964 interview with Oriana Fallaci,[2] twenty-year-old Geraldine Chaplin said that she and her brothers and sisters grew up with a father who loved them very much and a "saint" of a mother who gave them a lot of her attention. Children had a happy time in the Chaplin household, Geraldine averred, with lots of playing and laughing and singing. Children never were unhappy or lonely in the Chaplin house, and because they had that singular example of a happy marriage being played out before them, they always thought that marriage meant that you fall in love and you stay in love forever. (Thirty years later Geraldine Chaplin again spoke of "growing up with a fantastic example of a happy marriage.")[3] No wonder they believed this. Their parents' mutual passion had suffered no sea change in the passage from America to Europe. Oona and Charlie Chaplin remained mutually enamored and unabashedly and unselfconsciously demonstrated their affection. She would sit on his lap, and the two of them would hold hands and flirt like teenagers. James Bond's creator, Ian Fleming, brought to the Manoir by Noel Coward, watched the Chaplins in action during a visit and pronounced it "wonderful to see two people bask unaffectedly in each other's love."[4] Still, the delight that Oona and Charlie took in each other's company tended to isolate them in that self-sufficient world of love, an atmosphere which strangers and friends found utterly charming but which, as many observed, could be unintentionally exclusive for the children.

In addition to their parents' mutual exclusivity, the children had to deal with an extraordinary generation span in their ranks. Nineteen years separated the oldest from the youngest; the siblings matured at different times and had to face different circumstances. The oldest saw their parents interacting in the romantic fairy tale of an older Prince Charming dancing attendance on a fair young maid, whereas the youngest ones saw, at first, a fairly young woman struggling to keep a superannuated Little King on his throne, and finally, a worn-out middle-aged alcoholic tied to a sick old man. During their childhood the older set received the best from their mother because she was not yet completely burdened with looking after Charlie. When the Chaplin children grew up and wanted to do things on their own, conflicts arose. Oona had gone through a similar process in her adolescence—she declared her intention to become an actress, and her father smashed her down. Precisely because Chaplin picked up the pieces, she felt that she owed him everything even beyond what she owed her children. To a large extent, problems between the Chaplin parents and children arose not because Oona and Charlie were uncaring or disunited in their concern for their youngsters, but simply because he wanted her all to himself. Oona only could be there for her children within the confines set by her husband. Consequently "a certain reticence and evasion became characteristic of the relationship between the Chaplin parents and children."[5]

Even if Charlie Chaplin's streak of meanness occasionally did cross the border into cruelty, he was no Eugene O'Neill. He enjoyed being surrounded by his young ones—not while he was working, though, and never in that inviolate region he and Oona occupied. By all accounts he could be wonderfully amusing at home and delighted his children with tricks, such as the dancing rolls on the fork routine from The Gold Rush, or by standing behind a sofa and pretending to go downstairs as he bent further and further at the knees. He told them bedtime stories, many of which started out in a classic Hans Christian Andersen or Brothers Grimm vein and then in a vaudevillian turnabout became sparkling tales centering around the adventures of The Nice Old Man,[6] a character Chaplin invented and, surely, was. A far stronger, happier presence in the lives of the older siblings, Charlie tended to be less severe with the younger

European-born ones than the older American group. Without doubt, he dealt better with his daughters—the extensions of Oona—than he did with his sons.

Michael Chaplin described his mother as an oversensitive woman who, aware of the hard knocks, studiously avoided them. She was affectionate and attentive, and Michael especially responded to her love of animals.[7] Oona transmitted this enthusiasm to all her children, and not just for the run-of-the-mill dog or cat, either. Someone once gave Michael a tame rat as a gift, and though he was less than thrilled Oona encouraged him, saying that she once had kept rats and they were really smart and made interesting pets. Oona also was infatuated with everything mechanical. She carried a camera at all times and avidly took pictures at home and on vacation. She was equally enthusiastic about making home movies and recorded many of the plays that her children mounted and performed at the Manoir. She would be the first to spring to her children's defense, Michael felt; but loving and attentive as Oona was, he found her willingness to act as Charlie's mouthpiece her most glaring shortcoming. His mother thought and said what his father thought and said.[8]

In big families, big problems exist for the offspring. Not only do they have to scramble for parental attention, but they are caught up, sometimes unknowingly and unwittingly, in sibling rivalries that are played out daily. Vying for the attention of their parents was doubly difficult for the youngest Chaplins, because they had to break through their parents' barrier of exclusivity and negotiate with older brothers and sisters whose places already were established. Geraldine Chaplin learned early on how to placate her father, a skill that seemed to come easier to Charlie's daughters than to his sons. On one occasion "Charlie was reprimanding his five-year-old and would have gone on longer had Geraldine not thrown him a withering look, grabbed her baby sister's arm, and with a strong voice, 'C'mon. Let's get out of here,' dragged the barely toddling Josephine out the door. Chaplin's wrath could not withstand such an exit line."[9] By the time his youngest were lining up for attention, Charlie Chaplin already was doddering enough for the best exit line to get by him. While looking at pictures of the family in the early days, Christopher, the last child, was heard to remark, "I wish I'd been born then. You had all the fun."[10] As his children grew, Charlie, with Oona's constant help, directed whatever strength he could muster into his work. His patience shrank, and although Oona did her best she was too restricted by her overwhelming obeisance. Had all the Chaplins been placed on a sinking ship, the cry from Oona's lips surely would have been, "Charlie first!"

In time the children began to leave home. Geraldine departed at the age of fifteen to study at the Royal School of Ballet in London. Michael made his break a couple of years later and, in 1966, barely out of his teens, would recount his story in a candid autobiography, *I Couldn't Smoke the Grass on My Father's Lawn*. Title aside, the book is not a sensationalistic exposé; most of Michael's reminiscences smack of political correctness under the guise of rebellion.

In the late sixties Michael was supposed to be on a hiking trip and instead headed for London, where he hid out with Geraldine. Once it became obvious that Michael was missing, Oona became more and more agitated, and the more distraught she became, the more it upset Charlie. When at last the boy's whereabouts were revealed, a relieved though exasperated Oona wrote to her son that he was expected to return to school in Switzerland. Michael stood his ground and by return mail asserted that he would only attend school in London. He won. Michael was enrolled in the Stafford House Tutorial School in Earl's Court and almost immediately began goofing off. While Geraldine doggedly pursued a career—she switched to the drama school when it became apparent that she was not going to excel in ballet—Michael drifted. Occasionally he would drift over to visit Jerry Epstein, then living in London, and it was Epstein who convinced Michael to join the family for Christmas at a rented chalet in Crans-sur-Sierra.

Although the Chaplins always celebrated Christmas, Michael asserted that his father disliked the holiday and called it the most conceited, commercial day of the year. In Scrooge-like fashion, Charlie declared it a criminal waste to spend millions on fancy gifts and unhealthy cakes and drinks.[11] Oona thoroughly enjoyed Christmas; perhaps remembering her own catch-as-catch-can childhood, she put great emphasis on a holiday that traditionally brought families together. At any rate, Christmas definitely was *her* celebration. Michael believed that his father went along with it just because it made her happy. On Christmas Eve, Oona made everyone help decorate the tree and wrap the presents, most of which she had bought for the others to give. Convinced that Oona was spoiling the children, Charlie sat out the proceedings in another room. During that holiday at Crans-sur-Sierra, Charlie and Michael kept their distance; Jerry Epstein remembered that, inside and outside, the atmosphere was frigid. Father and son were estranged for some time, and it fell to Oona to keep the lines open. She remained Michael's staunch, if skeptical, ally until even her devotion was pushed over the limit.

Apprised that Michael had stopped going to classes, she wrote and told him that he would not be receiving any money from home. With his finances cut off, Michael Chaplin went to pot—literally—and became part of the drug culture. Meanwhile Oona, still unwilling to write him off entirely and hoping to establish some kind of détente between him and his father, asked Michael to join the family in Ireland for the Easter holiday. He arrived looking so unkempt that Oona suggested he leave before his father got a look at him. Michael left, but not without commenting that he found his mother's subterfuge rather farcical. Oona had sent him the plane tickets, and since she never kept secrets from his father, in Michael's opinion, Charlie damn well knew he was there.[12]

Enrolling at the Royal Academy of Dramatic Art, Michael continued to live a desultory life in London. Although his father remained unavailable, Oona wrote to him now and again. In December 1964, informed by a friend that Michael had a serious drug problem, Oona telephoned to say that they were coming to see him immediately. Michael asked her to talk to his analyst first. The analyst told Oona that Michael had to work things out for himself and that her presence would not be necessary. Oona accepted his words and did not go to London. Left to his own stoned devices, Michael decided to marry a young woman he had been seeing. She was twenty-four years old and did not need parental permission to wed; at age eighteen, Michael did. Charlie would not give his consent; accordingly, Michael obtained a special license, got married in Scotland, and settled in a top-floor walk-up in Belsize Park, Hampstead. Unemployed and in desperate need, he went to the National Assistance Board and was awarded ten pounds. Immediately the news that a Chaplin was accepting charity appeared in papers all over the world, and when reports reached Vevey, Oona, in a most dramatic break from her rule of privacy, issued a statement:

> Concerning my son Michael Chaplin: The young man is a problem and I am sorry he was given National Assistance. He has stubbornly refused an education for three years and therefore he should get a job and go to work. If I do not wish to indulge him as a beatnik, that is my privilege.—Sincerely, Oona Chaplin.[13]

Much amused at the byline, Michael Chaplin was certain that the statement, issued in his mother's name, actually came from his father.

Oona's unwillingness to indulge her son as a beatnik bears a superficial resemblance to Eugene O'Neill's refusal to indulge his daughter as an actress. The similarity, however, ends there. Justifiably irritated by Michael's immoderate behavior, Oona never completely severed her relationship with him, nor would she ever countenance a permanent break with any of her children. She never would do to them what had been done to her.

Perhaps the severest test came when eighteen-year-old Victoria ran off with Jean-Baptiste Thierrée, a French actor ten years her senior, who began his courtship by writing her a letter declaring his admiration. Generally speaking, Oona's affection for her children appeared to be proportionate; but Charlie's was lavished on his third daughter. Chaplin was in love with Victoria, said drama critic Francis Wyndham, quickly adding in a 1994 interview that not for one minute was this a sexual love. Judged by some family members as most like her father, Victoria was the inspiration for Charlie's last attempt at moviemaking, *The Freak*, and she was scheduled to star in the film. No surprise, Charlie did not approve of Jean-Baptiste Thierrée. After meeting secretly for a while, Victoria and the actor took off. By running away, she became the inadvertent source of Charlie's greatest disappointment. Once the shock of Victoria's leaving had been absorbed, Oona set about restoring the peace—a formidable task since Chaplin swore he would not let his daughter in the house. Once again, Oona succeeded in bringing about a reconciliation between father and child, and Victoria and Thierrée, by then man and wife, ultimately were received at the Manoir.

Geraldine and Victoria energetically pursued careers; the other Chaplins do not appear to have been as persistent or, perhaps, as fortunate. By far the most recognized Chaplin, Geraldine has had a steady and, in the opinion of some critics, stellar, career in international film. Victoria's fame has come through *Le Cirque Imaginaire*, now called *Le Cercle Invisible*, a performance act she and her husband devised. A charming, intimate theatrical piece, it brilliantly showcases Victoria's ingenious gift for pantomime.

Significantly, all eight Chaplin children have been drawn, at one time or another, in one way or another, to the discipline in which their father is an immortal. It is a rather intimidating path to follow since it is unlikely that any of them could hope to reach, let alone surpass, his standing. In general the eight Chaplins do not make headlines. The children of Oona and Charlie Chaplin had enough notoriety in their younger days to last many lifetimes and presumably are thankful to be out of the limelight.

seventeen

CAVIAR AND HOT PASTRAMI

Throughout the years of her self-exile, Oona's relationship with Agnes continued strong. They had had their fair share of run-ins during Oona's adolescence and Aggie's post-adolescence, but remained close even when they were an ocean removed. Oona loved to pamper her mother, and on one occasion, when she brought her to Switzerland, Oona sent Aggie a crocodile traveling case fully equipped with makeup and toiletries, an extravagance Aggie adored. Aggie's relationship with Mac Kaufman, however, did not fare as well; they separated in 1960 and eventually divorced. He went off to sea but continued to keep up with Shane's children through the mail. Near the end of his life Kaufman entered a nursing home in California, and until his death he corresponded with his former stepgrandchildren. Except for Eugene O'Neill, Agnes Boulton seemed to find gentlemen friends who actually liked and were kind to her children and grandchildren.

When Aggie and Mac separated, Shane, a pariah in the Point Pleasant community, moved his family back to New York City. With everyone out of the way, Agnes Boulton's eccentricities came into full bloom. She always kept a few cats around the house; now herds of them roamed freely, leaving in their wake abundant evidence as to their presence. Old House grew seedier and seedier, and Aggie grew thinner and thinner. She barely ate but loved going out to restaurants and frequented two local bistros, the Stanwell Inn and the Idle Hour; the latter, a tavern, became her haven. The Idle Hour kitchen, staffed by Chinese immigrants, turned out oriental cuisine rather than the usual tavern fare. This did not seem to bother patrons like Aggie, who were less interested in food than in idling away the hours over a glass.

One evening Aggie casually invited the indigent kitchen crew to come and live with her. At once Old House overflowed with the Idle Hour's Asian employees, none of whom spoke much English. Aggie endured the crowd for a couple of weeks until, realizing what she had done and unable to undo it, she called the police. Agnes Boulton may have been eccentric, but she was not crazy. Within hours the chief of police, George Beecroft Sr., cleared out the surplus boarders and Old House settled back into whatever Aggie considered normal—until the next episode.[1]

Oona believed that Aggie's exaggerated sense of drama kept her mother eternally young; she also believed that Aggie's outlandish nature and tendency to hyperbole was described best by Jim Delaney. In the late thirties Aggie left Jim for another man who, she announced grandly, was fabulously wealthy and connected to the Romanovs. Delaney mournfully told Oona that it was not the fact that her mother had fallen for someone else that bothered him so much; he himself had been attracted to others, but, he groaned, "Why, when it came to Aggie, did the Russian Crown Jewels always have to enter into it?"[2]

Living alone, and becoming more and more reclusive, Agnes Boulton continued to write. She had started work on a sequel to *Part of a Long Story* and asked O'Neill's biographer, Louis Sheaffer, to assist her in organizing the material. Sheaffer thought Agnes was a gifted writer but that she was unwilling to put in the kind of hard labor necessary to refine her work. In his opinion, Aggie either lacked the drive or just plain enjoyed living too much to concentrate on writing. Aggie kept at her work, and at the same time she stopped taking care of herself, or stopped caring about herself, and went deeper into seclusion and drink. Apprised of the situation (possibly by Barbara Burton), Oona arranged for a housekeeper, a woman who had known the family for years, to look after her mother. Accusing her of stealing, Aggie ran the woman out of the house two or three times. Though Oona tried to keep the peace over the transatlantic phone, matters accelerated until the housekeeper announced that between the cats and Aggie's mood swings, she had had it. Someone else was brought in.

While touring in a production of *The Little Foxes* in America, Geraldine Chaplin made arrangements to visit the grandmother whom she had not seen in years. She hired a car to take her to Point Pleasant, but when she arrived Aggie would not let her in. After much pleading through the door on Geraldine's part, Aggie relented. Shy at first, Geraldine soon was put at ease and she and Aggie chatted animatedly on a wide range of subjects. Geraldine was relieved to find her grandmother unchanged except for being so thin. Aggie's bearing and beauty, cheekbones, eyes, and smile completely captivated the young actress. Geraldine noticed that Old House was almost bare of furniture and was told that everything had been stolen. Convinced that she was being robbed blind, Agnes lamented the loss of her possessions, particularly the theft of her Space

Shoes. (Murray Space Shoes, a footwear phenomenon of the sixties, resembled a pair of catcher's mitts. Despite their decidedly chunky look and high price, they were highly prized for their comfort, especially by senior citizens.) The shoes were a hot item in America, not in Europe, thus Geraldine Chaplin had no idea what her grandmother was talking about. The conversation then turned to Shane and his family and his drug problem. Shane, Aggie disclosed, even sent his children to get his drug supplies.[3] Despite Aggie's distress, she related the story with gusto and characteristically appeared to relish the drama of it.

During their lively exchange, Aggie pointedly played down the stories of her own drinking, informing Geraldine that they were much exaggerated. Later, when told that Oona was worried because she had not heard from her, Aggie took Geraldine over to the typewriter where, curled around the platen, there was a letter to Switzerland. She was in the process of writing to her daughter, explained Aggie, but had not gotten around to finishing. All in all, the visit was a smashing success. Suitably dazzled, Geraldine Chaplin declared her grandmother "fabulous."[4]

Fabulous, Aggie Boulton was; prudent, she was not. In November 1967, Chief of Police Beecroft notified Oona that her mother was suffering from acute malnutrition and, although hovering near death, refused to be hospitalized. Agnes Boulton's grave condition brought Oona Chaplin back to the United States for the first time in fifteen years.

After flying to New York City, Oona went immediately to Point Pleasant and, with much urging, managed to get her drastically weakened mother into the hospital. Aggie still refused food and waved off Oona's pleas to eat. In desperation Oona offered to get her mother anything she wanted. Smiling wanly, Aggie looked up.

"Anything?" she whispered.

"Anything!" repeated Oona.

"Caviar," sighed Aggie.

And she got it; an extraordinary way to end a fast, except perhaps for Agnes Boulton.[5]

During her return Oona was faced with sorting her mother's effects. Too emotionally drained to go through the past, she decided to put everything, including Aggie's personal papers, in storage, but first she had to assess the situation at Old House. Oona asked Chief Beecroft (whose many years of courtesy to the Boultons made it easier to ask for his help) to accompany her. With the chief by her side Oona went to her childhood home, grit her teeth, and entered. The place was in shambles and littered with piles of papers, letters, and magazines all bearing ample evidence of the many cats in residence; despite two fumigations, the air was befouled with the stench of felines. Beecroft stood by as Oona decided what to save, what to put in storage, and what to burn. Discovering the pages to the *Part of a Long Story* sequel piled up on Aggie's desk, Oona decided to take them back with her to Switzerland—not, she later explained, because she believed they had any monetary value, but simply because she wanted to read her mother's work. She also took with her a bust of her mother commissioned at the time of Aggie's marriage to her father, and a few of Teddy Boulton's watercolors. Her duties finished, Oona took a long, last look and left the house, locking the door behind her.[6]

More work had to be done, and Chief Beecroft offered the services of his son, George Jr. Oona gratefully accepted. For the remainder of her stay, twenty-five-year-old George Beecroft, a reporter for the *Asbury Park Press*, willingly acted as Oona's factotum by running errands, keeping curious neighbors and the press at bay, and listening, enthralled, to her stories, including the saga of the money-lined mink coat. Oona put on no airs and spoke as a peer to the young man, yet Beecroft was impressed by her cultured and regal bearing, which, knowing the family as he did, seemed to come out of nowhere—"Aggie was very beautiful and had a certain style, but Oona radiated class."

Beecroft remained genuinely puzzled at the innate elegance that set Oona apart, especially from her brother. Oona and Shane had the same parents and grew up in the same surroundings, yet Shane, when Beecroft knew him, was definitely not cultured and could easily have been mistaken for a Bowery bum. George noted that Oona never referred to Agnes Boulton as Mother; she was always Aggie. He also noticed that she never mentioned her father.

Charlie Chaplin phoned his wife every day, and they would talk for hours on the transatlantic line. Several times George Beecroft was present when Charlie's call came in, and the two Chaplins sounded to the young reporter like dating teenagers chatting with each other from the next block rather than a long-married couple conversing from two continents. Charlie wanted to hear all about America, and Oona filled in the details of what had changed or stayed the same. Beecroft learned that Chaplin most missed hot pastrami sandwiches from the Stage Deli in New York City. (In July 1997, George Beecroft Jr. wrote a brief recollection of Oona for her daughter Victoria and included the story of the sandwiches. Victoria called to thank him for sharing the reminiscences but what, she inquired, was the Stage Deli, and what was hot pastrami?)

One evening, with Aggie on the mend in the hospital, Oona gave a small dinner party at her hotel (the Beacon Manor, the only hotel in Point Pleasant) and invited Shane and his family, George Beecroft Jr., and Betty Tetrick, who had flown east at Oona's request and expense. Shane and Cathy did not show up, but their children, Maura, Ted, Sheila, and Kathleen, came and maintained an apprehensive silence during the meal. Oona attempted to draw them out and in searching for topics of conver-

Charlie and Oona at a Hollywood political rally for Henry Wallace. Chaplin seems to be the only one amused by Mr. Wallace. *(AP/Wide World Photos)*

February 1950. Triumphant return of the Stork Club's Glamour Girl. Oona is flanked by her celebrated husband and movie star Charles Boyer. *(AP/Wide World Photos)*

Oona with Charlie and the first two of their eight children on the lawn of Charlie's Summit Drive estate in Los Angeles. *(© 1964 Asbury Park Press, All Rights Reserved)*

With nineteen-month-old Victoria in her arms, Oona and her family are bound for London. Josephine (3 ½), Michael (6) and Geraldine (8) are unaware that they are waving good-bye, permanently, to their native land. *(UPI/Corbis-Bettmann)*

Oona leaves New York International Airport on her way to Los Angeles, where she will close the Chaplin's home and secure the Chaplin fortune. *(Photofest)*

The "exiles" are interviewed on the roof of the Savoy Hotel, their home in London. *(UPI/Corbis-Bettmann)*

Sydney Chaplin joins his father, Oona, and his half siblings at the London premiere of *Limelight*. Oona seems more interested in Victoria than in the cameras.
(*UPI/Corbis-Bettmann*)

Still smiling as her irrepressible husband entertains some children at a London Airport.
(*UPI/Corbis-Bettmann*)

Charlie celebrates his sixty-eighth birthday as Oona takes unfeigned delight in his clowning.
(*AP/Wide World Photos*)

A Swiss resident and a mother for the fifth time, a still trim Oona takes a turn on the Lausanne skating rink with an instructor.
(AP/Wide World Photos)

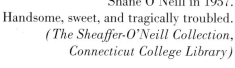

Shane O'Neill in 1957.
Handsome, sweet, and tragically troubled.
*(The Sheaffer-O'Neill Collection,
Connecticut College Library)*

Pregnant with their seventh child, Oona receives a tender kiss from her husband of sixteen years during a vacation in Majorca.
(Photofest)

Shane in 1962 after a suicide attempt.
His agony would continue
until his leap to death in 1977.
*(Dick DeMarsilo, The Sheaffer-O'Neill
Collection, Connecticut Library)*

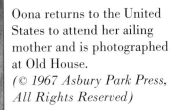

Oona returns to the United
States to attend her ailing
mother and is photographed
at Old House.
*(© 1967 Asbury Park Press,
All Rights Reserved)*

Oona sits on the sidelines
during the filming of
A Countess from Hong Kong.
(UPI/Corbis-Bettmann)

Charlie, about to cut into his eightieth birthday cake, is surrounded by Oona and their European born children, Jane (age eleven), Christopher (age six), Annette (age nine), and Eugene (age fifteen). *(Photofest)*

The Hollywood community applauds as Charlie receives his honorary Oscar in 1972. Oona, at his side, shares the moment. *(© Copyright Academy of Motion Picture Arts and Sciences)*

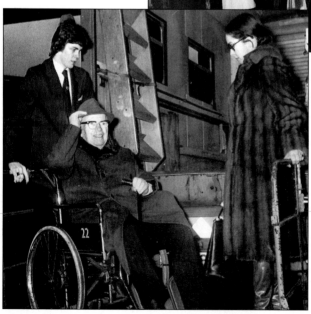

Charlie, about to be fork-lifted onto an airplane, the only way he could get on board. *(AP/Wide World Photos)*

Charlie is knighted by Queen Elizabeth. Clutching the K.B.E. Medal and a cane, he kisses a smiling, turbaned Oona.

Looking at Charlie's last book—realized through the efforts of Oona and writer Francis Wyndham. *(Photofest)*

Oona enjoys a sundae along with her "Boopsy," Betty Chaplin Tetrick. *(Betty Tetrick)*

Outside the Manoir, in the last months of his life, Charlie is feted by his family and friends. *(The Sheaffer-O'Neill Collection, Connecticut College Library)*

Charlie Chaplin is laid to rest. A bearded Eugene stands behind Christopher, Annette, their aunt Gypsy Chaplin, and Kay-Kay MacKenzie. Josephine holds an umbrella over her mother as Oona, looking remarkably like her father, stares numbly at the camera. Although she survived him by fourteen years, in a sense, Oona Chaplin died with her husband. *(AP/Wide World Photos)* sation latched on to bluefish, the special entrée that evening, as a subject du jour. Expressing her delight at finding bluefish on the menu, she went on to describe the Chaplin family's annual fishing trips to Scotland.[7] Oona's nieces and nephew had been told of the Chaplins' affluent lifestyle by their grandmother and listened in awe to their aunt's tales of vacations in Scotland. Aggie had always talked about the Chaplins' wealth. She once told George Beecroft that as each Chaplin child was born, Charlie transferred a million dollars in gold from his account to one in the child's name payable at age twenty-one—a story that might belong in the same apocryphal category as the tale of Charlie's buried million or the cash-lined mink coat. Oona did her very best to put her nieces and nephew at ease, yet how could they relax? How could they connect their forlorn, drug-dependent father with this elegant, famous woman? Although she was their aunt, and although she had been sending them gifts all along, Oona really was a stranger—a friendly, generous one yet still a stranger. How could they not be awed? The dinner was a valiant and generous endeavor to bring the family together, but in fact they were very far apart.

Presently, with Aggie's affairs somewhat in order and Aggie herself stabilized, Oona left for home. She never saw her mother again; a year later Agnes Boulton was dead at the age of seventy-seven. The headline of her obituary in the November 26, 1968, issue of the Point Pleasant *Leader* proved to be a wry precursor of what her daughter's would be like nearly twenty-five years later:

CHARLIE CHAPLIN'S MOTHER-IN-LAW

Ex-wife of Eugene O'Neill
Agnes Boulton Kaufman Dies.

Chaplin and O'Neill received top billing in both Aggie's and Oona's final notices. The *Leader* obituary went on to say that

Chaplin's mother-in-law and O'Neill's former wife had known fame and fortune, joy, and much sadness since her marriage to O'Neill at the end of the First World War.

> Just one year ago, she became ill in "Old House," the home she lived in with Eugene O'Neill at 2301 Herbertsville Rd., and was hospitalized. Her famous daughter Oona O'Neill Chaplain [*sic*] returned to the United States from a self-imposed exile to visit and make arrangements for her mother's care. Mrs. Kaufman's house was a haven for a dozen or more cats whom she cared for better than herself.

According to people who visited Old House, the obituary vastly underestimated the feline population; it should have read *dozens* of cats. Oona herself swore that at least two hundred of them were in residence.[8]

Not long before her death Aggie had complained to Betty Tetrick, "I'm so tired of hearing about O'Neill. I feel like I never want to hear his name again!" Now she took that name to the grave, and despite her expressed disdain Agnes Boulton Burton O'Neill Kaufman might not have been that annoyed at the final coupling with her second husband. Unlike her daughter, who never spoke of Eugene O'Neill, Aggie talked quite a lot about him. "When she got started on him," said Betty, "you felt that he hadn't married any other women, that it always was just the two of them."

Oona did not return for her mother's funeral. The absence was not due to indifference; she had not hesitated to make the journey the previous year when Aggie was alive, but with Aggie gone it would have been a hollow show to leave her own family simply to put in an appearance at the graveside. On a conscious level, that was Oona's rational approach; her subconscious, however, had something else to say. Shortly after Aggie's death Oona had a dream which so impressed her that she wrote it down. In the dream Oona was watching a movie that showed a young Aggie outdoors and next to her, on a rug, a baby. Oona recognized the baby as herself. As she watched, Oona found herself thinking how beautiful her mother looked and how much she wanted to speak to her. At the same time she realized that she must not say anything or the movie would stop. Unable to keep silent, Oona whispered something. Aggie looked startled and then laughingly said aloud that she thought the baby had spoken to her. Immediately the dream ended.[9] In the dream Aggie was alive. Clearly Oona wished she could bring her back to life, and perhaps she blamed herself for not doing more to save her mother. Realistically, Aggie was old and suffering from self-induced malnutrition and alcoholism—there was not much more Oona *could* do, a fact that did not keep her from feeling guilty.

Believing that neither her sister nor her brother was up to the task of arranging Aggie's funeral, Oona called on Betty Tetrick again, and once more the obliging cousin flew east. Betty made the funeral plans and, with the assistance of the Beecrofts, supervised the final dispensing of the estate. George Jr., one of the first to enter Old House after Aggie died, was given the unenviable task of emptying the refrigerator. Steeling himself against the possible sensory onslaught, he cautiously opened the door and found the shelves bare except for a couple of bottles of champagne and an unopened jar of caviar.

Since Aggie's affairs had been taken care of the previous year, and since any valuable items that remained in her possession were dispersed to her children, there was not much to do other than clean up and close up Old House. Regarding the outstanding matters of Aggie's estate, Oona was surprised to learn that her mother, so very legal-minded in her lifetime, died without leaving a will. Despite the fact that she had been married three times, divorced three times, was a property owner, signed contracts, took out loans, and made settlements and sales, the only official paper in Agnes Boulton's safe-deposit box was her birth certificate. Oona's main interest lay in the letters she herself had written to Aggie almost daily—letters full of family gossip and candid stories about the Chaplins' life in Switzerland, as well as advice for everything ranging from books Aggie should read, to medicine Aggie should take or not take. Agnes Boulton had saved every single one of her daughter's letters, and at Oona's request Betty Tetrick burned every single one of them.

After the funeral and burial, and with Oona's letters destroyed, Betty flew back to Los Angeles. It remained for Chief Beecroft to dispose of the remaining detritus of Aggie Boulton's life—old bills, household lists, various letters, and magazines. A bonfire was set in the yard, and the chief enlisted his son to carry the cartons out of the house and consign them to the flames. In the middle of the procedure George Jr., struck by the finality of his actions and concerned that papers of possible historical significance might be lost forever, put aside his father's directive and began grabbing random handfuls, saving what he could. Among the rescued material were the letters of James Delaney and two oversized sheets of paper containing photographic copies of articles Aggie had clipped from newspapers for over forty years. The articles included the obituaries of James, Ella, and Eugene O'Neill as well as the death notice of Ralph Barton, Carlotta Monterey's former husband. There were also accounts of Eugene O'Neill's professional achievements, including a Spanish production in Buenos Aires of *Anna Christie* in 1930 and the 1956 premiere of *Long Day's Journey into Night* in Stockholm, as well as articles about his personal life with Carlotta. Prominent among the clippings were pictures and blurbs about Oona's progress from her debutante days ("Oona O'Neill Goes Home to Her Famous Father—To Get Movie Job Okay") to her exile as Mrs. Charlie

Chaplin ("Chaplin's Wife Drops Status as U.S. Citizen"). For decades, Agnes Boulton had been tracking her former husband's and her daughter's lives.

Police Chief Beecroft long had admired Old House, and with Aggie gone and no one in the family interested in living there, Oona made it possible for him to purchase the property at a nominal fee. After three generations the Boultons' association with the quaint ramshackle dwelling on Herbertsville Road was over, and Oona Chaplin's long and predominantly happy association with her childhood home came to an end.

eighteen

DEAR LOU . . . POOR SHANE

On January 26, 1969, in response to a letter forwarded to her by Aggie's lawyer, Herbert Jacoby, Oona Chaplin wrote to Louis Sheaffer in Brooklyn Heights, New York. Oona's letter began, "Dear Mr. *Schaefer*" (proper names aside, Oona's spelling, like her mother's, was idiosyncratic; in fact, her correspondence is filled with schoolgirlish apologies for her poor spelling and is liberally sprinkled with *Sp?* signs). Sheaffer, a theatrical press agent and former film and drama critic for the now defunct newspaper the *Brooklyn Eagle*, began work on a Eugene O'Neill biography in the mid-fifties and spent some sixteen years capturing the story of America's Nobel laureate dramatist. The first volume, *O'Neill: Son and Playwright*, was published in 1968, and at the time Sheaffer received Oona's letter he was at work on the concluding volume.

In his quest for information Sheaffer painstakingly retraced Eugene O'Neill's long-ago routes from Connecticut to

New York, from Maine to Bermuda, from Sea Island to California, interviewing the dramatis personae in the playwright's life. He spent much time with Oona's family—her mother, her aunts, her sister and brother—and in the process became very close to the family, particularly to Agnes Boulton. Along with helping Aggie with her manuscripts, Sheaffer went to Point Pleasant to care for her on a few occasions when she became ill. Not until after the publication of his first volume, however, did he come into contact with Oona. In November 1968, Sheaffer wrote to Aggie's lawyer, Herbert Jacoby, inquiring about certain missing papers that he needed for his research. Jacoby, no longer involved with the late Mrs. Kaufman's affairs, forwarded the inquiry to Switzerland; hence the letter from Oona.

In clearing up the mystery of the missing papers for Sheaffer, Oona explained that on her trip to America, being overcome with emotion at returning to her childhood home and at seeing her mother so ill, she had not felt up to dealing with Aggie's multitudinous effects. Consequently she had them put in storage with the idea of sorting through them at a future date. Since her mother had died intestate and since Oona could not leave her husband for more than a couple of days, she hoped that the bank would take over, act as executor, and ship the papers to her. The cache was presumed to include letters from O'Neill as well as Aggie's diary of their life together, and therefore of possible value. Oona added that she had ordered her own letters to Aggie destroyed because in writing freely to her mother Oona had made a few remarks about Barbara Burton getting on her nerves, and knowing that Aggie saved everything, she feared that those letters might fall into Barbara's hands and hurt her unnecessarily.

The two half sisters stayed in contact throughout Oona's life, but there were ups and downs in the relationship. Oona later revealed that she sensed Barbara's ambivalent feelings about Oona's relationship with their mother, with Eugene O'Neill, and ultimately with Charlie Chaplin. That resentfulness caused Oona to withdraw from personal contact for many years; she found that dealing with Barbara from a distance was easier.[1] Whether she saw Barbara or not, Oona continued to steer any O'Neill funds that became available over to her half sister and her brother. Concerning her mother's papers, Oona did not know how to go about selling them, and though she was not interested in the money for herself, she was looking out for Barbara and Shane. Her generosity impressed Louis Sheaffer. He also was touched to learn that Oona even diverted some O'Neill money (which, despite her father's will, she had come into through various copyrights) to Carlotta's daughter, Cynthia.[2]

In closing her letter Oona briefly referred to *O'Neill: Son and Playwright*, and while terming the book very good she said no more other than to report being moved at finding a beautiful photograph of Aggie among the illustrations. Oona had few mementos of her early years and eagerly sought pictures of her family.

Louis Sheaffer wasted no time in replying. His answer is dated January 30, 1969, a mere four days after Oona wrote her letter. Opening with a formal "Dear Oona Chaplin," Sheaffer confessed that long before she contacted him, from all he had heard, he felt drawn to her. Promising to do his best for Shane and Barbara, Sheaffer indicated that he did not believe there was much money to be realized from the papers. Aggie had sold her O'Neill correspondence for $10,000 to Harvard University some ten years earlier, and that left Aggie's 1925 diary, which at best probably was worth a few thousand. Sheaffer assumed that the remaining lot consisted of letters to O'Neill from various friends and therefore not of extraordinary monetary value. Volunteering to look through the collection if it were made available, Sheaffer also offered to answer any further questions.

In her second letter Oona confessed that the idea of trying to sell private letters, particularly between husband and wife—and most particularly if they were your parents—was distasteful to her. She was relieved that Aggie had taken matters into her own hands and not left it up to her heirs. This time, Oona spelled Sheaffer's name correctly. Though he relaxed enough to address her, in his reply, as "Mrs. Chaplin" rather than "Oona Chaplin," the two of them continued to salute each other formally until, in a typewritten note dated February 27, Oona opened her letter with "Dear Lou" and went on to politely inquire if she could address him in that manner. She took the liberty of doing so, she added, because she knew that her sister called him "Lou." One can imagine the pleasure experienced by the biographer to have Eugene O'Neill's glorious daughter address him familiarly. A correspondence had begun, and although they would not meet each other in person for many years, they formed an easy and close alliance.

An attractive man of strong features—prominent nose, wide mouth, and deeply set dark eyes beneath thick brows à la Eugene O'Neill, Louis Sheaffer was born in Louisville, Kentucky, in 1913. After completing his education at the University of North Carolina he worked for newspapers, taking time out for military service in World War II. A self-proclaimed romantic, Sheaffer gravitated toward the ideal, and in Oona Chaplin he found the personification of his ideal. According to his niece, author Michelle Slung, the fact that Oona was married, as well as the great distance separating them, made it possible for Sheaffer to fantasize about her with no fear of sexual confrontation. For her part, Oona found in Louis Sheaffer an intelligent, willing, and friendly correspondent to whom she could freely express herself and who, unlike her aged husband, was vitally interested in her past.

Oona particularly wanted to know about her mother. What, for instance, did Aggie do between the time she left home at age seventeen and her meeting with O'Neill? Who was Barbara Burton's father? Neither she nor Barbara ever got a straight answer from Aggie. Whenever they questioned her, Aggie either burst into tears or made vague allusions to the reporter who had been killed in the war. Sheaffer was not able to come up with any solid information regarding Mr. Burton but proved knowledgeable about nearly everything else. Most important, the gentle, critical manner in which Louis Sheaffer had portrayed Eugene O'Neill allowed Oona to reconsider certain of her own long-standing assessments of her father. Living with Charlie Chaplin for twenty-five years had given her some comprehension of the nature of genius, and while she could understand that her father's ill treatment of others came out of his creative drive, the melodramatic self-pity and tendency toward self-dramatization in which her father indulged himself had thoroughly exasperated her. In a letter to her mother in April 1962, Oona said she chose to keep a vague idea of her father as someone who wrote a lot of plays and kept himself aloof, but when she read quotations from his letters she found them "absolutely embarassing." [sic] Her father was "BLOODY unsophisticated" and she hated his use of words; in fact, all the self-pity and exclamation points after trite sentences and banal sentiments made her despise him.[3]

Oona credited Louis Sheaffer with giving her insight into the way O'Neill's childhood and youth had reverberated throughout his whole life, and actually shaped his life; Sheaffer also showed her, for the *first* time, the intense autobiographical nature of her father's works. It seems odd that a perceptive woman like Oona had not noticed that long before; then again, disenfranchised as she was, she might not have known the facts of her father's life. It is odd too, in holding him up to the mirror of genius, that she did not see obvious parallels to her husband: the melodramatic self-pity, the tendency toward self-dramatization, and the capacity for cruelty—at least she does not mention them. Because Oona had no O'Neill lore to pass on to her children, they grew up with no knowledge of their grandfather's tortured history and were only vaguely aware of what he did. Indeed, after reading about O'Neill's life in Louis Sheaffer's book, the Nobel laureate's granddaughter Geraldine would exclaim, "No wonder he wrote such plays!!"[4]

For the next two decades the wife of Charlie Chaplin exchanged thoughts, opinions, remembrances, and confidences with the biographer of Eugene O'Neill. Since the bulk of Oona Chaplin's other letters were either scrapped at her request or saved in a scattershot manner, this block figures significantly as an example of Oona's considerable gift for words. While great letters do not necessarily a great writer make, one has to read just a few to realize that she was superbly capable of expressing herself. In order to assist Sheaffer, Oona revisited her past, a journey made easier because the writer either helped her look at events in a different light or actually shed light on certain situations—such as her exclusion from O'Neill's will. Sheaffer had heard that Oona and Shane *were* in a previous will, but after Eugene and Carlotta's breakup in 1951 Carlotta insisted as a condition of taking O'Neill back that she be named his sole heir and heiress. If it was Carlotta's doing, suggested Sheaffer, would it not modify O'Neill's position a little? The biographer also believed that O'Neill probably thought that disinheriting Oona and Shane did not mean much since the playwright's reputation was at a low point during his last years and he did not believe he had much to leave. He was not trying to whitewash her father, Sheaffer explained; O'Neill *was* an unforgiving man, but this was also part of his equipment as a dramatist.

Along with attempting to explicate, if not justify, O'Neill's actions toward her, Sheaffer brought Oona up to date on diverse characters in the O'Neill pageant. This included Carlotta Monterey, about whom Oona confessed to be "forever curious." Sheaffer likened Carlotta to a beleaguered Bourbon, one who did not belong in this century "but in the nineteenth—an adventuress in red velvet posed against purple draperies with gold fringes."[5] He dismissed a good percentage of Carlotta Monterey's own grandiose tales of her background, and he did not accept the more lurid stories in circulation; for example, her mother was not, as one story had it, the madam of a San Francisco bordello. In his dealings with her, Sheaffer never felt that Carlotta held a grudge against her stepdaughter. On the contrary, she spoke well of her. When Oona expressed surprise at hearing this, Sheaffer countered by saying that he was similarly astonished that Oona spoke well of Carlotta. Oona told him that in reminiscing about her visits to Tao House, she found it easier to focus on her stepmother than on her father. Carlotta dominated and was "gloriously in the air," whereas O'Neill remained quietly in the background. Nevertheless, Oona claimed to have realized from the first that Carlotta only appeared to dominate simply because it suited her father's purpose. "Things seemed to happen to Carlotta that only could happen to Carlotta," Oona explained; that was why she viewed her stepmother as an almost comic character,[6] a Margaret Dumont–like foil for O'Neill.

Oona was right; as long as he got what he wanted, Eugene O'Neill cared little how his home situation appeared to others. Read the playwright's letters to the women in his life, from his first love to his last, one sees that although their names change, the same signals—love me, take care of me—were sent. The Monterey/O'Neill alliance had its own share of squabbles, and in the waning years of their life together waging those monumental battles they would split up, get back together again, and repeat the process. But after the furious break that resulted in his hospitalization, when he begged her to take him back, she did—for when all was said and done, Eugene O'Neill was Carlotta Monterey's mission. She needed to care for him as much as he needed her to do so, and that was exactly what the young Oona sensed and the mature Oona noted. Carlotta Monterey literally had fashioned her own background and because of this, according to Sheaffer, constantly had to keep covering up. Her persistent subterfuge illustrated a basic difference between Oona's mother and stepmother. Except perhaps for Mr. Burton, Agnes Boulton had nothing to hide, looked dead-on at life, and was a woman of considerable intellect, which, for all her posturing, Carlotta was not. Oona felt that her stepmother's fear was not simply the result of trying to gloss over her past, but more the result of an awareness of her intellectual weakness. Carlotta remained terrified lest someone cut through the veneer of assurance and expose her for what she was: a beautiful shell. Despite her insight into Carlotta's shortcomings, and even as she saw through her, Oona swore that she liked, or possibly *sympathized with*, her stepmother.

Of invaluable support in reassessing the assorted personages of Oona's past, Louis Sheaffer also played a role in the present, especially by acting as an intermediary between her and Shane. Although they saw each other rarely, the love between brother and sister endured, if for no other reason than that they were united in being the objects of their father's contempt. O'Neill heaped the same hearty scorn on his second son as he had on his daughter. "Shane has a background all torn apart without inner or outer decency, the Boulton background—a laziness, a grafting, in which nothing is ever finished, a slow decay, spite, unscrupulousness, envy, ridiculous

social aspirations, a hatred of anyone who succeeds. Bohemi-
anism at its nasty silliest,"[7] O'Neill wrote to his eldest child,
Gene Jr., in May 1945. As usual, O'Neill cited the Boultons as
the source of degeneracy in his second and third born. But
how, then, to explain the eventual fate of Eugene Jr.? On September 25, 1950, his drinking out of control, divorced from
his third wife, jobless and living on his father's dole, he
climbed into a bathtub, slashed his wrists and ankles with a
razor, and bled to death, leaving a note which read: "Never let
it be said of O'Neill that he failed to empty a bottle. Ave atque
vale." No Boultons to blame here.

While her half brother's suicide upset Oona, he had not
been a vital presence in her life, just a vague figure who infre-
quently appeared throughout her childhood. He had never
made any attempt to get in touch with her after she grew up,
and Oona felt constrained about contacting him. The nearest
she got was during a weekend spent at Yale when she was fifteen years old. Gene Jr. was teaching classics, and although
Oona expressed interest in seeing him she was too shy to contact him out of the blue—perhaps she did not want to put herself in the position of being snubbed by yet another Eugene
O'Neill. Her sadness at her half brother's death, though sincere, was detached, a grief once removed. Barbara Burton had
been a more viable sibling but that relationship was somewhat
complex, which left Shane as the object of Oona's strongest
sibling alliance. He was the big brother she looked up to as a
child and whom she tried to look out for as an adult. Over the
years Oona was as generous with Shane as anyone could be
with someone who put every cent he could get his hands on
into feeding an all-consuming drug habit. Then, too, she had
to deal with Shane without bringing her husband into the picture. Chaplin viewed his intemperate brother-in-law as a
never-ending emotional, if not financial, drain on his wife;
Shane was a bother, and Charlie did not want Oona bothered.

Louis Sheaffer conceded that of all the characters in Eugene O'Neill's life, Shane was the one who gave him "a bit of trouble." He met the playwright's son on the same evening that he met Agnes Boulton in person. Sheaffer had been corresponding with Aggie for quite some time and had thoughtfully arranged for her to stay for a few weeks in the Greenwich Village apartment of a friend of his. Sheaffer met Aggie at the station, and after dropping off her luggage at the apartment they went out for dinner. On the way back Aggie stopped in a delicatessen to buy orange juice and coffee while Sheaffer waited outside. She exited the store, and at that moment an untidy-looking young man carrying some sort of shopping or shoulder bag happened along. It was Shane. Taken aback, Aggie introduced the two men and then chatted briefly with her son. Soon Shane was on his way. As Aggie watched him move off down the street, she turned and mused, "I wonder what he has in that bag?" Sheaffer was moved by Aggie's surprise at finding her son in the city; it was obvious that for the moment, anyway, she was not in touch with Shane and knew nothing of his comings and goings. A short time later Sheaffer met Shane for the second time, and this, he wrote Oona, remained his most vivid encounter with her brother:

> I was in Point Pleasant for a few days, staying with Aggie, trying to help her with her book. Shane joined us one day in going to the beach. After coming out of the water, we noticed a sea-robin (the first I'd ever seen) up on the sand, a touching sight to see the fish out of his element. I remember that it had bright, bright, bright blue eyes, and I took it as symbolic of Shane who was out of his element in the world, who never learned to cope, who never developed a protective hide, as most of us do.[8]

Before Louis Sheaffer entered the picture, Oona had relied on her mother, her sister, a few friends, and Jacoby the lawyer to keep her posted about her brother's doings. Shane covered a lot of territory and at different times lived variously and precariously in New York City, Bermuda, Florida, and New Jersey. In September 1952, just prior to the Chaplins' fateful sailing on the *Queen Elizabeth*, sister and brother were reunited in New York for the first time in seven years. According to Shane, Oona visited him at his top-floor apartment on East Twenty-second Street off Lexington Avenue, and the next day he and his wife, Cathy, attended a screening of *Limelight* and a party afterward at Lillian Ross's apartment.[9] The following day Cathy took their three children, Maura, Sheila, and Ted, to the Chaplins' suite at the Sherry-Netherland, where Oona arranged a children's party complete with cake, ice cream, and presents from FAO Schwarz. Maura and Sheila received little fairy princess dresses, and Ted was given a Teddy bear. And then Oona was gone, off to her castle in Switzerland. Shane rarely talked about his sister to his children. "We only knew about her from the papers, and whatever Aggie wanted to tell us," remembered Sheila O'Neill in a 1997 conversation. "Oona was always good to us, though. She sent notes to my mother and she sent us clothes, really nice clothes her kids had outgrown. I loved to get clothes from her."

In the winter of 1952–1953, while Aggie was living in Mexico with Mac Kaufman, Shane ran out of money. Having no place to go, he broke into Old House and, along with his wife and children, moved in. The O'Neills were scorned by most members of the conservative community, both because of Shane's disorderly behavior and because of their Tobacco Road-ish lifestyle. They kept animals—assorted dogs and cats, a rooster, and a donkey that, according to Sheila O'Neill, was purchased through a Sears catalogue. The dogs chased after trucks, the rooster bit the mailman, and when the mail-order donkey proved impossible to care for, he was given away. The animal's disappearance gave rise to a rumor that it had died and been interred on the grounds of Old House. The O'Neill children were mercilessly questioned by classmates as to why their father had buried a donkey in the backyard. More frightening than the disdain of the townsfolk and the teasing of the schoolchildren was Shane's constant battle with his addiction. Although he maintained that he no longer used drugs, New Jersey state law dictated that a convicted narcotics addict be registered, and in June 1953 Shane Rudraighe O'Neill was recorded as such by the Point Pleasant police.

A year after the Shane O'Neills took refuge in Old House, Aggie returned from her Mexican trip with Mac Kaufman. During his mother's absence Shane, assisted by daughters Maura and Sheila, had papered the walls of Aggie's studio with *National Geographic* covers. When Aggie saw what had been done she cried out furiously, "You've ruined the library!"[10] Shane walked away without saying a word. Aggie had someone come in and tear off all the covers; her troubles with her son, however, were not as easily removed. He continuously looked for jobs, but when he found them he was unable to hold on to them. Mac Kaufman, at work on a fishing boat, talked the captain into hiring his stepson. Shane grew a beard, wore a red stocking cap with a tassel, and acted strangely. The skipper found him "kind of queer" and after a few voyages let him go. In truth, Shane was taking an inordinate amount of Benzedrine, which probably accounted for his strange behavior. Shane could get by on Benzedrine, but "it only made life bearable." Heroin, on the other hand, "gave him something to live for."[11]

On October 2, 1954, Shane O'Neill was found lying in a ditch and when roused could not give coherent answers to the questioning police officer. Arrested on a charge of disorderliness, he was put in the county jail for observation; the authorities determined that he had overdosed on Benzedrine.

During Shane's inexorable descent, his family desperately tried to keep him afloat. Agnes helped Cathy with the children, while Oona sent a hundred dollars every month and continued to mail hand-me-downs and gifts to her nieces and nephew. Decades later, Sheila O'Neill would recall one such present which she never received. "My father was in New York and he was supposed to bring me a ballerina outfit. He got on the train and fell asleep and when he got off, he forgot the bag with my costume in it. I was about three and I really wanted that ballerina outfit. But that was Shane, he lost it, he'd always lose everything."

Although Aggie did what she could for her son, she could not live with him. In the fall of 1954 Shane, Cathy, and the children moved out of Old House into an apartment in downtown Point Pleasant. In February 1955 Cathy had another baby, a little girl they named Kathleen. Despite the fact that he now had four children and a wife to support, Shane O'Neill remained incapable of caring for himself, let alone his family. Often out of control, he was a physical wreck. His hair was long and uncombed, his teeth had fallen out, and he went for days without eating. Emaciated and unkempt, Shane looked as awful as the lowest character limned by his father. One evening Aggie and Sheila came home from a trip to the Stanwall Inn and found him waiting at Old House. "He was in a bad mood," recalled Sheila, "and Aggie was afraid. I was, too. She called the cops and they came and put him on the train to New York."

Shane spent many evenings wandering around New York City talking to himself and just as many evenings doing the same thing in Point Pleasant. In the early hours of one morning, he started banging on the window of an elderly lady's home; the police were called, and once more charged with being disorderly, Shane O'Neill was sentenced to twenty days in jail. Believing that his condition was exacerbated by excessive amounts of Benzedrine, the prison doctor recommended that he be committed to a psychiatric facility. Agnes asked if it was possible to get him psychiatric and medical assistance at home; Shane, however, would not accept any such plan. In May 1956 he was committed to the Ancora State Hospital for treatment as a Benzedrine addict. Aggie and Cathy saw him once a week, and by the end of the summer he was well enough to visit at home.

Meanwhile, in another twist reminiscent of an O'Neill drama, Cathy's mother had been murdered by her third husband and Cathy used the inheritance money to purchase a small house not far from Aggie's. Shane immediately felt at ease in his new home and pleaded to be allowed to stay. He certainly showed signs of improvement—fitted with false teeth, he had put on weight and neatened his general appearance enough to seem ready for the outside world. Cathy spoke to one of the psychiatrists and was told that while nothing really was wrong with her husband, it was absolutely necessary for him to give up *all* drugs, including Benzedrine. Released from Ancora on September 12, 1956, Shane O'Neill moved into his new home in Point Pleasant.

On October 16, 1956, the sixty-eighth anniversary of the playwright's birth, Eugene O'Neill's *Long Day's Journey into Night* was given its American premiere in Boston; eventually it would receive the Drama Critics Award and a Pulitzer Prize. Eugene O'Neill was news again, and tipped off that his son was living in New Jersey, the *New York Post* sent reporter Helen Dudar to see him. Tall, gaunt almost to the point of emaciation, Shane sat in a rocking chair and rocked slowly throughout the interview. He had misplaced his false teeth that afternoon and spoke haltingly in broken sentences. In his lap he held a child's doll, which he squeezed forcefully in order (the reporter felt) to hide the pronounced tremor in his hands.

Shane O'Neill seemed to be a stranger in his own home. As Helen Dudar saw it, "the deep crevices created by his missing teeth, the downward slope of the sad eyes, gave his face the look of an elongated Greek drama mask of tragedy."[12]

In 1966 Shane and Cathy O'Neill separated. Although she subsequently entered into a second marriage, they remained friends. Divorced, Shane continued his erratic ways, and following Agnes's death there was great concern that without her steadying presence he would crash. Surprising everyone, he went straight into Methadone treatment and even showed enough foresight to divide among his children the small inheritance left by his mother. Oona heard the news and was heartened by her brother's attempts to set his life straight. However bizarrely he acted, whatever he did, Oona saw beyond the awful reality of her brother's existence and responded to the innate sweetness of his nature.[13] She stayed in touch with him throughout his entire life, and considering his grievous condition, the connection probably was far easier to sustain from a distance—Oona had enough difficulties close at hand in dealing with her aging husband.

nineteen

OUT OF THE SHADOWS

The *Countess from Hong Kong* fiasco and its devastating effect on Chaplin's professional standing were accompanied by adversities in his personal life. Death had claimed his beloved older half brother, Syd, and his younger half brother, Wheeler Dryden, as well as colleagues such as Edna Purviance and Mack Sennett. Then, in March 1968, Charlie Chaplin Jr. suffered a fatal thrombosis. In this, as in all the afflictions of Charlie's later life, Oona was there, not only to comfort but to urge him into new endeavors, or at least to keep him working at something, anything. Fortunately Chaplin had that built-in safety net; at a loss for something fresh, he could take refuge in and draw inspiration from his vast output of the past.

After the *Countess from Hong Kong* debacle he began working on a musical score for his silent success, *The Circus*. At the same time ideas for possible films came to him; maybe he would play a dual role as a mad Roman emperor and his slave, or maybe he would make a movie about the early days of motion pictures, or maybe he would do a prison film, and on and on. One by one the story lines were presented to Oona, who listened in her accustomed rapt mode to each and every proposal. One by one the scenarios were abandoned as Charlie lost enthusiasm. Chaplin continued composing for *The Circus*, but then, late one afternoon as he sat outside the Manoir watching birds fly over the lawn, he got the idea for *The Freak*, the story of a girl born with wings. Not only was Chaplin elated at finding a vehicle, he was equally exhilarated that the role of the winged girl perfectly suited his daughter Victoria. This film, the old man was convinced, would make her a star. Galvanized into action, Chaplin soon was back at Shepperton Studios making tests of his daughter and supervising the construction of a pair of wings. At the comedian's request Jerry Epstein came in to assist, and the two of them worked on a budget to present to potential backers. Alas, it proved not to be like old times; Chaplin, formerly brimming with vitality, had markedly slowed and during discussions about the financing would sometimes nod off.[1] Hard as it was for Jerry Epstein to see Charlie Chaplin failing, it was agonizing for Oona.

The Hollywood dictum "You're only as good as your last picture," soon was brought to bear on one of the industry's most illustrious architects. In trying to sell *The Freak*, Epstein contacted United Artists. A pair of executives, accompanied by their wives, flew to Vevey to view the script and discuss matters with Chaplin. Oona graciously showed the visitors around the grounds and served them lunch on the patio. After the meal Epstein read the screenplay aloud. With assurances that Charlie would hear from them directly, the executives, carrying a copy of the screenplay for further study, departed. Many, many weeks later a package containing the script of *The Freak* was delivered to Jerry Epstein's house. No cover letter was enclosed, just a form note inscribed, "With the compliments of . . ." Charlie Chaplin had been given the brush-off by representatives of the very studio he had helped to found.

The setback hurt but did not stop Epstein. He made the rounds and, after obtaining financing, returned to Vevey and prepared to give Charlie the good news. Carrying a storyboard of *The Freak* under his arm, Epstein was on his way to Charlie's room when Oona stepped into the hallway. She wanted to speak to him, she whispered. Drawing him into the doorway, Oona said quietly but forcefully, "There's no picture." Epstein listened in amazement. "I have to make a decision," Oona continued; "he'll never survive this picture. If *The Freak* was an easy film I would let it go ahead. But you know how impatient Charlie is on the set. Can you imagine what he would be like waiting for the special effects people to get the flying right? If it was the prisoner film or a simple comedy, I wouldn't object. But this picture would kill him."[2]

Heretofore, Oona had kept to herself whatever fears she may have had about Charlie's ability to function, but in that defining moment she moved out of the shadows, stated the case, took action, and then retreated into her fixed position in the background, allowing her husband to continue to operate in a world of creative possibilities which no longer really existed. Unaware that Oona had squelched the project *before* Victoria ran off with Thierrée, Charlie continued to talk about replacing his daughter and making *The Freak*—but it was only talk; to all intents and purposes, the film was shelved. The realization that her husband no longer was equal to the task of creating a film, no longer able to do what she knew kept him going, impelled Oona Chaplin to wrest control from the guardian and caretaker of her life. Their positions were reversed; now Oona was guardian and caretaker. She would do for him in his dotage what he had done for her in her prime; she would take care of him.

The changes in the condition of her own marriage turned

Oona's thoughts to another May-December union, that of the Irish dramatist Sean O'Casey and his much younger wife, Eileen. O'Casey, blind and enfeebled in his last years, lived in virtual isolation in the country and his wife faithfully tended to him. After his death she moved to London, where (her friends assumed), relieved of the burden of caring for the old man, she would have an opportunity to enjoy life. The Widow O'Casey, however, did *not* enjoy life and was miserable without her husband.[3] Perhaps Oona Chaplin gave considerable thought to Eileen O'Casey's story because she recognized in it a possible scenario for her own future—no matter how difficult life with Charlie might be, life without him could be worse.

Searching for something to do, Charlie Chaplin once again looked backward and pressed forward with a plan he had been mulling over for some time. Realizing that his old movies were a source of present income, he decided to sell the distribution rights, a move that would allow him to get money up front while putting the burden of circulating the films on someone else. Chaplin had spoken about this to his son Sydney and promised the rights to him. However, when Sydney brought in a potential partner to discuss terms, Chaplin peremptorily dismissed both of them. Other candidates were proposed and dropped, and then Rachel Ford suggested Moses Rothman, a crackerjack publicist and, in Ms. Ford's opinion, the smartest man ever employed by United Artists. Oona agreed with Rachel Ford's choice and urged Charlie to make the deal. During all the negotiations between Charlie and the man she called "Mighty Mo," Oona was present. Impressed by her understanding of the proceedings as well as her devotion to Charlie, Rothman subsequently described Oona as both a good businesswoman and a terrific lady. The deal was made, the rights were passed to Rothman, and he proceeded to make a fortune for himself and the Chaplins. A grateful Oona sent a thank-you note to the entrepreneur, and, adding her husband's gratitude to her own, wrote that Charlie thought very highly of him—which may or may not have been the case. The fact that Mo Rothman made a great deal of money from the films irked Chaplin, but when he grumbled that he should have realized more himself, Oona gently reminded him that Rothman had been the one to take the chances and market the films. Furthermore, in Oona's opinion, while they were very well off they were never *that* rich until they had sold the rights to Mo Rothman.[4] Rothman always retained a soft spot for Oona Chaplin—he had her handwritten thank-you note enlarged and prominently displayed in his office.

The Chaplin-Rothman distribution deal also called for Charlie to make personal appearances, ones that would not tax his strength, and with Oona alongside him the aging comedian reveled in the adoration and acclamation of a new generation of fans. About this time Mo Rothman came up with an idea. He contacted Martin Segal, founder and director of the Lincoln Center Film Society in New York, suggesting that the Film Society honor Charlie. Segal thought it a terrific plan but wondered whether Chaplin would return to the States. Rothman believed that Oona wanted to come back and would be helpful in getting Charlie to agree. With this in mind he arranged for Chaplin and Segal to meet in London (ostensibly to view a new print of *The Kid* for which Chaplin recently had composed a score, but actually in order for Segal to propose the Film Society tribute). Segal and his wife, Edith, flew to London, checked into Claridge's, and then went to the Warner Bros. screening room, where they were introduced to Oona and Charlie. When the movie ended Segal immediately complimented Chaplin on the score. He had seen the movie many times before and, of course, it was great; but the music was new and wonderful. Chaplin was very pleased and asked the Segals to join him and Oona for dinner. They had a thoroughly enjoyable evening.

Just as they were parting Chaplin said quietly to Segal, "Weren't you supposed to ask me something?" In the excitement Martin Segal had forgotten about the Film Society honors. Charlie laughed and said, "It's all right, Oona told me. I know what you were going to ask me, and I'll come."

Once word got out that Chaplin was returning, the Academy of Motion Picture Arts and Sciences in Los Angeles decided to offer him an honorary Academy Award. This, too, Charlie accepted. To make the return to the States easier, Rothman and Segal suggested that the Chaplins stop first in Bermuda, clear customs, and then go on to New York, which they did.

On April 2, 1972, Charlie and Oona Chaplin arrived at Kennedy Airport. Twenty years after departing for their self-imposed exile, Charlie was making his first return, and Oona her third—her last visit to tend to her ailing mother had been some five years earlier. That visit had engendered little press. And whereas her trip in 1953 had given rise to a few scattered notices, the joint return with Charlie became a media bonanza. The *New York Times* reported that a crowd of nearly 300 people gathered at the airport, 100 of whom were members of the press. The plane door opened and Charlie, with Oona right behind him, stepped onto the ramp and looked down at the mob of photographers and reporters on the tarmac. Throwing kisses to them and to observers looking out from the sweeping glass panes of the Eastern Airlines Terminal, he walked slowly down the collapsible staircase. The *New York Times* reported that "Chaplin's 46-year-old wife, Oona O'Neill Chaplin, stood behind and gently guided him toward a limousine waiting in the shadow of the jet's tail." Under the heading "Wife Stands Behind," the article went on to say that Oona seemed delighted to let all the attention focus on her husband.

The Chaplins were whisked off to the Plaza Hotel, where another large crowd had gathered. With Oona at his elbow the old man made his way haltingly into the Plaza through the Fifty-ninth Street entrance, no doubt to avoid the many stairs fronting the entrances on Fifth Avenue and Central Park South. That evening Oona's longtime friend Gloria Vanderbilt, now Mrs. Wyatt Cooper, gave a dinner in the Chaplins' honor at her town house on East Sixty-seventh Street. Oona hovered about her husband while he received his admirers, and though he felt "a little bit in slow motion," Charlie warmly greeted each of the guests. Frail as he was, Charlie Chaplin, an instinctive performer, could rise to the occasion.

The next evening, Wednesday, April 5, the Salute to Charlie Chaplin took place at Philharmonic Hall in Lincoln Center. Charlie and Oona entered through the rear entrance of the hall and were led to their box above the orchestra. Someone cried out "There he is!" and the entire audience (which included Paulette Goddard) rose to its feet applauding and cheering. Smiling broadly, Charlie responded to the welcome by throwing kisses and waving and doing a few quick comic motions. He turned to Oona, who was dressed in white, looked at her quizzically for a few seconds, and then turning to the audience, shrugged his shoulders as if to say, "Who's this?" Oona smiled. After *The Idle Class* and *The Kid* were shown, Chaplin stood up and spoke for the first time since his arrival. Filled with emotion, he said he was glad to be among so many friends. As cries of Bravo rang out, Charlie pointed to his ring finger and then to Oona. Implicit in the brief pantomime was his desire to let everyone know that his wife shared in this moment.

The press treated Chaplin kindly; articles concentrated on descriptions of his rosy, round face or wisps of white hair rather than his seriously curtailed mobility. With Oona always at hand ready to cue him, only those who got very close saw how weak he was, and no one chose to make it an issue. Covering the event for *LIFE* magazine, actress/photographer Candice Bergen found the Chaplins "conspicuous in their simplicity" and was struck by the obvious depth of their feelings for each other.[5] The New York celebrations came to a close and they were about to move on to the West Coast when Chaplin got cold feet. Increasingly nervous about returning to Los Angeles, he questioned why he had accepted an invitation to go where he was hated and declared that he had a bad feeling about Hollywood. Eventually he simmered down and philosophically observed that Hollywood, in fact, could not have been too awful a place because he had met Oona there.[6]

Like Gloria Vanderbilt Cooper in New York, Carol Marcus Matthau, Oona's other girlhood friend, planned a celebration on the West Coast. In preparation for the party, banks of hyacinths were placed along the driveway of the Matthaus' home. When she heard rumors that Charlie might not be coming, Carol immediately called Betty Tetrick to find out the truth. "Look," she told Betty, "we've planned a luncheon but if they can't make it, well, nothing's lost except for the fucking hyacinths."[7] The hyacinths were not lost. The Chaplins arrived and were feted at the Matthaus' home. Once again Oona was kept busy standing guard and identifying people as they approached her husband. An oft-reported anecdote about the luncheon concerned a somewhat portly bald gentleman who walked up and said, "Hello Charlie, don't you remember me? I know I've changed, but it's me, Jackie Coogan." Coogan, the brilliant child actor, had appeared in *The Kid*. Chaplin just looked vague, sank deep into his chair, and gave no sign of recognition. Oona leaned over, nudged him, and said, "Charlie, you know who this is, it's Jackie Coogan, the little kid that you directed." Charlie would not look up; Coogan shrugged his shoulders and went away. When he was out of earshot, Oona spoke. "Charlie, what was that all about? You know who Jackie Coogan is; you've often talked about him." Charlie looked up. "I know who he is," he answered, "and I'm not talking. He probably wants residuals." That was *one* version of the meeting of Chaplin and Coogan; in another, when

Coogan reached Charlie the old man took one look, burst into tears, and embracing him cried, "What a pleasure to see you . . . little boy."[8] Either version could be true; the first a perfect illustration of Chaplin's legendary stinginess, and the second, of his unfailing sentimentality.

During the Academy Award ceremony, Oona and Charlie sat in a backstage dressing room and watched the show on a television monitor. At the appointed time, as snips from *The Gold Rush* and *City Lights* were projected on the screen, Charlie was wheeled onto a darkened stage and assisted to his feet. Once he was positioned, the spotlight was turned on him. Bathed in the lustrous glow, with his snow-white hair forming a halo around his head, Charlie Chaplin stood behind the podium and received the cheers in what has been called the single most emotional incident in Academy Award history. Overcome, Charlie thanked the "dear, sweet people" for honoring him and softly murmured, "Words seem so futile"—a phrase he had uttered first in *Monsieur Verdoux*. He recovered enough to do a bit of shtick with a bowler hat, demonstrating that no matter how futile his words, Charlie Chaplin could say everything in mime. At the end of the ceremonies Oona, wearing a long white skirt and a white jacket, stepped out from the wings and took her place beside her husband. Charlie made a number of pointed jabs in her direction, which clearly meant, there she is, honor her, she's the reason I'm here. "It almost made me cry," said Chaplin in a follow-up interview, ". . . and *this* one," he added, nodding his head toward his wife, "this one kept saying, 'Oh, don't snivel.' " The interview ended. Chaplin stood up and, with twinkling eyes and feigning impatience, said, "Let's go celebrate, for God's sake!" He took Oona's arm, began humming his song, "Smile," and made his way gallantly out of the room.[9] With Oona at his side, Charlie Chaplin had come home.

twenty

LIVE AND LEARN

After they returned to Switzerland, Charlie suffered a fall. Oona called his injury more painful than serious, but had to be his nurse day and night. Moreover, she wrote to Louis Sheaffer, the irony of his coming through a 12,000-mile journey with flying colors and *then* suffering an accident was not lost on her. Surprisingly, Oona's New York stay had not included a meeting with the biographer. Later she explained that she simply was too wrapped up in getting Charlie through the ordeal to make any extra excursions on her own. Disappointed at not seeing her, Sheaffer nonetheless immediately wrote to commiserate over Charlie's accident. "Must keep you on tenterhooks all the time, worrying about his health and welfare," he commented. "From the articles I read on your recent visit here and from seeing the Oscar program on TV, it was evident that you were always on the qui vive to give Charlie a hand if he needed it." Sheaffer had no way of knowing that *if* was not an adequate appraisal. Charlie *always* needed a hand. In her reply Oona told Sheaffer that Charlie was not exactly ill, rather, after being x-rayed two months following his accident, it was discovered that a central vertebra in his back had been severely fractured. He had been in a lot of pain, and compounding his agony was the fact that it took so long to determine the cause of his suffering. Aside from being nervous about falling again, Charlie, according to Oona, was in good shape. Still, she could not leave him alone at all—*not*, she quickly added, that she wanted to.

Five months after the visit to America, at the request of the Italian government Charlie was off to Venice to receive the Golden Lion of the Venice Film Festival and to participate in a benefit to save the sinking city. Surprised that Charlie accepted the invitation, Oona was amazed as well that he actually made the trip. He, Oona, Jane, and Christopher along with their nannies and Betty Tetrick and Rachel Ford were flown by private jet to Marco Polo Airport and then put up at the Gritti Palace. On the final day of the festival the Piazza San Marco was cordoned off and turned into an open-air theater. Some 3,500 chairs were set up, and a giant screen was placed in front of St. Mark's Church. Plans called for Charlie to appear on the balcony of the Doge's Palace and receive his award from the wife of the president of Italy, and then for the screening of *City Lights* to begin. The floodlights were turned on. Drenched with light, Charlie rose to the cheers and cries of the wildly enthusiastic crowd. He blew kisses and took his seat as the movie began. The plan now called for the Chaplins to slip away to avoid problems with traffic. Accordingly, Oona and Rachel Ford stood up and made ready to depart, but Charlie stopped them. "Where are you going?" he said; "I want to see the fight scene, it's my favorite part." He sat and watched the entire movie as the Italian officials grew more and more agitated at the prospect of getting him through the crowds. When the film ended the Chaplin entourage was hustled into gondolas and taken down the side canals, which were lined with people who reached out their hands and literally pulled the boats along. Betty Tetrick remembered that there was some apprehension about things becoming too unruly, and although she and Rachel expressed their concerns, Oona remained calm. "The city had gone mad," recalled Betty in a 1994 interview, "but Oona never blew her cool. Then again, she never did." They reached the Gritti, and Chaplin retired to his room. This time Oona, who always left parties and celebrations early because her husband did, stayed up all night. According to Betty, the two of them "drank champagne like it was water." That evening in Venice was, in his cousin's estimation, "the most wonderful night of Chaplin's senior years."

Protecting and handling Charlie was now a full-time job, and Oona was under constant pressure. Yet she continued to gloss over the situation in her letters to Louis Sheaffer. In those letters she also shared thoughts about her father; thoughts, she wrote, that she had allowed herself since reading *O'Neill: Son and Playwright*. Now she clearly saw the parallels in the lives of her father and her husband. She felt that O'Neill's life ended when he was unable to work; thus she determined that Charlie had to be kept working at whatever was possible for him to do. Unfortunately the prospects and possibilities continued to shrink. Someone came up with the idea of having Charlie speak into a tape recorder and relate why he had composed the music for his films. Excited, Oona found the proposal appealing on two counts; not only would this keep her husband occupied, he also would be able to make money. When Charlie was told of this plan he answered, "I don't *know* why I composed the music" and the project was dropped.[1]

In May 1973, Louis Sheaffer mailed the galleys of *O'Neill: Son and Artist* to Oona, telling her that he was most eager to hear what she had to say about his portrayals of her parents and Carlotta. Since he had considerable respect for her editorial and literary judgment, he requested she let him know if she found any passages that struck her as careless or bad writing. On May 15, 1973, Oona sent a telegram advising Sheaffer that she nearly was finished. Although she had been calling him *Lou* for several years, the telegram began "Dear *Louis*," almost as though the importance of the work precluded her addressing him familiarly. The telegram soon was followed by a letter, once again to "Dear Lou," in which Oona told Sheaffer of the trials and tribulations of trying to read the galleys. She had alerted her husband that she was going to immerse herself in the manuscript and told him not to expect her to be around. She thought Charlie accepted her plan only because of her upcoming birthday; in other words, his present was to leave her alone. Classifying herself as a medium fast reader, Oona spent all Saturday afternoon, all of Sunday and Monday—with a couple of breaks to be with Charlie—reading. By Saturday evening, however, Charlie was getting edgy. To keep himself busy, he took up a book and soon was deep into his own reading. What book did Charlie choose? His autobiography, which, he advised Oona, was damn good and worthy of her reading again.[2] No matter how his faculties diminished over the years, Charlie Chaplin's ego remained remarkably intact.

Oona extolled Sheaffer's manuscript. Even allowing for her lack of objectivity, she truly believed that it was a great biography, well worth the years of effort. Reading the galleys had triggered many emotions in her, some of which were generated by the photographs as well as the text. Among the pictures, Oona particularly liked one of her as a baby with Aggie. Oona, appreciative of Sheaffer's delicate and compassionate handling of her parents' divorce, was moved to tears by a poignant quote from her mother: in discussing O'Neill's desertion, Aggie once said, "But of course Carlotta is so much more beautiful than I am." The idea that her beautiful mother felt inferior to Carlotta deeply touched Oona. Protective as she was of Aggie, Oona also could look dispassionately at the manner in which Carlotta Monterey was treated in the book. She complimented Sheaffer on the well-rounded way in which the third Mrs. O'Neill emerged, the good being there as well as the bad. Oona agreed with Sheaffer's theory that her parents likely would have separated even if Carlotta had not been involved. Her father needed someone else, Oona stated candidly, and Carlotta answered his needs.

Sheaffer was relieved to hear that Oona approved of his characterizations, especially that of her mother. He found Agnes to be the most elusive of the three principals, he explained, and comparing her with Carlotta, he told Oona he saw the two women as jigsaw puzzles. Carlotta was made up of large, bold pieces in primary colors, whereas Agnes, a far more complex personality, was composed of hundreds of small parts done in subtle hues.

Carlotta Monterey's large, bold pieces fell apart in her last years. She had dedicated herself to O'Neill and his work while he was alive and to putting on his last works after he was gone. Later, with nothing left to do, she deteriorated. Accustomed to a life of activity and accomplishment, with her mental state aggravated by idleness as well as medication, the once fastidious Carlotta, now disheveled in body as well as mind, went from living alone in a hotel suite to a nursing home where she received good care—but with a sardonic catch. The home was staffed by blacks, and Carlotta, who had long harbored fears of and aversions toward minorities,[3] could not bear to be touched by them. Oona never could abide Carlotta's pronounced racist sentiments; nonetheless she was moved by Carlotta's fate. Expressing her sadness in a letter to Louis Sheaffer, Oona wrote, "It must have been a nightmare . . . for the nurses as well as Carlotta." Carlotta Monterey died on November 18, 1970, and her ashes were interred next to O'Neill's grave in Boston's Forest Hills Cemetery. She survived her husband by seventeen years. Louis Sheaffer reported that over those years Carlotta continued to ease up on her judgment of Oona and confided to friends that she actually had come to admire Lady Chaplin.[4]

Although she was lavish in her praise of Sheaffer's manuscript, one inclusion did distress Oona. Years earlier Sheaffer had come across an interview quoting Oona Chaplin's personal thoughts about her life with Charlie and had been surprised that she talked so openly. From the little he had heard of Oona, it did not seem likely that she would go public with her emotions. Not knowing her at the time, however, he accepted the contents at face value and included references to the interview in his book. Oona now took the opportunity to clarify the story.

When she and Charlie moved to Vevey, Frederick Sands, an English journalist living in Switzerland, started publishing newspaper articles focusing on their *palatial* way of life. The Chaplins dismissed the writing as the contrived product of yet another reporter trying to make his name by impugning theirs. A friend told them that Sands really was a nice enough fellow who probably wrote what he did because he did not know the truth. Eventually Oona and Charlie met Sands at a party and found him to be pleasant, although Oona did think him a terrible gusher.[5] Following that meeting Sands made an about-face and wrote a number of effusively complimentary pieces. The three of them continued to bump into each other at various social events, and while Oona and Charlie were polite, as far as they were concerned Sands was simply another face on the Swiss party circuit.

A while later a former secretary of Chaplin sold a series of articles about the comedian to the London *Express*. The secretary had been fired, and the articles consisted of nasty peeks into the private life of The Little Tramp. Charlie was familiar with such treatment, but this time—and Oona could not recall why—he decided to do something. He telephoned Frederick Sands and asked the journalist if he would write a piece for the *Daily Mail* debunking the *Express* stories. Sands eagerly assented and in subsequent articles did succeed in taking the heat off. The journalist was on good terms with the grateful Charlie—and, by default, Oona. Several years later Sands telephoned Oona, pointedly reminded her of what he had done for her husband, and explained that he had been asked to do an article about her. He did not expect to interview Oona in person or anything bothersome like that; oh no, he believed that he was well enough acquainted with her and with the Chaplin lifestyle to use his knowledge in a proper manner—that is, if she did not object. The sell was soft. Had Sands asked for a private interview Oona would have refused, but because he did not seek face-to-face contact she gave her permission. Immediately Mr. Sands was off and running, leaving in his wake a piece of reportage that purported to expose the innermost thoughts of Mrs. Charles Spencer Chaplin.

"That most revolting sort of reporter," as Oona referred to Sands, betrayed her trust; worse, she could do nothing about it because she had granted her imprimatur. Unable to defend herself, she felt like a fool. "We live and learn," Oona wrote Sheaffer. "That bloody 'interview' was printed all over the place, and I had to live with it and go blue in the face trying to explain." Dismayed as she was, Oona recognized at least one humorous consequence. Everyone at the Manoir knew she had had nothing to do with the interview; nevertheless, after poring over the piece, Kay-Kay MacKenzie sought out her employer and bitterly complained. Why wasn't *her* name mentioned as a contributing member of the Chaplin household? Why had she been overlooked? Oona could laugh at this foolishness, but there was another assertion that could not be

sloughed off; Frederick Sands made reference to Oona's unhappy childhood, which greatly offended Agnes Boulton.
What did Oona mean by calling her childhood *unhappy*? She
never had said that to her; in fact, Aggie remembered that
when Oona was around fifteen years old, she specifically told
her mother that she had had a happy childhood, especially
during her growing-up years in Point Pleasant.[6]

Did Oona really think her childhood was unhappy? Her intimate friends believed that she did, but whether or not Oona
felt that way, she quickly moved to reassure her mother. If her
childhood was unhappy, it probably had more to do with her
father, she said. Anyway, Oona often declared that she never
knew happiness until she married Charlie, and that statement
may have been misinterpreted by Frederick Sands. She never
even spoke to Sands, let alone made comments about her
childhood. After reading Oona's version of the story, Louis
Sheaffer immediately made corrections to the galleys.

Another item in the O'Neill manuscript amused rather
than annoyed Oona. She told Sheaffer that at great expense her
daughter Geraldine had obtained a copy of the silent film of
James O'Neill's *The Count of Monte Cristo* and presented it to
her mother. Oona viewed it, found it embarrassingly bad, and
put it in the vault. She then read in Sheaffer's galleys that her
father, too, had owned a copy. But he went his daughter one
better and never even looked at the film!

Oona hoped to reread the galleys while on holiday. However, Michael Chaplin informed his mother that he had written a novel that had, he felt, a marvelous story. Before she left
on the visit to Scotland he sent her the manuscript, told her
that she was the first person to whom it was being given, and
asked for her comments. Oona did not relish the possibility of
having to criticize her son, and while expressing the hope that
the novel *was* marvelous, she could not refrain from interject-
ing an "Oh dear" in a letter to Louis Sheaffer. Her son's book

took precedence over Sheaffer's galleys on that trip, but she did not mention Michael's novel again.

As the summer of 1973 approached Oona continued to dash off letters, giving Sheaffer further thoughts on his book. A sense of urgency pervaded her correspondence as Charlie became more and more needy. She was no longer attempting to disguise Charlie's state of health, and admitting that he was unsteady on his legs and dependent on her, she confessed to finding it difficult, if not impossible, to leave him on his own.

By the end of 1973, *O'Neill: Son and Artist* was published and favorably reviewed, thus concluding the ostensible need for correspondence between Louis Sheaffer the biographer and Oona O'Neill Chaplin the indispensable source. However, the two were committed to their exchange of letters and continued to write for many years thereafter. At Oona's request, copies of *O'Neill: Son and Artist* were mailed to Claire Bloom, Jerry Epstein, Rachel Ford, Herbert Jacoby, Carol Matthau, Mo Rothman, Ella and Donald Ogden Stewart, Betty and Ted Tetrick, Gloria Vanderbilt Cooper, Syd Chaplin's widow, Gypsy, George Beecroft, and those of her children who were not living at the Manoir—Geraldine, Michael, Josephine, Victoria, and Jane. Sheaffer arranged for Oona to get his 40 percent discount from the publisher, which pleased her. She herself received a bound copy and wrote that she got a great kick out of seeing Sheaffer's photograph on the inside back cover flap. Her face was very familiar to him, but this was Oona's first real look at Louis Sheaffer, and she told him that the photograph was very *nice.*

While Oona praised the book, some members of the Boulton clan took umbrage at certain passages. Aunt Margery Boulton was touchy on the subject of her father and resented Sheaffer's statement that Teddy Boulton had a hard time supporting his family. Nor did she like the fact that E. W. Boulton was referred to as "Teddy." Oona pointed out that everyone called him Teddy, and as far as making a living was concerned, she reminded her aunt that obscure artists often have trouble supporting families, as did many *great* artists, and there was no reason to be ashamed.[7]

Oona read and reread Louis Sheaffer's book. In the end she announced that as far as her father was concerned, she felt that all the nonsense should be forgiven and forgotten in the face of his heroic battle to become an artist. This was a generous statement, but even if Oona the adult actually had reached that kind of resignation, the realization came too late. In her efforts to get away from the specter of her father, Oona went directly to Charlie. She never stood on her own.

twenty-one

LADY CHAPLIN

Charlie's increasing frailty curtailed their travels, but the Chaplins still entertained at home and Oona always had Charlie dressed and ready to receive guests. At one dinner party, actress Cybill Shepherd was seated next to the host; also at the table was Geraldine Chaplin, home for a visit. The conversation was lively; Chaplin, however, did not say a word during the meal but simply ate slowly and kept his gaze on his plate. Then, just as they were about to get up, he tugged at his dinner partner's elbow. The actress leaned over to hear what Charlie Chaplin had to say, and he whispered in her ear, "You know, my daughter's a very wealthy woman."[1] Increasingly, his conversations were filled with non sequiturs.

In 1974, having successfully worked with Charlie ten years earlier, Francis Wyndham was sent by Max Reinhardt to assist Charlie in a follow-up to the comedian's autobiography, an as-told-to picture book. Oona saw it as a godsend, something that would interest her enfeebled husband and keep him occupied. She was very eager for the book to happen. Arriving at the Manoir, Wyndham immediately saw the change in Chaplin, now essentially confined to a wheelchair. The project was not particularly demanding. Charlie was supposed to do captions for the photographs, yet Wyndham found the going difficult. He recalled in December 1994 that while "Charlie was 'on the spot,' he would wander and sort of couldn't remember. We brought up batches of photographs from the basement for him to go through and we tried to get him to make comments. There were a great many photos of Paulette Goddard and he'd point and say, 'Who's that girl? I never saw her.' And Oona and I got the giggles. It was nice that she could laugh." Oona did not go into details about Charlie's incapacity in her letters to Louis Sheaffer; rather, she told him that the process was difficult simply because Charlie did not want to discuss his old movies, he just wanted to talk about *The Freak*. Meanwhile she tried everything to keep Charlie focused, but even with a lot of prodding, as with the photos of Paulette Goddard, he often could not make connections. "Charlie could talk," said Wyndham, "but he did repeat himself. He was very sweet and he wanted to please one by remembering, but then he would sort of forget."

If Wyndham found Charlie's company exhausting, he found time spent with Oona exhilarating; the two of them would sit and talk for hours, especially about books. Although she was not a writer, she impressed Wyndham with her perception of all things literary and with her appetite for reading. The two got along famously, but their pleasant moments together came to an abrupt end when Charlie demanded her presence. "He would not let her out of his sight," Wyndham remembered. "If she moved or looked as though she might be going out of the room, he became frightened." By the time of Wyndham's last visit, Charlie's world had narrowed to the confines of his upstairs bedroom where the three of them—Oona, Wyndham, and Charlie—worked and dined. Lavish dinners were brought up and placed on a rickety card table around which the trio gathered.

Ultimately the photographs were pulled together and the book, *My Life in Pictures*, did come out; rather than featuring any text by Chaplin, it was almost entirely pictures with an introduction by Francis Wyndham. Appreciative of Wyndham's efforts, Oona wrote to thank him. He was touched by her thoughtfulness; "I was just a journalist, you know, and she was so shy and reserved but I think she knew I liked her."

For a while Francis Wyndham attempted to keep up with Oona through the mail and, on one occasion, sent her a biography of Trotsky. In her thank-you letter Oona confessed that she had given the volume to Charlie, explaining that she always was on the lookout for new books that he might like since he tended to reread his favorites. She would not get to the Trotsky biography for a while because Charlie was a slow reader. Eventually Oona's correspondence with Francis Wyndham ended, but, as was so often the case with people whom she met and liked, his name was added to the family Christmas card list.

Although Francis Wyndham came away from the Manoir de Ban with the sense that the sweet, frail old man he had met might not have been so nice in the past, he remained unstinting in his praise for Oona and the way she handled the situation. In recalling his time with the Chaplins at his London home in September 1994, Wyndham spoke admiringly of Oona. "She lived with a very exacting person who could not bear to have her out of his sight for a minute, and however much she may have loved him, this was a terrible burden. She was so tactful and unassuming that many people tended to overlook her in their attempts to get to Charlie. She, of course, did nothing to alter the situation. She never put herself before

him and actually endeavored to steer things his way." Wyndham also believed that for many years visitors went to the
Manoir de Ban more for Oona's sake than for her husband's.
"I know Graham Greene found Chaplin tiresome, didn't like
him, but he liked Oona. Put it this way," concluded the English
writer, "although one ostensibly traveled to Vevey to see Charlie, one came away remembering Oona."

Harold Clurman viewed the situation in a similar light. In
his 1979 oral history interview for Columbia University, Clurman said that Oona knew exactly how to handle her husband—"not in a bad sense," he stated, "but through love: she
understood him." Clurman also was struck by the irony of the
situation: Eugene O'Neill had regarded his daughter and her
marriage with contempt, and "she was the one person in the
whole family who turned out quite well."[2]

In the winter of 1974, William Phillips, another literary
gentleman, was added to Oona Chaplin's list of correspon-
dents. Phillips, Louis Sheaffer's editor at Little, Brown, was
working on the photographs for the O'Neill biography at the
author's apartment when he came across a stack of Oona's
letters. "While Lou was fiddling with the pictures he let me
read them, and I just fell in love with this extraordinary
woman." Struck not only by the "gentleness, warmth, loyalty, straightforwardness and lack of pretension" in the letters,
Phillips thought Oona an incredibly gifted writer. "She had a
wonderfully easy style and in these delightful charming letters, she told marvelous stories that were funny and touching." Bill Phillips decided that Oona should write a book, and
he wrote a letter to her pitching the idea. He suggested that she
do something along the lines of Lillian Hellman's *Pentimento*.
Oona took her time in replying. When she at last responded,
she told the editor that his suggestion had resulted in an immediate writer's block which included her ability to answer

him! She had not thought of doing a book, except perhaps about her mother, who, Oona felt, never had received her due.[3] If that wish ever turned to reality, Oona promised to contact Phillips; meanwhile, she added his name to the Christmas card list. Phillips, in turn, began sending her books and occasional memorabilia. He had a print made of the photo of Eugene O'Neill as a young man which appeared on the paperback edition of *O'Neill: Son and Playwright* and sent it to Switzerland. Thrilled, Oona had it framed, and placed it in a corner of her bedroom. She took a picture of the scene with her latest toy, a Polaroid camera, and sent it to the editor. The snapshot showed two photographs standing side by side on a bookcase shelf: the one of O'Neill and the other of Charlie Chaplin. (Louis Sheaffer believed that the placement of those photographs indicated that Oona had forgiven her father.) Bill Phillips continued to send things to Oona and she always wrote to thank him, hence, they stayed in touch. The young editor used these opportunities to keep prodding her, subliminally, about doing a book.

Around this time Oona's journalistic nemesis, Frederick Sands, launched a fresh round of annoyances. Intimating that he was Oona Chaplin's ghostwriter, Sands managed to collect an advance for a book entitled *Charlie and Oona*, an expansion of the infamous interview with her. When it was discovered that the book was *by* Frederick Sands and not, as the publisher had been led to believe, *by* Oona Chaplin *as told to* Frederick Sands, the publisher withdrew. Sands then brought his project to Max Reinhardt. Reinhardt attempted to dissuade him, still the journalist would not give up and tried to interest a number of London newspapers and magazines in serializing his opus. Meanwhile Max Reinhardt advised Oona that the best way to stop Frederick Sands from going ahead with his unauthorized book was for her to let Reinhardt announce that she was doing a book for his publishing house, Bodley Head. Desperate to keep her privacy, Oona agreed. A version of that release was picked up by the *New York Times*, and Oona immediately heard from both Louis Sheaffer and Bill Phillips. The former congratulated her, wished her well, and offered to help; the latter wanted to know what was up, since it was his understanding that if ever she did a book, Little, Brown would be the publisher. Oona wrote back advising both men that there was no book and no contract, just Max Reinhardt carrying out his plan to block Frederick Sands—with the possible hope that she indeed would someday publish a memoir. She never did. (Oona did keep a daily journal, which she wanted destroyed after her death. The diary might be in the hands of her children.)

Eugene O'Neill: Son and Artist was nominated for a National Book Award but lost to Douglas Day's *Malcolm Lowry: A Biography*. Though she had not read the latter, Oona wrote to Sheaffer telling him she thought he deserved the prize instead. When it was announced that Sheaffer's second volume had received the Pulitzer Prize, Oona immediately cabled congratulations and followed the wire with a letter full of praise as well as more anecdotes about Eugene O'Neill. She had been contacted by Yale University and asked to pay half the yearly upkeep of her father's grave. Willing to pay the entire cost, a whopping sixty dollars, Oona was vastly amused that the university was bothered by such a pittance, especially since her father and Carlotta had given Yale an incredible number of papers and manuscripts for the Eugene O'Neill Collection. Later, asked by the Eugene O'Neill Memorial Theatre Center to contribute to the renovation of the Monte Cristo Cottage on Pequot Avenue in New London, Oona sent a check for a thousand dollars. First her father's grave, then his childhood home; little by little, the disinherited daughter was becoming unofficial keeper of the Eugene O'Neill flame.

Despite his Pulitzer Prize, Louis Sheaffer wrote to Oona

that he was feeling down in the dumps and suffering from post-publication blues. The book had done well, but not well enough for the man who had spent so long in writing it. Oona wrote back that she understood his dejection and remembered how let down she had felt when Charlie's last four films were reviewed with less than critical acclaim. The films were her husband's creative works, but Oona's passionate involvement with everything he did and the fact that they were done during her reign as Mrs. Charlie Chaplin made their failure all the more painful for her. Agnes Boulton at least had had the satisfaction of knowing that she was Mrs. Eugene O'Neill during the time acknowledged as the playwright's greatest period of productivity. Oona's association with Chaplin covered the comedian's creative dusk.

In the summer of 1974, Louis Sheaffer was invited to a reception at the Manoir de Ban following the private wedding of Eugene Chaplin on August 10, 1974. He could not make the trip but was flattered and delighted to be included in a family celebration. The epistolary link with Oona had drawn him into the O'Neill/Chaplin circle, and Sheaffer's absolute veneration of those two men made that inclusion especially sweet. To show his appreciation Sheaffer occasionally mailed Oona some small treasures. One time he sent an original edition of *Part of a Long Story*. Her thank-you letter began with the requisite apology for having waited so long to respond, after which she went on to say that she cherished the gift. Her own copy of Aggie's book had been given to an overzealous bookbinder who returned a leather volume that looked like a "red and gold prayer book."[4] Oona thanked Sheaffer for restoring to her *Part of a Long Story* in its original form.

For as long as he was able, or could be made able, Oona continued to do the things with Charlie that they had always done. Although long journeys were out, she felt that Charlie welcomed a change in scene. Despite the difficulties, they continued to visit London. Each time they made the trip they were driven up to the plane and Charlie was assisted out of the car and into a wheelchair. The chair was pushed onto a platform, which was raised level with the plane's door to allow Charlie to be wheeled onto the aircraft and to his seat. Oona settled in next to him and, as the plane taxied down the runway, took his hand in hers. In years past they had hugged and kissed during the flights; now their ritual was reduced to holding hands.

On January 1, 1975, Charlie Chaplin's name appeared on the Queen's Honors List. Charlie had told Oona many times that a title did not go with his character and that the idea of *Sir* Little Tramp was silly.[5] A number of people thought that Charlie Chaplin retained his British citizenship for just such a possibility. Oona said that by accepting the knighthood he proved himself to be more thoroughly an Englishman than she ever had imagined. The Manoir immediately was stormed by the English press and television, but Oona turned them away, saying that Charlie, who was ill in bed with the flu, could see no one. On January 2 Oona showed Charlie a headline that read "Arise Sir Charlie," at which point, according to his wife, Chaplin actually arose from his bed, got dressed, announced that he was taking Oona out to dinner, and then, spirit yielding to flesh, fell back into a chair.[6]

In March, Chaplin managed to get to London for the investiture. He and Oona checked into the Savoy, where they were formally addressed by the hotel staff as Sir Charles and Lady Chaplin. Oona was certain Aggie would have gotten a kick out of hearing her daughter called My Lady, and equally sure that her father was "shuddering in his grave." She had a hard time with Charlie on that trip and had to assist him in everything. Charlie liked to take long baths in the Savoy's oversized tub, but getting him in and, especially, out was a formidable task. One day Oona simply could not lift him from the water. She called the floor manager, who came into the bathroom and with total aplomb put his arms around Chaplin's chest in a gentle, firm embrace, and with a cry of "Upsadaisy, Sir Charles,"[7] raised the naked knight-to-be from the tub.

Oona's main concern was whether or not Charlie had enough stamina to make it through the investiture ceremony. Charlie desperately wanted to walk the ten yards to the Queen, but it proved impossible; he simply did not have the strength. Pushed down the aisle by a palace steward, Charlie sat in a wheelchair as the Queen tapped him on the shoulder with the sword. He could not rise to that august occasion and himself recognized that the fact that he got to the ceremony at all was a small miracle. "I was determined to go in person to receive the honor," he told the *Daily Express*, "and I did, but I would never have got there without Oona's help."[8] For many long years Charlie Chaplin would not have gotten *anywhere* were it not for Oona's help. Oona's efforts on Charlie's behalf were generally admired; after his death, though, an opposing sentiment was expressed by Georgia Hale. "Oona, I believe, really loved Charlie, but her endeavour to shield him from the world was not only feeble but it seemed to me—weaken[ed] the one she smothered with her love."[9]

twenty-two

THE LONE SURVIVOR

During the summer of 1975 the Chaplins returned to London for a week's stay and Charlie fell on his back. The doctor told Oona that her husband needed at least a couple of weeks to convalesce and that it would best be done at home, not in a hotel. As soon as he was able to travel Chaplin was given painkillers and, clad in bathrobe and pajamas, was flown back to Switzerland. Thereafter he was attended by a twenty-four-hour nurse as well as by Oona, whose hours were no less demanding.

Meanwhile, awards kept pouring in for the old comedian. Charlie was made an honorary member of the American Academy of Arts and Letters and the National Institute of Arts and Letters, and the American ambassador wanted to come to the Manoir to present the citation. Oona welcomed the prospect of the ambassador's visit even though Charlie had suffered a slight stroke some months earlier and was now hesitant about seeing people.[1] They had to remain at the Manoir that summer because Charlie was not able to travel. Late in September he rallied enough for them to take a trip to London. While Charlie "never complained," Oona sadly mused in a letter to Louis Sheaffer, "it's hard to grow old."

In January 1977, Sheaffer told Oona that he had gone to the Museum of Modern Art to see *A Woman of Paris* and was impressed with the new score as well as the old film. Oona wrote back proudly that Charlie had composed the music in less than a month in 1975 and had recorded it in 1976. She continued to encourage him to work on more musical scores but, she confided, Charlie got "bored" with the idea. Indeed, he was "bored" with almost everything—even his obsession with *The Freak* had faded. Reading between the lines, one can see Oona's attempts to make her husband sound more capable of activity than he actually was. Chaplin was not bored; he was becoming more and more infirm.

At their Sag Harbor home in the summer of 1993 Kathy and Robert Parrish, friends from Hollywood days, recalled seeing the Chaplins on one of Charlie's last trips to London. "He was kind of dotty, by then," said Parrish. "Oona was wheeling him into Trader Vic's, they went there a lot, and Kathy and I were walking toward them. Oona spotted us, leaned over Charlie, who was crumpled down in the wheelchair, and cried out, 'It's the Parrishes, Charlie! It's Bob and Kathy!' Charlie raised his head and said, 'Oooh, Bob. Ooh, Kathy.' He used our names but you knew if she hadn't roused him, he'd have sailed right by."

In *Eugene O'Neill: Son and Artist*, Louis Sheaffer described the diminishing of the playwright's powers: "For more than thirty years, with incorruptible integrity, he had dreamed of and fought for effective utilization of his works; now he was letting go." The sentence had moved Oona to tears. If *thirty* were changed to *sixty,* that sentence summarizing the end of her father's life could have been applied to her husband. Charlie, Oona confided to Sheaffer, was letting go. Recently they had watched *The Gold Rush* on Swiss television, and through some error an entire scene had been eliminated. She was furious at the sacrilege, and whereas a few short years ago Chaplin would have been enraged, now he said nothing. Touched that Oona thought of the lines from his book about O'Neill's letting go in regard to Charlie's changed attitude about his own life's work, Sheaffer answered immediately: "I can easily imagine how you feel about his indifference now, but at the same time I'll always think of Charlie Chaplin as one of the most fortunate of mortals, not simply because of his international fame and his fortune but because at a time when you'd think his life's pattern was crystallized and he was on the downward slope of his life, he had you and his life began a second Springtime. Won't say more because it might sound mushy, except that he was very fortunate to find you—and you him."[2]

Early in April, Frederick Sands (a man it would seem with the hide of an elephant) sent a letter to Oona announcing that his book *Charlie and Oona: The Story of a Marriage* would soon be published and that he hoped to have a copy available for Charlie's birthday. The book had been serialized in *France Dimanche,* and the author apologized for some stupidities that had been added to his straightforward piece. To set things right, he wrote a letter to the editor citing three of the most glaring errors, to wit: when Charlie watched his old movies, he would cry and request that he be taken to his room; that Oona had white hair; and that Charlie was sixty-one and she twenty-five when they married.[3] While there was some truth to the first two statements—Charlie did get weepy on occasion, and Oona had been dyeing her hair since her mid-thirties when it began to gray[4]—Sands denied saying any of them. A week later he sent an advance copy of the German edition of the book, explaining that the English publishers were lagging behind. With staggering gall, Sands added that he hoped to drop by the Manoir to say hello. Despite all Oona's efforts, *Charlie and Oona* was published in Germany, serialized in Spain, and later translated into English. Upset and frustrated that she could do nothing to prevent the publication of his book, Oona could and did keep Sands out of her home.[5]

On April 16, 1977, Charlie Chaplin celebrated his eighty-eighth birthday, and though all eight of his children were present, his condition precluded anything other than a simple gathering. A stroke in 1976 had left Chaplin partially paralyzed, and for many months Oona had been housebound, not daring (or, as she put it, *wanting*) to leave her husband. The three youngest children were living at home—not a pleasant situation considering that their father was fading fast and their mother was fully absorbed with him. Dinner was served at an hour that suited the invalid, and after Charlie was in bed for the night Oona holed up in her suite. Evenings, formerly a time to bask in the company of her husband, now stretched before her bleak and empty. Photographs taken at this time show a decided difference in Oona's appearance. She looked far nearer in age to her husband, almost as though she were willing herself to diminish the age gap. She even had begun to *look* like him—her face was losing its classic angularity, deep circles appeared below her eyes, her cheeks had an anile ruddiness, and though her smile remained warm and open, a palpable sadness seemed etched into her features. More than anything, these photographs suggest that Oona Chaplin already was drinking too much, as indeed she was. Before his complete collapse, it was rumored that Charlie and she had terrible battles over her drinking.

In the past, no matter what the provocation, they had not fought. Now Charlie's absolute abhorrence of alcoholism took over. Reportedly Oona would lock herself in her room and Charlie would bang on the door insisting that she come out.[6] Whether or not these scenes actually took place, family and close friends knew she was drinking and some tried to help. Oona would have none of it; she would do as she wished and she wished to drink—as her father and brothers had done. Her alcoholism did not keep her from her absolute service to her husband, and eventually he grew too weak and dependent to make an issue of it; regardless of her condition he just wanted her near.

Charlie Chaplin, so fastidious throughout his life, became terrified of wetting his bed and no longer would sleep alone. During the day a manservant helped move him around, but the burden of lugging him in the early hours fell to Oona. She would get into the other twin bed in his room, lie there until he fell asleep, and then wearily pull herself up and return to her room. One of the servants set up an alarm system, and if Charlie stirred during the night a bell would ring in Oona's bedroom. She would rise, go to her husband, and assist him into the bathroom. Sometimes the bell rang and rang, and Oona ran and ran. The sheer physical strain took its toll. She injured her back severely, and the pain of her injury coupled with the agony of watching Charlie disintegrate made her seek liquid peace. Unable to sleep, her back paining her, Oona would pour a little tea and a lot of whiskey into a cup. Later she said that she got into the habit of lacing her tea to fortify herself for those hellish nights.[7]

On Friday, June 24, 1977, Oona Chaplin received a telegram from Herbert Jacoby informing her that Shane had "passed away" on the previous day. Jacoby expressed his sympathy and promised to write in more detail later. Stunned, Oona immediately tried to get in touch with the lawyer, reaching him only after repeated attempts. Pressed for more details, Jacoby said that he knew little else other than that Shane had fallen or had thrown himself from the window of a fourth-floor apartment and, with his former wife, Cathy, at his bedside, died a few hours later in the hospital.

At first Oona wanted to believe that it might have been an accident. Shane reportedly was in good shape, and his money problems had ended when royalties started coming in from his father's plays—royalties that through some legal proceedings had reverted to O'Neill's surviving children. Oona had diverted her share to her sister and brother[8] and was unaware that the money had created a new set of problems for him. The funds were administered by Herbert Jacoby, and when Shane began spending at an accelerated rate—some $2,000 per week—the lawyer correctly suspected that his client was back on drugs. In fact, the day before his death Shane had intimated to the lawyer that he planned to enter a rehabilitation clinic.

Later Oona reached Barbara Burton, who corroborated Jacoby's story about the drugs and about Shane leaping out of a window. Barbara also reported that a girlfriend supposedly was with him when he jumped. Confused and agitated at being so far away, Oona contacted Louis Sheaffer and asked if he could find out more. Sheaffer went to a Brooklyn police station, informed them that he represented the deceased's sister, spoke to the detective who had handled the case, and uncovered the last unhappy moments of Shane O'Neill's life.

"From the start," wrote Sheaffer, "I was careful not to let them know Shane was the son of a famous man, but they already knew that. However, they were not curious about you, so of course I said nothing about your being married to Chaplin." Shane still was conscious when the detective arrived at the scene. When asked why he had jumped, Shane answered that he was tired of this world, tired of his life. He also told the detective that he did not live there but had been visiting a girlfriend. The detective actually thought that Shane was not badly hurt and would survive. Sheaffer then spoke to another detective, a man who knew something of the decedent's history. Apparently, "Shane had been feeding half the neighborhood" for quite a while and the detective was curious as to the source of his income. When Sheaffer offered no answer, the detective went on to say that Shane, in a drug-induced frenzy, had jumped out of a police station window several years earlier—only that time it was a first-floor window. On the basis of Shane's history, both detectives agreed that there was no mystery; it was an open-and-shut case of suicide.[9]

While Sheaffer was doing his sleuthing, Oona learned that Jacoby, knowing that Charlie was very ill and not wanting to add to Oona's troubles by burdening her with the sordid details, had been withholding facts about Shane's condition. Oona confided that being left in the dark and not knowing had in fact *added* to her troubles. She was glad that Aggie had not lived to hear of Shane's death and glad, too, that Shane knew that his niece Geraldine, then living with the Spanish director Carlos Saura, had named their son after him.

Shane's funeral was attended by his former wife, his children and grandchildren, and his half sister, Barbara. They recited a Hail Mary and Our Father, walked around the coffin, and then went out the door as the two floral arrangements were quickly removed; the entire ceremony took five minutes. When she was told by Barbara of the funeral's brevity, Oona mourned that her brother seemed to have "died like a stone sinking without a ripple." She unburdened herself to Louis Sheaffer in a lengthy letter telling him of her thoughts.

She last had seen Shane during Charlie's triumphant return in 1972 when he brought his daughters and his grandchildren to Chaplin's suite at the Plaza Hotel. Oona was touched to see that her brother was wearing a cheap dark suit in an obvious attempt to look presentable for her. Yes, his life had been wasted, yet she was certain that those who knew him really loved him. Nothing Shane did could erase the sweetness in his nature, and she had not wanted his death to be casually dismissed. Oona felt relief in knowing the truth about her brother's last days and expressed her gratitude to Sheaffer for filling in the details.[10]

After years of agony Shane Rudraighe O'Neill took his own life. Ironically, this was one instance in which he was able to emulate his older brother. With Shane's death Oona Chaplin became the only surviving child of Eugene O'Neill. Grief would follow grief. In a few short months the man responsible for her surviving the childhood that had destroyed her brother would be gone. And when that time came, Oona would find herself, like Shane, in a world and in a life that had less and less meaning for her.

twenty-three

CHRISTMAS 1977

Every twenty-five years the village of Vevey celebrates the Fête de Vignerons, a two-week fall festival in honor of the vineyards and wineries of the region. A joyous time of parades, dancing, drinking, and feasting, the quarter-century holiday occurred in 1976 and the Chaplins took part in the revelries. Even Charlie managed to get out and was photographed with daughter Annette attending the Knie Circus on October 15. It was his last public appearance.

Oona had been fighting to keep Charlie going for many long years. Despite the gossip about her drinking, those who witnessed her heroic efforts could not help but be impressed. Like other visitors to the Manoir Chaplin's biographer, David Robinson, was struck by her unwavering dedication. "Oona was always there, a charming, gentle, smiling presence, and the marvelous thing of seeing them at that stage was the way she carried on." In Robinson's opinion, for a long time Charlie's mind had been working perfectly, but because he found communicating difficult, many people assumed he was senile and treated him that way. Eventually the condition matched the treatment. According to Robinson, "however fragile he was, however difficult he found it, Oona treated him as if he were as he'd always been, nor would she acknowledge to him or anyone else that he was not as he had been. This was really wonderful for him, and I believe he became very dependent upon that."

Early in 1976, when Chaplin was taken to the film studio to supervise the recording of the music he had written for *A Woman of Paris*, Robinson saw the drastic change in the comedian's behavior and spoke of it in a conversation with the author in June 1994. "Oona left the room because she had something to do and he become so anxious, so terribly, terribly anxious, he literally went to pieces until she came back. She rarely left him, though; I mean not at all." At the Manoir, Oona "continued to be a most wonderful hostess except that she would disappear for a large part of the day." Although everyone knew that behind the locked door of her bedroom she was drinking, nothing was said. In later visits Robinson saw that Oona's illness had progressed, but he also noticed that "her powers of recovery were marvelous."

While Charlie was still ambulatory Oona would walk with him around the grounds, holding him by the arm and propping him up as he balanced himself on his cane. When he could no longer walk Oona would wheel him down to the lake and push him along the embankment. On one promenade a British reporter recognized Oona and spoke to her. "I wouldn't have changed a thing," she said. "All of the trauma and difficulties and heartbreak I have been through with Charlie—it was worth every minute of it."[1] Later on, as Charlie's condition weakened further, the chauffeur or the butler would drive both Chaplins to the water's edge and leave them sitting there for an hour or so. At other times she would just sit with him, holding his hand and not saying a word, sharing what son Michael had termed their "strange solitude." With her hair pulled back in a bun, often clad in a simple housedress, perhaps with an apron thrown over it, Oona Chaplin looked more like a bourgeois Swiss hausfrau than a onetime Glamour Girl of the Year.

Charlie Chaplin was up and dressed and downstairs until the last three weeks of his life. He grew weaker and weaker and still was brought to the table for meals. Oona assisted him, sometimes feeding him so deftly that the illusion prevailed that he was lifting the spoon to his lips by himself. After the evening meal Oona would announce that it was time for the "telly" and wheel him in front of the set, where he would watch news broadcasts and American movies. He spent a lot of time looking at television or his old movies. Oona continued to fashion his life as he had liked it long after he had any real sense of like or dislike. His speech became slurred, and she seemed to be the only one who could understand what he was saying. When he no longer was able to speak, clad in shirt and tie he would sit in his wheelchair, his eyes following Oona around the room. Although it was not altogether clear that he knew who she was, he would reach for her hand as she passed by and press it to his lips.[2] Early on Christmas morning of 1977, Charlie Chaplin died in his sleep. Despite his deteriorating condition Oona was taken by surprise. She had thought he would live at least until age ninety, if not one hundred.[3]

How had those years of painful service—of seeing the powerful core of her life slowly decay and become the powerless center of her life—affected Oona? She must have felt relief when the burden was lifted, and with that relief there must have been an accompanying guilt. The old ruin whom she so faithfully attended obscured the vibrant man whom she had so worshipped. Oona's loyalty and love match any myth of devotion, but what did she do to *herself* in those trying, terri-

ble years?—Or, had it been done long years before? Her relationship to her father never was resolved, and in the last years
of her marriage, in dealing with the unresponsive old man that
Charlie had become, was not the awful story of her childhood
in some way being retold? How utterly distressful it must
have been to once again try to relate to someone who could
not relate to her. One thing is certain: when at last death came
to Charles Spencer Chaplin, the era of the teacup ended—Oona
stepped out of her protective shelter and emerged as a full-
fledged alcoholic.

PART THREE

twenty-four

CHARLIE'S WIDOW

Charlie Chaplin's funeral was held on a gloomy rainy Tuesday, December 27, 1977, at the Anglican Church in Vevey. The burial took place in the cemetery high on the hill overlooking Lake Leman. At the graveside Oona stood beneath a canopy of umbrellas, dark glasses shielding her eyes, a black kerchief covering her pulled-back hair. Framed in black, her face pale and haggard, her mouth drawn tight, Oona was caught by an intrusive cameraman. In the resulting photograph she gazes numbly into the lens, looking remarkably like her father. After the burial the funeral party gathered at the Manoir.

For Oona, the impossible had happened. Charlie had left her, and needing to get away from a house filled with his remembered presence, she soon went alone to the chalet in Crans where the family had frequently vacationed. There she tried to recuperate—and to drown her sorrows. First she had been deserted by her father; now the man who had rescued her was gone forever. The adult Oona was overwhelmed by the same sense of loneliness, abandonment, and despair that had plagued her childhood. A half century on, she seemed no better able to handle the inevitable loss of Charlie Chaplin than she did Eugene O'Neill's cruel withdrawal.

On her return to the Manoir, Oona was confronted with a bizarre crisis; dead and buried for over two months, Charlie Chaplin made headlines again when his coffin was dug up and stolen. The body snatchers telephoned, demanded money for the return of the cadaver, and further threatened that unless they were paid the youngest Chaplin children would be maimed or worse. In his lifetime Charlie had said he never would yield to the demands of kidnappers and never, under any circumstances, was ransom money to be paid by any member of his family. Oona resolutely followed his mandate and refused to pay. "A body is simply a body. My husband is in heaven and in my heart,"[1] she told the family lawyer. The police, however, urged her to pretend to negotiate with the grave robbers, thereby making it easier to apprehend them. She complied, and the Chaplins went under police protection as Oona and Geraldine dealt with the body snatchers over the phone.

Charlie's coffin was discovered in a cornfield near the village of Noville, about fifteen miles from Vevey, and was removed and re-interred in the cemetery. The criminals, Roman Wardas and Gantcho Ganev, two auto mechanics, were apprehended, tried, and sentenced, and the ghoulish brouhaha ended. The farmer in whose cornfield Charlie was buried put a wooden cross decorated with a cane on the spot where the coffin had been found, a setting Oona reputedly called even lovelier than the official grave and one that she was said to have visited on several occasions. Until the matter was resolved the tension and activity related to solving the crime, although nerve-racking, probably helped distract her from dealing with the cold hard fact of Charlie's death. Once the grotesque diversion ended Oona had to move forward, but having been on idle for so long, she could not shift gears easily. Her life had been tailored to the needs and demands of someone decades older, and in the process she was not only anchored by his presence but weighed down by his years.

At age fifty-two Oona Chaplin was alarmingly alone. For weeks—in some instances, months—she did not respond to letters of sympathy. However, true to her epistolary fashion, she eventually answered them all. Someone once commented that the surest way to stay in touch with Oona Chaplin was through the mail. She did not always return phone calls but always answered letters. Her notes were redolent of her sorrow, and many allusions were made to the impossibility of being without Charlie. "It's so sad," she wrote to Francis Wyndham, "unbearable really." She was lost, and in the opinion of some friends her state of confusion was partly a result of the passivity that had been nurtured during all those years of being looked after. Robert Parrish believed that Oona *had* to be passive with a man like Charlie, or else leave him. Calling Oona someone who allowed things to be done for her, or to happen to her, rather than initiating action on her own, Kathy Parrish swore that Oona did not know how to rent a car or even how to make a phone call. "She was utterly cosseted and cocooned by Charlie," said Oona's Hollywood friend in September 1992. "It was like she had been in a cast all her life and suddenly the cast had been removed and she did not know how to walk." Betty Tetrick, invited to visit in Switzerland, watched as Oona moved forlornly through the Manoir almost as though she were expecting Charlie to appear. Betty accompanied Oona on a trip to London, the widow's first without her husband. As the plane took off, Betty glanced over to see how Oona was doing. "She wasn't aware that I was watching and I saw her open her purse, take something out and then hold on to it. At first I thought it was a hanky or something like that, but I looked closer and I saw that it was one of Charlie's gloves. She held it in her hand for the entire flight, just the way she used to hold on to his hand."[2]

Oona continued to hold on to Charlie. No one could draw her from *his* shadow as he had pulled her from her father's shade. Dead and buried, both men still influenced her life. Eugene O'Neill's sway was deeply embedded and most people did not bring up his name, but she never appeared in public without being asked about Charlie. Some of the queries took her by surprise. She told Jerry Epstein that after a flight to New York City the plane's captain politely inquired if he could ask her a question. Oona agreed, and the captain said, "Was your husband Jewish?" Taken aback, Oona recovered and answered yes. Epstein interrupted, saying that Chaplin had told him he was not Jewish. Oona then explained that Charlie had told her that whenever people asked such a question, she had to say yes, otherwise she would be playing into the hands of anti-Semites. "Anyway," Oona laughed, "he was part Jewish, wasn't he? Oh, I really don't know, but who cares. . . . What does it matter?"[3]

In the summer of 1978 Oona accepted an invitation from Carol Matthau to stay at the Matthaus' beach house at Trancas Beach right above Malibu. Before she left Switzerland Oona wrote to Louis Sheaffer and, expressing the hope that they would at last see each other in person, informed him that she was coming to America. She enclosed the Matthaus' address and advised Sheaffer that upon her return from the West Coast and after visiting Claire Bloom in Connecticut, she would be staying at the Carlyle Hotel in New York City where she hoped they could meet. (Bloom, coincidentally, lived in the same town in which Aggie Boulton resided before she met Eugene O'Neill.)

Oona arrived in Los Angeles and joined Carol at Trancas. Her hostess had arranged for them to be alone so they could spend the days "listening to music, reading, talking, not talking, laughing, cooking, walking on the beach, catching up on everyone we ever knew."[4] Oona never seemed to give way to her emotions, and knowing the depth of her friend's grief Carol questioned the restraint. She purposefully avoided tears, Oona explained, because of a remembered incident. Years ago, she and Charlie had visited his recently widowed sister-in-law, Gypsy, and the bereaved woman was completely inconsolable. She cried for days, and her immoderate behavior made an indelible impression on Oona and Charlie, both of whom felt helpless and awkward in the face of Gypsy's uncontrollable flood of tears. Oona resolved, then and there, that when Charlie died she would not let her grief manifest itself in a torrent of tears; she would control herself, and she did. In the month that Oona spent in California, she sometimes took long solo walks along the beach. On one of those strolls Carol watched as her friend headed toward the water's edge. "With the sun slanting in as it did and the glare of the water and the shadows, it looked almost as if she was only one-half a person, and that was the truth of it."

Oona received many invitations but accepted few; she did go for lunch at Merle Oberon's because the Chaplins had been quite friendly with the onetime screen star and her then husband, Alexander Korda. Neither woman had much to say to the other, however, and the luncheon was not uplifting. "Merle always was a fucking bore," Oona sighed when she and Carol returned to the beach house.[5] Oona also accepted a luncheon invitation from actress Jennifer Jones, now Mrs. Norton Simon. The wealthy art collector was Jones's third husband, and the happiness of that union was a prime example of getting on with life after the loss of a great love. Having been widowed by David O. Selznick, the actress vividly described the first year after he was gone as one etched in sorrow, and she confided that she might not have come through had she not sought professional help. Oona appreciated Jones's words of encouragement but could not apply any of the actress's recuperative experiences to herself.

"Oona made a try at living after Charlie died," wrote Carol Matthau, "but it didn't work. She simply could not stand the pain of being alive without him."[6] Most other friends felt the same. "It was a great love story," asserted Norman Lloyd in February 1993, "and then it was over. You couldn't have someone like Charlie go out of your life and just pick up another life, not with what their relationship was. I dare say she felt that her own life was finished."

The adored wife had become an immutable widow. Although various opportunities to do something constructive presented themselves—she could have participated *actively* in Chaplin film festivals or established foundations—Oona did nothing other than *sanction* a few projects, such as David Robinson's biography and Richard Attenborough's film, *Chaplin*, which was based on Robinson's book. Sorrow stifled her, loneliness overwhelmed her, and she drank to escape.

By contrast, it is interesting to compare the manner in which another woman dealt with a similar situation nearly a century earlier. Like Oona Chaplin, Cosima Wagner was the daughter of a genius, Franz Liszt, and the wife of another genius, Richard Wagner. Also like Oona, at her husband's death Cosima entered a long period of intense grieving. She, however, eventually emerged from mourning, took over the music festival in Bayreuth, and brought it to a level of success which had eluded the composer himself. When asked why she had not run the festival during her husband's lifetime, Cosima famously replied, "Because then, I served."

Oona also served, but once the object of her veneration was gone she was unable to rally. Although these two women lived in different times and different worlds, the basic ingredients in their lives were quite similar—with a notable exception. Like O'Neill, Liszt had walked out on his family when his daughter was young, but unlike the playwright, Liszt never cut his daughter off. Despite their relatively infrequent personal contact, he kept a caring eye on her all his life. Cosima's self-esteem had not been ravaged by her father; Oona's had. Charlie's death, his *involuntary* leave-taking, reactivated somber memories of her father's *deliberate* abandonment, and Oona was overpowered by grief. Unlike Cosima Wagner, she could not move past mourning.

twenty-five

NO WAY OUT

Following her visit to California and a brief stay in Connecticut, after nearly a decade of correspondence Oona met Louis Sheaffer in person at her suite in the Carlyle Hotel. Both were shy, and in their guardedness it must have become obvious that the intensity of their relationship on paper could not be sustained. Whatever Oona might have been expecting—and she may have fantasized a bit about her longtime pen pal—it was not to be found in the repressed personage of Louis Sheaffer. Sheaffer's niece, Michelle Slung, believed that her uncle's correspondence with Oona had been a quiet refuge for her while Charlie and children were still around her, but that suddenly, in the wake of Chaplin's death, Oona's zest and energy for such things departed. They were extraneous to her, but not to Lou Sheaffer, who, his niece further asserted, never saw Oona as a real woman with flaws, neuroses, and needs but simply idealized her. He desired nothing more from her than an affectionate friendship from afar and could not handle her womanly presence. And, added Ms. Slung in a letter to Brian Rogers, curator of the Sheaffer/Chaplin letters at Connecticut College, while Oona exhibited a fair flirtatiousness at first, she too had been protected by the distance.

In a letter dated October 9, 1978, concerning their long-awaited get-together Sheaffer wrote, "It goes without saying, that I enjoyed meeting you—you have a very responsive nature, you were just as I had expected." Hardly a passionate declaration, and at this point Oona Chaplin probably needed a more enthusiastic validation. It was not until November 27 that she responded to Sheaffer's letter. Telling him that she felt awful not to have written sooner, she made a brief reference to their meeting and said she regretted that their time together had been so brief. Her tardiness in answering, she explained, was due to her state of health and mind.

She complained of pains in her stomach and bemoaned her inability to write or read; she could not even listen to classical music because it made her too sad. She felt that the Manoir was inhabited by ghosts, a ghost; yet when she took short jaunts to Paris and London to get away, she immediately wanted to return home. Unhappy at the thought of spending Christmas at the Manoir, she expressed relief that the Matthaus had offered their beach house to her over the holiday. Although she said that she did not like California very much, the ocean meant everything to her; thus, she planned to go and to take Jane, Annette, and Christopher with her.[1] The three youngest were living at home, but Oona's aptitude at parenting, long held in check by her need to tend to her husband, continued to be stymied by her need to drink. She was unable to derive the satisfaction and solace from children which many widows experience; indeed, it seemed that she could no longer derive any satisfaction at all. With Charlie, life had form and meaning for Oona. Life without him was formless and meaningless. Although there were children and grand-children to consider, and although she eventually would enter into a series of affairs in an effort to seek a measure of comfort, nothing really helped. After Charlie Chaplin's death, Oona's closest relationship was with the bottle.

twenty-six

LIKE MOTHER, LIKE DAUGHTER

The daughter of Eugene O'Neill and the widow of Charlie Chaplin continued to manifest an extraordinary mystique. On a tour of Europe in the late eighties the strange (but not yet nefarious) Michael Jackson declared that Oona Chaplin was the person he most wanted to meet. Oona's old friend Sophia Loren, "something of a Jackson groupie,"[1] had been attending Jackson's concerts, and when the singer came to Switzerland the Italian actress did arrange for them to meet. He went to the Manoir and was given a tour of the estate by Oona. At one point she told him that he and Charlie "had a lot in common: you were born poor and had to strive to achieve all that you have."[2]

Many men were dazzled by Oona, and not a few were chosen. In that respect one only can think back to Aggie Boulton. Some with whom Oona became involved were highly unlikely prospects, and one of the earliest, Ryan O'Neal, was one of the most unlikely. Oona met the actor at a Hollywood soirée at a time when she was, in her words, "still very sad about losing Charlie."[3] Finding O'Neal terribly sweet, she was highly flattered when he called her the day after the party and proclaimed, "If I'd met you a few years ago my whole life would have been different." Oona reported that her children were stunned when she told them that she was being courted by this movie star. She went out with Ryan O'Neal and was with him until three in the morning, along with Jane, Annette, and Christopher. "It was one of the greatest moments in my life, and there I was with three chaperones," she later told an interviewer from *The Sunday People*, a Sunday London newspaper. In the May 11, 1981, issue of the magazine, in an article subtitled "The Truth about Her Friendship with Ryan O'Neal," a rather startling portrait of the woman thought to be in perpetual grief was presented. According to the newspaper, "less than a mile from the resting place of the world's best-known comic, Charlie Chaplin, his house rings with the laughter of his widow as she talks about the other men in her life. Although Lady Chaplin reveres the memory of her late husband, the black veils of widowhood are not for her." Oona, previously so private, so quiet about her life, now allowed herself to be presented to the public.

Oona and Ryan O'Neal became so much "an item" that his daughter, Tatum, allegedly wrote a poison pen letter telling Oona to stay away. Oona did not acknowledge receiving such a letter and also declared that hearing such gossip did not upset her. She brushed it off—her time with Ryan O'Neal, she said, was just something very, very nice in her life. "It was fun and it gave me such a lift after a long period of being so sad."[4] Despite the frequent use of the word *platonic*, the romance with Ryan O'Neal was presumed to be intimate. Allegedly Oona told some acquaintances that O'Neal "wanted to be with her," and when she said that she could not give him any children he joked, "I'm sure you've got a couple still up there."[5] Besides upsetting her lover's daughter, the affair caused Oona's family and friends concern; she was, after all, sixteen years O'Neal's senior. Gloria Vanderbilt questioned how she could be with a man so much younger. "Good God, he doesn't even know the same songs!" exclaimed the heiress. While denying that she made that statement, Ms. Vanderbilt admitted telling gossip columnist Liz Smith that "Ryan wanted to marry Oona just to make her an O'Neal again." Whether or not Tatum O'Neal influenced the proceedings, the affair had a brief run and then ended, apparently amicably. Oona was quoted as saying that "If Ryan phoned me today and said, 'I need you,' I'd be there. I really liked him."[6] Oona's opinion of her paramour vastly differed from that of a journalist in the *Sunday Telegraph* who, in commenting on the Widow Chaplin's embarking on a series of unsatisfactory affairs, cited the one with Ryan O'Neal as "surely a sign of desperation."[7] For his part, O'Neal remained respectfully closemouthed about their romance.

Oona was introduced to her next swain through her second son. Eugene had become friendly with David Bowie and asked his mother to entertain the rock musician and a group of his friends at the Manoir. Oona agreed, and while she intended only to be around for a minute before making herself scarce, she found herself quite taken with the "very charming, very intelligent, very sensitive fellow—who came from the same part of London as Charlie."[8] The charming, intelligent, and sensitive Bowie was twenty-two years younger than Lady Chaplin, which did not keep them from becoming very close, very quickly. Soon the captivated musician bought a house not far from the Manoir. In another interview, this time for the *Evening Standard*, Oona told the respected journalist and author Alexander Walker that she liked Bowie very, very much. When Walker asked why so extroverted and publicized a figure as the pop star should have an affinity for her, Oona replied that Bowie had a quiet, serious side to which she responded. At his urging Oona considered taking a role in a movie being made by a young producer, Keith Rothman. It had been nearly forty years since Oona had tried out for a film part, and she was very nervous.[9] Bowie told her that if she did the movie, he would do a stage play he had been offered. Oona called their bargain "a kind of mutual dare," but while David Bowie scored a triumph on Broadway playing John Merrick in *The Elephant Man*, Oona Chaplin's movie evidently was not realized.

For a while Oona kept busy with what her former daughter-in-law, Patrice Chaplin, rather ungenerously termed as school-girl crushes on sexy younger men.[10] The irony of Charlie's widow being involved in well-publicized December-May affairs was not lost on the public. Pictures of her and Ryan O'Neal, or of her and David Bowie, could have been those of mother and son, just as long-ago photographs of Charlie and Oona could have been those of father and daughter. Oona's crushes may have been pursued in a capricious manner, yet viewed compassionately they can be seen as sincere if desperate efforts to reaffirm her desirability. For many years Oona had been shielded from time because of Charlie, in whose eyes she could not fade, in whose eyes she was forever fair. His adoration was part of what made it possible for her to live with the notoriously difficult man. How hard it must have been, after all those years, to cease being the object of such devotion. And how eagerly she must have reacted to the ardor of someone from another generation.

Two years following Charlie's death, Oona once again met someone at a party given by the Matthaus. This time it was a contemporary, not a macho young movie or rock star. Walter Bernstein, a director and screenwriter, was doing a remake of

Little Miss Marker starring his friend Walter Matthau. "Oona and I met, at a certain kind of time in both our lives when we were important for each other—however temporary it was always going to be," recalled Bernstein. "Obviously, no one was going to take the place of Charlie Chaplin. She was never going to get married or anything like that."[11] From the beginning of their affair the screenwriter sensed something rootless about Oona; she did not want to stay at home, consequently she often was on the go. Though they saw each other steadily, Bernstein was unaware of her drinking for the first two years of their relationship; he had very little experience with alcoholics, and Oona was skilled in the art of cover-up. "We'd go out for dinner, have a drink beforehand and maybe wine with the meal, and that was all. I never saw her drink." Bernstein was impressed by Oona's intelligence. "She was uneducated, really an autodidact, and in that respect her omnivorous reading was very important to her." Like Louis Sheaffer, Max Reinhardt, Bill Phillips, Francis Wyndham, David Robinson, and others, he recognized Oona's gift for writing. She sent him excerpts from her journal, and years later he still remembered especially liking one entry in which Oona wrote of viewing her father with *weary contempt.*

In general Oona upheld her rule of silence about her father, but she did talk to Bernstein about Aggie—and with real affection. It was obvious to him that she cared a great deal about her mother and about her childhood home. She spoke of the happy times at Point Pleasant, and according to Bernstein, when she talked of leaving there she made it sound like the expulsion from Paradise. Several times Jim Delaney's name came up, and she mentioned how guilty she felt at turning him away when he was in Los Angeles. Charlie had forbidden her to see the beloved friend of her childhood, she explained, and she had obeyed him—she always obeyed him.

According to Bernstein, Oona had had only two bona fide

affairs before Charlie—one with Peter Arno, the other with Orson Welles. In Bernstein's opinion Oona had come into something very imposing with her marriage, and that *grandness* caused her to take a backseat, especially in Switzerland. As he saw it, dinner parties at Vevey were opportunities for Charlie to hold forth with the movers and shakers of the world while Oona sat at the foot of the table not saying a word. Despite her assertions that she had begun drinking when Charlie was old and ill, Bernstein felt that she had been drinking a little for years earlier in order to fortify herself.

Bernstein did not minimize the love between Charlie and Oona, yet he thought that another component had to be factored in—safety. In Charlie's harbor the demons which had driven Oona's two brothers to suicide could be controlled, and her appreciation of his refuge was such that even after he was gone she still defended him fiercely. Once, Oona showed Bernstein a version of *The Gold Rush* for which Chaplin had been forced to do a narration in order to protect the copyright. "The sound track was terrible, it really hurt the picture and I told Oona so. She just jumped all over me. 'No, it's great, it's even better!' She just had to defend, publicly at any rate, anything he did." Walter Bernstein regarded the Chaplin marriage as an extraordinary symbiosis in which Oona and Charlie lived for each other—again, to the exclusion of the children, who "really suffered."

While Oona did not want to talk about why she and Charlie had so many children, she did tell Walter Bernstein that it was *she* who wanted them. And while Bernstein never talked directly to Oona about her relationship with Charlie, he pieced together a scenario from little things that she said. "I think Chaplin was extremely Victorian and Oona was the absolute image of what he wanted. He didn't want a woman, he wanted a girl. She could be a girl and she could be a mother, but he didn't want a fully developed sexual independent in any kind of way." The marriage easily lent itself to analysis, yet

Bernstein was quick to point out that "whatever it represented, for whatever crazy reasons, it worked for the two of them. Who knows in what direction she would have gone had not he closed off the area for her. That marriage was made in heaven."

Bernstein met Oona's children, and in watching them interact with their mother he felt that she spent a good deal of time appeasing them. They, of course, had to have harbored some grievances against her. When the majority of them reached adolescence she was immersed in her drinking, and whereas their father could not help growing old they must have felt that their mother *could* and *should* have exercised control. Why did she *allow* herself to become a substance abuser? Whenever Walter Bernstein visited Vevey, or when he saw them in New York, the Chaplin offspring were friendly toward him, although he did feel that no one quite knew what he was doing there—including himself. One thing he was doing was accepting Oona Chaplin's largess.

"It was like being in a toy shop in a funny kind of way, but she was so genuinely generous, I don't mean just with the money, she was a generous person, warm, smart, and . . . shrewd. Charlie had taught her well about money, and she was always going to this banker who handled this part of the money and that banker who handled the other part of the money. She used to say to me, 'You know, every day I get richer' and I'd say, 'that's nice.' But I really kept after her to do something with her writing. She kept saying she would and she never did. She didn't have to. She wrote in her diary, but it's one thing to write a journal that no one's going to see and quite another to write. She was never going to compete overtly in anything."[12]

Oona did have a measure of expertise in one area, and she had been taught by a master. Early in their marriage Charlie had tutored her in the ins and outs of wealth. Reportedly he always gave her a substantial sum of money on her birthday, often in blue-chip stocks; and as an incentive for her to save, if she still had the money on her next birthday he would double it. Protective of her growing nest egg, Oona took a genuine interest in the workings of finance. In later years that interest, combined with what she had learned during her apprenticeship, paid off. *She* got the money out of America, *she* championed Mo Rothman, and after Charlie died *she* made millions by taking a large chunk of money out of Switzerland and investing in the Dreyfus Fund, whose board she consented to join. She did little more than attend the annual meetings but was treated royally. Oona said that she did not know exactly what was happening, but she enjoyed holding a position on the board. When Bernstein asked why she bothered to attend the meetings, she answered bluntly, "I just love sitting next to all that money."

Unlike their mother or their father, the Chaplin children apparently showed little interest in finances. "Oona got really mad because not one of the kids paid attention to the family fortune," remembered Betty Tetrick. "They didn't care. She did. She got a kick out of making money with money."[13]

Oona continued to treat Walter Bernstein lavishly and among other lagniappes sent him round-trip tickets on the Concorde. He would join her in London or Paris, where they would meet at the Savoy or the Ritz. A yacht was hired in the summers, and they would cruise the Mediterranean or the Aegean, usually with Bob and Kathy Parrish; sometimes they were joined by one or another of Oona's children.

In March 1980, Oona was introduced, through Bernstein, to Frances "Frankie" Schuman, wife of composer William Schuman, the director of the Juilliard School of Music. During a fund-raising campaign for the MacDowell Colony, a non-profit organization that funds creative artists, Bernstein suggested that Mrs. Schuman, a board member, call Oona Chaplin. "You'd better hurry up," he added, "she's leaving for Switzerland." Taking him at his word, Mrs. Schuman dropped off a note at the Carlyle Hotel. "I did not see her, then," she recalled, "but she did send me a check, along with a lovely note saying that Walter and Louis Sheaffer had told her how much they were helped by the MacDowell Colony. I think she wrote the note on the plane going back to Switzerland. Well, I really was astounded by the size of the check. We were looking for something like five hundred dollars and she sent us an obscene amount of money, ten or twenty thousand dollars. It was unbelievable. I remember asking Walter what made her do that, and he answered, 'She probably thinks that's what it costs.' "[14]

In part because of her relationship with Bernstein and also because she wanted a base in the States, in the early eighties Oona purchased a duplex apartment on East Seventy-second Street in New York (the very same apartment for which former president Richard Nixon had been turned down). It was Oona's first American home in over thirty years, and the very first that was completely hers. Because of tax reasons, she could stay in the States for only three months at a stretch; thus, for the next several years, using the Concorde as though it were a branch of the IRT, Oona commuted between New York and Europe. After fixing up the apartment Oona held a housewarming. "Oona gave the party, but I think it was probably Walter's idea to let people know she was in town," commented Frances Schuman. Guests arrived and milled around the apartment for quite some time with no sign of the hostess. "It got to be quite late and she still hadn't appeared," recalled Ms. Shuman. "Ordinarily, I would have left, but I hadn't yet met her in person and I wanted to see Mrs. Chaplin. Finally she came into the room wearing what looked like a rumpled linen negligee. I wondered if this was the latest European chic and then I realized it *was* a nightgown. She'd been sleeping and had just roused herself . . . but, her hair and face were groomed, she'd put on her makeup, and except for her odd attire, she looked okay."

Oona moved to the center of the living room, and the guests lined up. Frances Schuman was introduced and complimented her hostess on the lovely apartment. Oona immediately offered to show her around. "We walked out onto the terrace, which was beautifully landscaped with banks of potted shrubs and flowers—an abundance of roses, as I recall. The way Oona pointed things out, I got the feeling that she was sort of seeing it for the first time. Maybe I was wrong, but I didn't think that the terrace meant anything to her except for the sunlight. The living room was large and opened into a library, which created a really big space. A quite marvelous staircase led to the second floor; she never had to use it, though; her bedroom was on the living room floor, as was a second bedroom that she'd turned into an office. She sent me upstairs on my own to take a look. I believe there was a guest suite, and I distinctly remember a wall of family photographs. I'm pretty sure I saw one of her father." Frances Schuman genuinely admired the apartment, yet she got a distinct impression that whoever had designed it for Oona had a lot of entertaining in mind. "For me, it wasn't the sort of place that you came into and felt cozy. The library, for instance, had this books-by-the-yard look, you know, just to have them there. A really beautiful desk stood in the middle of the room and there wasn't even a pencil on it. I'm sure the desk was there for her to work at, but it hadn't been touched; it just stood there like a reproach." Oona Chaplin, who had surrounded herself with books all her life—books that she read and treasured—now had a library of decorative convenience.

Walter Bernstein had urged Oona to buy the apartment, and he continued to encourage her to do something about her writing. "I wanted her to go to Columbia School of Journalism; I thought it would be good for her. Also, I was always trying to cook up schemes whereby she could stay in the States longer, and a student visa would have solved the problem. She came close, but she couldn't deal with sitting in a classroom with other people, and the plan was dropped." Because of the limited amount of time that Oona could spend in America, there was a limited amount of time she could be with Walter Bernstein. They talked about living together, but his children were in America and he did not want to be away from them for any great length of time. "Once, she thought of buying a house in Bermuda. She was born there and always had a fond spot for the island, and, it was close enough so that I could fly there easily. I think she would have bought a house anywhere if I had said I'd be there. She was perfectly willing to do that, but it never happened; she would just send me the Concorde ticket and I'd go off and be with her."[15]

On certain occasions, though, Oona's travels did not take her as far away as Bermuda or Europe. One spring Sunday afternoon, George Beecroft Jr. was making chili for a family dinner when the doorbell rang at 2301 Herbertsville Road in Point Pleasant, New Jersey. He went into the hall, opened the front door, and came face to face with Oona Chaplin. Behind her he saw an automobile parked at the curb; he also made out the figure of a man sitting in the car. Oona smiled and held up a camera. "Hi, remember me? I'm Oona Chaplin, my family used to live here. I hope I'm not disturbing you but I'd like to take a look around. I was hoping to make a video." Beecroft asked her to step in but she declined; she did not want to go inside the house—"too many memories"; she just wanted to film the property and visit her grandfather's studio, that is, if it had not been torn down.

The chili bubbled on the stove while George Beecroft accompanied Oona around the grounds of her childhood home.

She videotaped the interior of Teddy Boulton's old studio and then, handing the camera to her host, asked him to film her. Beecroft followed Oona as she walked about and described what she saw. He could see by the fixed, sad smile lingering on her face that she was moved at being back home. The brief visit ended, Oona thanked Beecroft for making her welcome, returned to the car, and drove off.

Walter Bernstein maintains that during their affair he and Oona never talked about marriage, only about living together; Oona, however, told some of her friends that the matter *had* come up and that it was he who broached the subject. Again, there are discrepancies; some who knew the couple insist that Oona *never* wanted to marry and that Bernstein did, others say the opposite. One evening, at the William Schumans' Park Avenue apartment, Bernstein left the room and the hostess, not one to beat around the bush, spoke up. "I was curious about why they weren't talking marriage," admitted Frances Schuman. "Walter's perks were obvious, but he genuinely seemed to want to help Oona and bring her out. He'd had a couple of marriages and had been prolific and so, of course, was she and between them they had something like thirteen or fourteen kids. And, I knew that Walter's kids stayed with her when they went to Europe, so it was all very comfortable and I wondered why they hadn't legally tied the knot. Anyway, I remember putting the question to her, and she said 'Because he just hasn't asked me,' or something like that, which meant to me that she was ready and he wasn't."[16]

Other friends, among them the Parrishes, the Lloyds, and Betty Tetrick, did not believe that Oona sought marriage. "Walter was an adorable man, terribly bright, persuasive and very sexy in his own way," commented Kathy Parrish, "and, while it was all very glamorous for him, Oona didn't want to be Mrs. Walter Bernstein living on Central Park West. She was

Lady Chaplin, and I don't think she could give it all up." "Walter Bernstein was a fine, upright, brilliant man," said Peggy Lloyd, "but after all those years with Charlie, it was too late for her to fall in love with him." Norman Lloyd forthrightly stated that "no guy was ever going to fill that vacuum." Lloyd also had something to say about Bernstein urging Oona to attend Columbia Graduate School. "To take a woman who's been with every important personage in the world and stick her in a classroom? What was in his mind? It was totally inappropriate."[17]

Marriage or not, a strong physical attraction drew Oona and Bernstein together. Oona had adored Charlie openly and was just as demonstrative with Walter Bernstein. At one MacDowell Colony benefit, the two of them were seated with Frances Schuman, and she was shocked at the way they carried on. "Their hands were all over each other. They were touching, touching, touching. Then Walter got up and went out, obviously to the gents' room, but another friend of mine said, 'I'm not sure whether Walter has left the table or is under it.' " "They'd leap into bed at every given moment," recalled Kathy Parrish, "but then, she'd get hostile and say, 'Charlie was better' or something like that." Betty Tetrick would make only one concession to the affair—"Oona found sexual gratification, period!"

Oona, it seems, had confided to a few close friends that she had not experienced complete sexual satisfaction with her husband. Perhaps the long years of Charlie's decline, coupled with her drinking, had clouded her memory, or perhaps Chaplin's amorous technique really was unsatisfying—the wham, bam, thank you ma'am variety as reported by a few former lovers. On the other hand, given the particulars of Oona's life, it would not be surprising if areas of her sexual development had not been fully realized. She loved Charlie, she had eight children by him, but being rejected by her father and then being viewed as a kind of woman-child by her husband indeed might have affected her sexually.

On their third summer cruise Walter Bernstein found out about Oona's drinking. The ship's captain observed her forays into the liquor cabinet and, based on her behavior, told Bernstein he thought she was an alcoholic. "My mother is one," confided the captain, "and I know one when I see one." Once he became aware, Bernstein started seeing the signs himself and, among other things, discovered the telltale bottles hidden away. During that voyage of enlightenment Kathy Parrish noticed a strain between the lovers and tried to lighten things up. "Her name was Oona Ella and Walter had an awful middle name, something like Arthur, and I told them that I was not going to pay any attention to them and would call them Ella and Arthur. We laughed about that, and it took off some of the edge. He kept calling Oona, 'Ella' and at the same time that she hated it, she thought it was fun."[18]

They did have fun together, and even those who saw him as a bit of a fortune hunter agreed that Walter Bernstein— who, to a great degree, was responsible for the apartment, the yacht trips, and the travels—energized everything in Oona's life. Despite this, as her drinking accelerated, Oona's relationship with Bernstein became increasingly combative. "When she did get drunk, overtly drunk," he recalled, "her anger would come out and underneath, she was a very angry lady. She still was angry at her father and she was angry at Charlie. But her anger at him was for his dying, or at least that was the manifest reason; what the latent one might have been I don't know . . . I think she was angry at men."[19]

twenty-seven

THE CURSE OF THE MISBEGOTTEN

Recent studies in the understanding of alcoholism have shown that whereas men are apt to drink to feel more powerful, the disease in women appears to be in response to life events; women usually drink to medicate anxiety and depression. Oona Chaplin, dealing first with her husband's lingering illness, then with his death, and finally with her own sense of abandonment and loss, desperately "medicated" herself. Compounding her misfortune was the family penchant for alcohol which had infected her grandfathers, her father, and her brothers. Aware of what could happen if she drank, she could not help but drink, and no one could stop her.

The frustrating spectacle of seeing their mother slide further and further into alcoholism had a demoralizing effect on the Chaplin family. In such a situation even the most loving children such as Oona's can find excuses not to be around. Although it does not appear that an official intervention took place, and although all of them (to varying degrees) had to deal with her problem, some were more involved than others. Betty Tetrick remembered big fights in Vevey with Geraldine, Josie, and Vicky trying to get their mother into different treatments. "Oona kept saying, 'I don't need it!' and the girls would get so frustrated with her and with her doctors. They wanted to keep Oona a paying patient and wouldn't go along with the children." Eventually Oona did enter a few detoxification programs. She would sign herself in and sometimes come out dry yet never was able to sustain a program of abstinence. The children had to face the fact that their mother was determinedly and hopelessly ill. A housekeeper was hired to look after her in New York, and the Manoir's staff did the same in Vevey.

In the mid-eighties Gloria Vanderbilt, dealing with her own substance abuse, suggested that Oona go into therapy with psychiatrist Christ L. Zois, with whom Gloria was in treatment; Oona began seeing him. Her association with Zois flourished even as her relationship with Walter Bernstein came to an end. Whether she or Bernstein initiated the separation is unclear. Ted Tetrick did say that Oona asked him to get back the key to her apartment from her former lover. The affair had run its course, and at this point its conclusion was secondary to the issue of the psychiatrist and his growing influence.

Despite the fact that she was his patient and he was a married man, Oona and Christ Zois had a social as well as professional relationship. According to Betty Tetrick they displayed openly affectionate behavior in public. Particularly vulnerable at this point in her life, Oona became very dependent on the doctor, and he became the willing beneficiary of her generosity. Betty Tetrick also related that the intensity of Oona's and Gloria's association with the doctor eroded the friendship between the two women and resulted in a permanent estrangement. Eventually Dr. Zois's treatments and motives were brought into question and into the courtroom. In 1993 he was sued by Gloria Vanderbilt, who won a $1.5 million judgment against him for preying on her wealth and emotional fragility.[1] In Oona's case, Dr. Zois "had borrowed half a million dollars to buy a house in New Jersey on the strength of a promissory note bearing Oona's signature. Her estate successfully sued in the U.S. District Court in Manhattan, disclaiming the note."[2]

As dependent as she was on alcohol, many who met Oona Chaplin during her years of unbridled drinking were unaware that they were in the presence of someone very much under the influence. If they noticed anything at all, it was her flushed face and her neglected grooming. Jeannie Bach, an award-winning documentary filmmaker, met Oona at an Upper East Side dinner party. "She wore a loose-fitting dress, used no makeup, and faded into the background. Her drabness was quite conspicuous because everyone else was dressed beautifully. All rather sad when you consider that the party was given for her, and guests of honor usually rise to the occasion. She did have magnificent jewelry, though," added the filmmaker.

Howsoever she appeared, Oona remained a much-sought-after guest; Lady Chaplin's presence was considered a coup. Jacqueline Onassis, herself a social icon, extended a couple of dinner invitations. Ms. Onassis, an editor at Doubleday, also very much wanted to publish Lady Chaplin's autobiography and purportedly sent Oona a blank check to be filled in with any amount. Although Oona accepted the dinner invitations, she never showed. Ready to give up, Mrs. Onassis was persuaded to tender one more request. This time Oona actually was dressed and on her way to the party when she slipped and fell in her apartment, fracturing her shoulder. She had to be put to bed, and in the confusion no one thought to inform the waiting hostess. This was the last known invitation extended to Lady Chaplin by Jacqueline Onassis.[3]

Maureen Stapleton, the legendary stage and screen actress, met Oona through their friend Carol Matthau, and the two women struck up a brief acquaintance. One evening they were going out together and Oona came by Stapleton's Upper West Side town house. Pretending to be not quite ready, the actress told Oona to come in and wait for a minute. As Oona stood in the entrance hall, Stapleton called up to her young son and told him to come down and say hello. "He appeared at the top of the stairs, shouted, 'Hi,' and then disappeared back into his room," recalled Maureen Stapleton, who was trying to set up a more meaningful exchange. "Oona was living history as well as one helluva fine lady," explained the actress, "and I thought it would be kind of nice for my son to be able to say years later that he'd met the daughter of Eugene O'Neill and the wife of Charlie Chaplin." [4]

Eventually most friends and acquaintances gave up trying to reach Oona; a few, like Frances Schuman, remained loyal. Ms. Schuman frequently telephoned Oona's apartment and often spoke to the housekeeper. "Because she heard everyone call me by my nickname, the housekeeper assumed I was a member of the MacDowell staff rather than a patron," laughed the composer's wife. "She got chummy and started calling me *Frankie*, which was fine—it was a great bond. She'd tell me things about Oona's drinking and her life in general in a kind of *Upstairs-Downstairs* way and kept me apprised of Oona's condition."

Following the breakup with Walter Bernstein, Oona skipped the annual MacDowell benefit. The next year, Frances Schuman called and told Oona that not only was she welcome at the benefit, she would be provided with an escort. "I really wasn't fixing her up; I just wanted her to be able to come to the party and I knew that she needed someone at her side. My friend Jack fit the bill; he was very easy to talk to and a charming gentleman." Oona did attend the benefit and appeared to enjoy herself. The next day, her escort called Frances Schuman to see if she thought Oona would come to his house for dinner. "Jack lived in a small apartment and when he made dinner it was usually macaroni, but I told him to give it a try. He asked if Bill and I would join them and I said sure. I really was surprised when Jack called to say that Oona had accepted." As it happened, William Schuman became ill and the Schumans had to cancel. Later, they were flabbergasted to learn that Oona went on her own. "It was so unlike her; most of the time she'd accept invitations and back out at the last minute."

Oona's pattern of accepting and then not showing up grew more conspicuous. A bit later, Frances Schuman introduced her to another friend and for a while the four of them used to go out to dinner. "One evening, he called and said he'd found a new restaurant and we had to go. I phoned Oona and she said okay, and I told her that Bill and I would pick her up. Later, I spoke to the housekeeper and she said flat out, 'She'll never make it. She'll never go.'" That evening when the Schumans arrived at East Seventy-second Street the housekeeper opened the door and triumphantly declared, "She's not going!"

Soon, Oona almost never went out in the evenings, although she did keep a few lunch dates. "We went to some nice places," remembered Ms. Schuman, "but I always had to choose them." Oona managed to see a few of her longtime friends and, of course, her children, but gradually she withdrew further and further into her own liquid world of memories.

From time to time Oona allowed people to use her apartment for meetings or parties, and on one occasion she threw a party for her daughter Victoria. The Thierrées brought their *Cirque Imaginaire* to New York City for a two-week run in

1986, and Jed Wheeler, a young theatrical manager, handled the arrangements. Rehearsals for the show were held in the cafeteria of a Manhattan day school, and according to Wheeler, Oona, closely attended by a uniformed driver, visited on a number of occasions. "The driver was a bodyguard type," remembered Wheeler, "a really large man. He'd park the car, a ten-year-old black Cadillac, and then follow Oona into the cafeteria. She'd sit there surrounded by children, which seemed to please her. It was a racially mixed group and she was fascinated by the kids." Oona was so taken with the schoolchildren that she arranged for them to see her daughter's show. "She bought thousands of dollars worth of tickets," said Wheeler, "which was fine except that the kids were not interested. We couldn't give the tickets away. We'd hand them out, but then no one would show up." Wheeler also remembered that Victoria was very affectionate toward her mother and concerned about where Oona was and what she was doing.[5]

Around twenty people were invited to the party Oona gave on the opening night of the *Cirque Imaginaire*. The guests arrived and went to the top floor of the duplex, where they were surrounded by Chaplin memorabilia, pictures, props, and so on, but no food or drink. When it became clear that no preparations had been made, Victoria took over. She went into the kitchen and scrounged up some food while someone else brought out champagne. Meanwhile the tardy hostess came in and sat on the couch next to Jed Wheeler. She was polite, quite regal in her bearing, and still beautiful, yet the young theatrical manager did think Oona looked a lot older than her years. She was gracious and spoke intelligently, but Wheeler soon realized that she had been drinking—the first he had seen of her condition. They spent about an hour chatting together, and Wheeler later was told that Oona had been very impressed and wanted to see him again. While he doubted that she even remembered him, he never forgot her.

The MacDowell Colony board held a few of their meetings at Oona's penthouse and at their first gathering found the exact opposite of Jed Wheeler's experience—abundant provisions. Oona called a fancy East Side purveyor, and luxurious food baskets, including tins of fresh caviar, were sent up. She lent her home and provided food and drink, yet the MacDowell committee never saw her; they went about their business and she remained sequestered. At one gathering the housekeeper walked into the living room and called out, "Frankie, she wants to see you."

"I got up and followed her into the hallway," recalled Frances Schuman, "and I remember how beautiful that day was. The sun was pouring in from the terrace and the sky was clear and blue." Led to the door of Oona's bedroom, "Frankie" was given a knowing look by the housekeeper and then let in.

The shades were drawn, and it took a minute for her eyes to adjust to the darkness. She saw Oona stretched out on the bed, went over, and sat down next to her.

"Oona, what are you doing? Why are you in here in the dark?"

Oona did not respond. She lay quietly until, looking up at the ceiling, she giggled and said, "This is how it must be where Charlie is."

Frances Schuman stayed for a while and listened to a lot of embarrassed giggling and aimless chatter. "I told her I had to get back to the meeting, but I promised to come back and visit the next day. I was really upset. I couldn't get it out of my head, here was this woman with everything, millions of dollars coming in every day, and she couldn't do anything but lie there in the dark."

The next morning Frances Schuman called to see if it was all right for her to come over and was told to please do so. She arrived and was ushered into the sun-filled living room where Oona waited. "Considering the way she had been the day be-

fore, she looked remarkably put together. She had amazing recuperative powers." The two women greeted each other and,
without mentioning the previous day, talked a bit. Then the
visitor got to the point.

"Why do you come to New York?" asked Ms. Schuman.
"You just stay in your apartment. Why don't you get out?"

"I love to walk," Oona ventured.

"Well then, get out and walk," came the reply. Oona mum-
bled something about having to be in town to deal with the
O'Neill family and to do some writing, but neither excuse impressed Frances Schuman. She knew that Walter Bernstein and
others felt that Oona had great potential, but what was potential alone? "Talent is a dime a dozen; the difference between
talent and achievement is the ability to do it. Maybe Oona
never would have had the ability to write cold sober. We just
don't know. It was foolish to talk about something she *wasn't*
doing."

On a more constructive level, Frances Schuman told Oona
that rather than thinking about writing, she should do something beneficial for others. Why not, for instance, do something
wonderful with her money? "Look, your whole life has been in
the theater and film. You could set up a foundation. You don't
have to make it fancy and you don't have to have a lot of people involved." All the time the older woman spoke to her, Oona
listened attentively. Their visit ended and Frances Schuman got
up to leave. Oona walked over, put her arms around her, and
hugging her close said softly, "I know what you're trying to do,
Frankie, and thank you."

"She was so sweet and so sincere, but there was no way,
no way. She was miserable without Chaplin. No matter what
we all heard or read about him being an impossible person, she
was crazy about him and she simply never got over his death,
EVER. I remember a MacDowell benefit when I happened to
look over at Oona. Her head was thrown back and a look of

sheer agony was on her face. I knew she was thinking of Chaplin, and after all those years she still was absolutely consumed with terrible, terrible grieving. And of course the drinking exacerbated her pain."

In September 1984 Louis Sheaffer wrote to Oona that he intended to sell his collection of O'Neill papers to a university library. This, he quickly added, did not include her letters to him, which he was bequeathing to the New York Public Library Theater Collection at Lincoln Center. Three months later Oona responded. Rather than opening with the usual apology for her tardiness, she informed Sheaffer that she had not written to anyone in two years, including her children. Oona expressed surprise that her letters had been kept and claimed that had she known this she might have been more careful about what she wrote, particularly about some of her surviving family members. And, while she did not think her correspondence important enough to go anywhere except into the wastebasket, she told Sheaffer that if that was what he wanted to do, it was fine with her. She was coming to New York in early February to have a minor operation and recently had gone through a bout of hepatitis. Her recovery had been slow, all of which was depressing since, as she wrote, she had been healthy all her life. She closed by saying she was almost back to normal and sent her love.

Louis Sheaffer had no idea what *normal* had become for Oona Chaplin. He never learned of her dissolution into alcoholism or of the sad circumstances of her last years. For him she remained the tender, witty, delightful, and intelligent lady of letters—letters still in his possession when he died in August 1993.

twenty-eight

THE LAST YEARS

Oona Chaplin's life continued aimless and empty as she journeyed back and forth from New York to Switzerland in an odyssey of desperation and resignation. New York's energy and zest, once so loved, proved too difficult to handle—social demands were made, like the invitations she accepted and then reneged on; furthermore, too many people pressured her to dry out. Oona had reached the point where she did not want to be bothered. Her New York social life became almost nonexistent; her main activity consisted of strolling over to the Carlyle Hotel, where she would have her hair done, after which she might go for a walk along Madison Avenue. Oona loved to walk and in the past had roamed all over the city; now her strolls were brief and inevitably ended in her darkened bedroom.

Frances Schuman still tried to keep up. "If you could get Oona talking, she would talk, but her conversation had become less interesting. She chatted a lot about her friend Carol, and how they still were like kids together. One time the two of them were on the phone for hours making girl talk and, inadvertently, the entire conversation was recorded on an answering machine. Somebody played it back and said to Oona, 'The two of you are crazy.' Well, she liked that; it tickled her that she and Carol could act like giddy teenagers and be called 'crazy,' she really thought it was funny."[1] Although Oona mentioned her children and grandchildren, Frances Schuman observed that it was on an occasional rather than a regular basis. "In the beginning those grandkids amused her a lot, but she didn't go on and on about them. She wasn't that kind of grandmother, nor do I think she ever could have been." Her drinking made it virtually impossible for her children to reach her; they could not get close to her.

Betty Tetrick still made the trips to Switzerland and she, too, was dismayed at Oona's state. On one of the last visits Betty stayed at the Trois Couronnes. On the first morning Oona sent the car to retrieve her cousin. "I went out of the hotel and the driver was standing by the Rolls. He held the door and as I started to get in, I discovered Oona sitting scrunched up in the corner. 'I decided to come and pick you up, myself,' she said. She apologized for her appearance and then giggled. I could tell she'd been drinking, but what stunned me more was the way she was dressed, or rather was undressed. She'd gone out in her nightgown."

In those last doleful years Oona's physical as well as emotional health deteriorated. A small growth on her nose turned out to be a cancer, which she put off having removed until the doctors said it had to be done. She was upset at having surgery on her face, and the attending nurse told friends that it was difficult to get her through the operation. Oona recuperated at East Seventy-second Street, and Frances Schuman paid a visit. "She was all alone. I asked the housekeeper where her kids were; she said Oona didn't want them around because they told her to stop drinking." Plagued by severe headaches, Oona turned out to have a blood clot in her brain and, once again, had to undergo surgery. Then a hysterectomy was performed—the psychological implications of which can be well imagined.

Her surgeries notwithstanding, Oona's trips across the ocean continued at a more accelerated pace. "One minute I'd be talking to her in New York," remembered Frances Schuman, "and the next minute she'd be back in Vevey without letting me know. That was okay; there was no reason for her to call and tell me she was going, it's just that she would do this all the time, just all of a sudden turn around and fly back to Switzerland. She told me that the apartment had become a burden for her. There had been an awful fire—due to some faulty wiring, I believe, and even though the place was fixed up, it really bothered her. I think there was even another fire; I'm not sure. All I know is, she wasn't happy there. How could she be? She never went out anymore. She just stayed there in the dark."

Finally Oona made her decision. Avowing that it "broke her heart," she told her friend Frankie that she intended to sell the duplex. "But, I'll come to the MacDowell benefit," Oona promised. "I'll stay at the Carlyle." She never came; instead, she sent a letter expressing her regrets and, as always, enclosed a large check.

Frances Schuman continued to mail invitations and on November 24, 1990, received a note from Switzerland. "Frankie darling," the letter began. Oona went on to relate how happy she was to hear from her but that she no longer would be leaving Vevey. City life got her down, she wrote, and even though her children could not understand it, she was happy to be alone at the Manoir and found it very difficult to leave her dogs, ponies, cats, and goldfish in the garden. Oona enclosed a check and ended the letter by saying how much she had loved the MacDowell galas and how touched she was by them. That was her last communication to Frances Schuman. "I think back about those days, and while I wouldn't say that Oona was always drunk when I saw her, I don't think I ever saw her when I didn't think that alcohol was lurking. I felt terribly sorry for her and I thought what a terrible waste. Not her life, though, just those last years."

Oona Chaplin retreated to the home of her exile; the sameness of life in Switzerland now suited her, but nothing could hold her interest for long—not even the gadgets and machines with which she surrounded herself. Once she had delighted in all forms of mechanical and electronic equipment, whether a new camera, a kitchen appliance, a typewriter, a photocopier, or a VCR. "She loved her cars, she loved her Walkman, she really enjoyed her machines," recalled a longtime acquaintance. "I remember one Christmas she was so thrilled because she'd found cards that were musical—she sent them to everyone." After Charlie's death, her interest in things electronic and mechanical gradually had taken on another, darker side. She used the duplicating machine to run off letters that she had received, particularly letters that she did not like, and mailed copies to everyone. The telephones throughout the Manoir were rigged so that she could listen in surreptitiously on private conversations; sometimes she would just listen, at other times she would listen and begin talking, or even shouting, into the receiver.

Something spiteful and small had been poured into Oona Chaplin's life, and her last years were marked by nasty scenes of substance abuse and desperate attempts to find answers to questions she never wanted to ask. "Charlie was a great man . . . wasn't he?" she demanded of one visitor to the Manoir, and even when he replied positively she was not soothed. Shaking off the "Yes, he was a great man," Oona cried out suddenly and terrifyingly, "What the fuck did I do with my life!" In a world distorted by alcohol, an utter hopelessness took hold and made her scream vindictively about her husband, her children, herself—but these were the sodden outbursts of a very miserable, very ill woman to whom nothing meant anything any longer.

Finally the pain of drinking was augmented by the pain of another disease, pancreatic cancer. Nothing could be done. The children who were far away kept in touch by phone, while those who were nearby visited often. Sometimes Oona was glad to see them, at other times she wanted to be left alone. The prolonged torment was excruciating, and after two months of suffering intensely Oona Chaplin died, mercifully, on September 27, 1991.

EPILOGUE

With all her children, except for Josephine (who was in India at the time), and some fifty relatives and close friends in attendance, Oona was buried beside her husband in the peaceful hillside cemetery overlooking Vevey and Lake Leman. After the fifteen-minute ceremony, as the mourners left, a truck pulled up to the site and nearly half a ton of cement was poured over her coffin. There would be no grave robbing. Today, two large solid square blocks of granite about three feet in height stand side by side in the quiet pastoral cemetery; one stone is engraved *Charles Chaplin 1889–1977*; the other, *Oona Chaplin 1925–1991*. Significantly, although it had determined her life's course, her father's name, and all it stood for, did not accompany Oona to the grave. In her death, she was able to obliterate the *O'Neill*; alive, she never completely freed herself from the constraints embodied in the man who disdained, disowned, and haunted her. Yet despite him she managed to find shelter.

Charlie Chaplin reversed in every way Eugene O'Neill's manner of treatment, and during their felicitous union she saw herself reflected not in the gloom of her father's frown but in the radiance of her husband's approving gaze. They found salvation in each other; the security their marriage afforded gave Charlie a second life and made it possible for Oona to function for many exhilarating and productive years as wife and mother. But everything was dependent on Charlie's presence, and his death completely crushed her. She felt abandoned once again, and in her half-life of widowhood there were no foundations established, no festivals overseen, no exploration of her own talent, and no sustained happiness with children and grandchildren. But that was at the end.

In her childhood Oona was told by a fortune-teller that it was impossible to predict her future because the lines in Oona's hand were too jumbled to read. In looking back it would seem that mixed up as they were, all those lines led to Charlie Chaplin. "She is my friend, my lover, my wife," said Chaplin, and at the conclusion of his autobiography he paid her a lasting tribute: "As I live with Oona, the depth and beauty of her character are a continual revelation to me. Even as she walks ahead of me along the narrow sidewalks of Vevey with simple dignity, her neat little figure straight, her dark hair smoothed back showing a few silver threads, a sudden wave of love and admiration comes over me for all that she is."[1] He grew old along with her; she, however, could not grow old along with him. Still, she did share in an extraordinary partnership, and surely it was that glorious *first* of her life with Charlie Chaplin for which the lamentable *last* had to be endured.

At the close of *Long Day's Journey into Night*, Mary Tyrone, the dramatic incarnation of Ella Quinlan O'Neill, wanders onto the stage. Drug-dazed, her mind adrift, Mary reflects upon the past and recalls her senior year in school. As the curtain falls she speaks the final words of Eugene O'Neill's finest play: "Then in the spring something happened to me. Yes, I remember. I fell in love with James Tyrone and was so happy for a time." Following *her* senior year in school, Oona O'Neill went to Hollywood. She fell in love with Charlie Chaplin and was so happy—not ever after, but for a long, long time.

NOTES

CHAPTER ONE
1. Louis Sheaffer, *Eugene O'Neill: Son and Playwright* (New York: Paragon House, 1968).
2. Ibid., 4.
3. Ibid., 50.
4. Ibid., 221.
5. Croswell Bowen, *The Curse of the Misbegotten* (New York: McGraw-Hill, 1959), 65.

CHAPTER TWO
1. Agnes Boulton, *Part of a Long Story* (New York: Doubleday, 1958), 293.
2. Jeff Heim, "Eugene O'Neill's Local Winter of Discontent," history term paper published by Point Pleasant Historical Society, September 1997.
3. Boulton, *Part of a Long Story*, 140.
4. Ibid., 21.

CHAPTER THREE
1. Sheaffer, *O'Neill: Son & Playwright*, 407.
2. Ibid., 416.
3. Ibid., 411.

4. Boulton, *Part of a Long Story*, 318.
5. Ibid., 331.
6. Louis Sheaffer, *Eugene O'Neill: Son and Artist* (New York: Paragon House, 1973), 247–48.
7. Travis Bogard and Jackson R. Bryer, eds., *Selected Letters of Eugene O'Neill* (New York: Limelight Editions, 1994), 195.

CHAPTER FOUR
1. Arthur Gelb and Barbara Gelb, *O'Neill* (New York: Harper & Brothers, 1960), 583.
2. Bogard & Bryer, eds., *Selected Letters of E.O.*, 196.
3. Ibid., 207.
4. Ibid., 210.
5. Sheaffer, *O'Neill: Son & Artist*, 217.
6. Bogard & Bryer, eds., *Selected Letters of E.O.*, 274.

CHAPTER FIVE
1. Sheaffer, *O'Neill: Son & Artist*, 311.
2. Bogard & Bryer, eds., *Selected Letters of E.O.*, 261.
3. Ibid., 287.
4. Ibid., 302.
5. Letters of James Delaney.
6. Ibid.
7. Ibid.
8. Ibid.
9. Ibid.
10. Ibid.
11. Ibid.
12. Gelb & Gelb, *O'Neill*, 695–96.

CHAPTER SIX
1. Sheaffer, *O'Neill: Son & Artist*, 391.
2. Bogard & Bryer, eds., *Selected Letters of E.O.*, 394.
3. Letters of Louis Sheaffer and Oona Chaplin, 1969–1991. The Sheaffer-O'Neill Collection at Connecticut College. (Hereafter cited as Sheaffer/Chaplin Letters.)
4. Ibid.
5. Telephone conversation with Walter Hance, November 1996.
6. Bogard & Bryer, eds., *Selected Letters of E.O.*, 415.
7. Sheaffer/Chaplin Letters.
8. Ibid.
9. Sheaffer, *O'Neill: Son & Artist*, 608.
10. Sheaffer/Chaplin Letters.

CHAPTER SEVEN

1. Kenneth S. Lynn, *Charlie Chaplin and His Times* (New York: Simon & Schuster, 1997), 429.
2. Sheaffer/Chaplin Letters.
3. Lynn, *C.C. & His Times*, 429.
4. Gelb & Gelb, *O'Neill*, 843.
5. Lynn, *C.C. & His Times*, 429.
6. Joyce Milton, *Tramp: The Life of Charlie Chaplin* (New York: HarperCollins, 1996), 409.
7. Aram Saroyan, *Trio* (New York: Linden Press/Simon & Schuster, 1985), 10.
8. Ibid., 134–54.
9. Carol Matthau, *Among the Porcupines* (New York: Random House, 1992), 6.
10. Sheaffer, *O'Neill: Son & Artist*, 531.
11. Ibid., 537.
12. Ibid., 531.
13. Bogard & Bryer, eds., *Selected Letters of E.O.*, 533.
14. Ibid.
15. Ibid., 534.
16. Sheaffer, *O'Neill: Son & Artist*, 549.
17. Ruth Reynolds, "Oona O'Neill Goes Home to Her Famous Father—To Get Movie Job Okay," *Sunday News* (New York), 25 October 1942.

CHAPTER EIGHT

1. Sheaffer/Chaplin Letters.
2. Sheaffer, *O'Neill: Son & Artist*, 537.
3. Ibid., 538–39.
4. Matthau, *Among the Porcupines*, 41.
5. Sheaffer/Chaplin Letters.
6. David Robinson, *Chaplin: His Life and Art* (New York: McGraw-Hill, 1985), 518.
7. Charles Chaplin, *My Autobiography* (New York: Simon & Schuster, 1964), 420.

CHAPTER NINE

1. Alistair Cooke, *Six Men* (New York: Knopf, 1977), 16.
2. Robinson, *Chaplin: His Life and Art*, 519.
3. Charles Chaplin Jr., with N. Rau and M. Rau, *My Father, Charlie Chaplin* (New York: Random House, 1960), 270–71.
4. Ibid., 272.
5. Milton, *Tramp*, 410–11.

6. Milton Berle, *B.S. I Love You* (New York: McGraw-Hill, 1988), 203.
7. Chaplin, *My Autobiography*, 420.
8. Lynn, *C.C. & His Times*, 432.
9. Chaplin, *My Autobiography*, 420.
10. Sheaffer, *O'Neill: Son & Artist*, 175.
11. Marjorie Loggia and Glenn Young, eds., *The Collected Works of Harold Clurman* (New York: Applause Theatre Books, 1994), 977.
12. Georgia Hale, *Charlie Chaplin: Intimate Close-Ups*, ed. H. Kiernan (Metuchen, N.J. and London: Scarecrow Press, 1995), xxvii.
13. Bogard & Bryer, eds., *Selected Letters of E.O.*, 545.
14. Robinson, *Chaplin*, 327.

CHAPTER TEN
1. Arthur Gelb has a copy of this letter and spoke of it to the author on 19 January 1998.
2. *Sunday News* (New York), 25 October 1942.
3. Robinson, *Chaplin*, 596.
4. Patrice Chaplin, *Hidden Star* (London: Richard Cohen Books, 1995), 188.
5. Lita Grey Chaplin, with Morton Cooper, *My Life with Chaplin: An Intimate Memoir* (New York: Bernard Geis Associates, 1966), 207.
6. Lora Heims Tessman, "A Touch of the Poet: A Discussion," paper presented at the American Repertory Theatre, Cambridge, Massachusetts, 13 March 1994.
7. Ibid.
8. Brooks Peters, "The Perils of Paulette," *Quest* magazine, May 1993.
9. Julie Gilbert, *Opposite Attraction: The Lives of Erich Maria Remarque and Paulette Goddard* (New York: Pantheon Books, 1995), 66.
10. Chaplin Jr., *My Father*, 75.
11. Robinson, *Chaplin*, 590.
12. Chaplin Jr., *My Father*, 272.
13. Chaplin, *My Autobiography*, 431.
14. Mary Ellin Barrett, *Irving Berlin: A Daughter's Memoir* (New York: Simon & Schuster, 1994), 229–30.
15. Salka Viertel, *The Kindness of Strangers* (New York: Holt, Rinehart Winston, 1969), 290.
16. Interview with Norman Lloyd, February 1993.

CHAPTER ELEVEN

1. Lester Middlehurst, "I'm Proud of My Dad, Charlie Chaplin. But I Still Hate Being His Son," *Daily Mail* (London), 26 January 1998.
2. Robinson, *Chaplin*, 596.
3. Shelley Winters, *Shelley II* (New York: Pocket Books, 1989), 29–30.
4. Letter to Jim Delaney, August 1943.
5. Kathy Parrish, "The Champ and the Tramp," *World Tennis*, February 1990.
6. Christopher Isherwood, *Diaries, Volume I: 1939–1960*, ed. Katherine Bucknell (New York: HarperCollins, 1997), 378.
7. Chaplin Jr., *My Father*, 99.
8. Milton, *Tramp*, 525.
9. Letter to Jim Delaney, August 1943.
10. Sheaffer, *O'Neill: Son & Artist*, 554.
11. Sheaffer/Chaplin Letters.
12. Gelb & Gelb, *O'Neill*, 852.

CHAPTER TWELVE

1. Epstein, *Remembering Charlie* (London: Bloomsbury, 1988), 49.
2. Ibid., 52.
3. L. Chaplin, *My Life with C.*
4. Robinson, *Chaplin*, 543.
5. Sheaffer/Chaplin Letters.
6. Chaplin Jr., *My Father*, 352.
7. Epstein, *Remembering Charlie*, 66–67.
8. Claire Bloom, *Limelight and After* (London: Weidenfeld & Nicolson, 1982), 98.
9. Ibid.
10. Quoted by critic and film historian Scott Eyman.

CHAPTER THIRTEEN

1. Lillian Ross, *Moments with Chaplin* (New York: Dodd, Mead, 1978), 20.
2. Robinson, *Chaplin*, 574.
3. Chaplin, *My Autobiography*, 466.
4. Bloom, *Limelight & After*, 74.
5. Reported by Scott Eyman.
6. Epstein, *Remembering Charlie*, 105.

CHAPTER FOURTEEN

1. Epstein, *Remembering Charlie*, 119.

2. Michael Chaplin, *I Couldn't Smoke the Grass on My Father's Lawn* (New York: Ballantine Books, 1966), 31.
3. Sheaffer/Chaplin Letters.
4. Ibid.
5. Ibid.
6. M. Chaplin, *I Couldn't Smoke*, 29.
7. Epstein, *Remembering Charlie*, 109.
8. James P. O'Donnell, "Charlie Chaplin's Stormy Exile," *Saturday Evening Post*, Part 1, 8 March 1958.
9. Epstein, *Remembering Charlie*, 115.
10. Gelb & Gelb, *O'Neill*, 939.
11. Sheaffer, *O'Neill: Son & Artist*, 672.
12. Sheaffer/Chaplin Letters.
13. Ibid.
14. Ibid.
15. Ibid.
16. Matthau, *Among the Porcupines*, 177.
17. Sheaffer/Chaplin Letters.
18. Epstein, *Remembering Chaplin*, 112.
19. Lynn, *C.C. & His Times*, 493.
20. Epstein, *Remembering Charlie*, 141.
21. Robinson, *Chaplin*, 590.
22. Ibid.

CHAPTER FIFTEEN
1. Robinson, *Chaplin*, 595.
2. Epstein, *Remembering Charlie*, 159.
3. Charles Chaplin, *My Life in Pictures* (London: The Bodley Head, 1974).
4. Epstein, *Remembering Charlie*, 167.
5. Ibid., 175.
6. Joan Collins, *Second Act* (New York: St. Martin's Press, 1996), 62.
7. Ibid., 64.
8. Epstein, *Remembering Charlie*, 190–91.
9. Robinson, *Chaplin*, 619.
10. Lynn, *C.C. & His Times*, 318.
11. Marlon Brando, with Robert Lindsey, *Songs My Mother Taught Me* (New York: Random House, 1994), 318.
12. Epstein, *Remembering Charlie*, 193.

CHAPTER SIXTEEN
1. Epstein, *Remembering Charlie*, 152.

2. Oriana Fallaci, *Limelighters*, trans. Pamela Swinglehurst (London: Joseph, 1967).
3. Ivor Davis, "Coming Home," *U.S. Airways Magazine*, May 1997.
4. Robinson, *Chaplin*, 596–97.
5. Ibid., 600.
6. M. Chaplin, *I Couldn't Smoke*, 54–55.
7. Ibid., 51.
8. Ibid., 58.
9. Robinson, *Chaplin*, 601.
10. Epstein, *Remembering Charlie*, 228.
11. M. Chaplin, *I Couldn't Smoke*, 115.
12. Ibid., 121.
13. Robinson, *Chaplin*, 601.

CHAPTER SEVENTEEN
1. Interview with George Beecroft, June 1993.
2. Letters of James Delaney (from G. Beecroft Collection).
3. Sheaffer/Chaplin Letters.
4. Ibid.
5. Beecroft interview.
6. Beecroft interview; interview with Betty Tetrick, May 1994.
7. Ibid.
8. P. Chaplin, *Hidden Star*, 188.
9. Sheaffer/Chaplin Letters.

CHAPTER EIGHTEEN
1. Sheaffer/Chaplin Letters.
2. Ibid.
3. Ibid.
4. Ibid.
5. Ibid.
6. Ibid.
7. Bogard & Bryer, eds., *Selected Letters of E.O.*, 569.
8. Sheaffer/Chaplin Letters.
9. Bowen, *The Curse of the Misbegotten*, 354.
10. Sheaffer/Chaplin Letters.
11. Bowen, *The Curse of the Misbegotten*, 480.
12. Ibid., 367.
13. Sheaffer/Chaplin Letters.

CHAPTER NINETEEN
1. Epstein, *Remembering Charlie*, 201.
2. Ibid., 203.

3. Sheaffer/Chaplin Letters.
4. Ibid.
5. *LIFE* magazine, 21 April 1972.
6. Robinson, *Chaplin*, 623.
7. Tetrick Interview.
8. Robinson, *Chaplin*, 624.
9. Ibid., 625.

CHAPTER TWENTY
1. Sheaffer/Chaplin Letters.
2. Ibid.
3. Ibid.
4. Ibid.
5. Ibid.
6. Ibid.
7. Ibid.

CHAPTER TWENTY-ONE
1. Conversation with Cybill Shepherd in Los Angeles, 1996.
2. Loggia & Young, eds., *The Collected Works of H.C.*, 977.
3. Sheaffer/Chaplin Letters.
4. Ibid.
5. Ibid.
6. Ibid.
7. Ibid.
8. Ibid.
9. Hale, *Chaplin: Intimate Close-Ups*, xxvii.

CHAPTER TWENTY-TWO
1. Sheaffer/Chaplin Letters.
2. Ibid.
3. Ibid.
4. According to Betty Tetrick.
5. Sheaffer/Chaplin Letters.
6. Lynn, *C.C. & His Times*, 519.
7. Tetrick interview.
8. Sheaffer/Chaplin Letters.
9. Ibid.
10. Ibid.

CHAPTER TWENTY-THREE
1. Milton, *Tramp*, 519.

2. Tetrick interview.
3. Sheaffer/Chaplin Letters.

CHAPTER TWENTY-FOUR
1. Robinson, *Chaplin*, 630.
2. Tetrick interview.
3. Epstein, *Remembering Charlie*, 221.
4. Matthau, *Among the Porcupines*, 257.
5. Ibid., 259–60.
6. Ibid., 263.

CHAPTER TWENTY-FIVE
1. Sheaffer/Chaplin Letters.

CHAPTER TWENTY-SIX
1. Warren Harris, *Sophia Loren: A Biography* (New York: Simon & Schuster, 1998), 351.
2. Christopher Anderson, *Michael Jackson Unauthorized* (New York: Pocket Books, 1994), 238.
3. *The Sunday People*, 11 May 1981. (Hereafter cited as Sunday People.)
4. Ibid.
5. P. Chaplin, *Hidden Star*, 193.
6. Sunday People.
7. Review of *Hidden Star*, *Sunday Telegraph*, 16 July 1995.
8. Sunday People.
9. Ibid.
10. P. Chaplin, *Hidden Star*, 123.
11. Interview with Walter Bernstein in New York City, 1992.
12. Ibid.
13. Tetrick interview.
14. Interview with Frances Schuman in New York City, March 1993.
15. Bernstein interview.
16. Schuman interview.
17. Parrish, Lloyd, and Tetrick interviews.
18. Parrish interview.
19. Bernstein interview.

CHAPTER TWENTY-SEVEN
1. *New York Times*, 29 October 1993.
2. Milton, *Tramp*, 521.
3. Schuman interview.

4. Maureen Stapleton and Jane Scovell, *A Hell of a Life* (New York: Simon & Schuster, 1995), 170.
5. Interview with Jed Wheeler in New York, August 1992.

CHAPTER TWENTY-EIGHT
1. Schuman interview.

EPILOGUE
1. Chaplin, *My Autobiography*, 497.

SELECTED BIBLIOGRAPHY

Alexander, Doris. *Eugene O'Neill's Creative Struggle: The Decisive Decade, 1924–1933.* College Station, Pa.: Pennsylvania State University Press, 1992.

Alleman, Richard. *The Movie Lover's Guide to Hollywood.* New York: Harper Colophon Books, 1985.

Anderson, Christopher. *Michael Jackson Unauthorized.* New York: Pocket Books, 1994.

Barrett, Mary Ellin. *Irving Berlin: A Daughter's Memoir.* New York: Simon & Schuster, 1994.

Bego, Mark. *The Best of Modern Screen.* New York: St. Martin's Press, 1986.

Berk, Laura E. *Child Development: Fourth Edition.* Boston: Allyn & Bacon, 1989.

Berle, Milton. *B.S. I Love You.* New York: McGraw-Hill, 1988.

Bloom, Claire. *Leaving a Doll's House.* Boston: Little, Brown, 1996.

———. *Limelight and After.* London: Weidenfeld & Nicolson, 1982.

Bogard, Travis, and Jackson R. Bryer, eds. *Selected Letters of Eugene O'Neill.* New York: Limelight Editions, 1994.

Bordman, Gerald. *The Concise Oxford Companion to the American Theatre.* New York: Oxford University Press, 1987.

Boulton, Agnes. *Part of a Long Story.* New York: Doubleday, 1958.

Bowen, Croswell. *The Curse of the Misbegotten.* New York: McGraw-Hill, 1959.

Brando, Marlon, with Robert Lindsey. *Songs My Mother Taught Me.* New York: Random House, 1994.

Brinnin, John Malcolm. *The Sway of the Grand Salon.* New York: Delacorte Press, 1971.

Brownlow, Kevin. *The Parade's Gone By.* New York: Alfred A. Knopf, 1968.

Callow, Simon. *Charles Laughton, a Difficult Actor.* London: Mandarin Paperbacks, 1987.

Chaplin, Charles. *My Life in Pictures.* London: The Bodley Head, 1974.

————. *My Autobiography.* New York: Simon & Schuster, 1964.

Chaplin, Charles, Jr., with N. Rau and M. Rau. *My Father, Charlie Chaplin.* New York: Random House, 1960.

Chaplin, Lita Grey, with Morton Cooper. *My Life with Chaplin: An Intimate Memoir.* London: Bernard Geis Associates, 1966.

Chaplin, Michael. *I Couldn't Smoke the Grass on My Father's Lawn.* New York: Ballantine Books, 1966.

Chaplin, Patrice. *Hidden Star.* London: Richard Cohen Books, 1995.

————. *Albany Park.* New York: Viking Penguin, 1987.

The Chronicle of the Movies. New York: Crescent Books, 1991.

Clymer, Floyd. *Cars of the Stars and Movie Memories.* Los Angeles: Floyd Clymer Publications, 1968.

Collins, Joan. *Second Act.* New York: St. Martin's Press, 1996.

Comden, Betty. *Off Stage.* New York: Simon & Schuster, 1995.

Cook, Blanche Wiesen. *Eleanor Roosevelt.* Vol. 1. New York: Penguin Books, 1992.

Cooke, Alistair. *Six Men.* New York: Alfred A. Knopf, 1977.

Cresswell, Julia. *Tuttle Dictionary of First Names.* Boston: Charles E. Tuttle Company, 1992.

Dardis, Tom. *The Thirsty Muse: Alcohol and the American Writer.* New York: Ticknor & Fields, 1989.

Eastman, John. *Retakes.* New York: Ballantine Books, 1989.

Epstein, Jerry. *Remembering Charlie.* London: Bloomsbury, 1988.

Eyman, Scott. *The Speed of Sound: Hollywood and the Talkie Revolution 1926–1930.* New York: Simon & Schuster, 1997.

Friedrich, Otto. *City of Nets.* New York: Harper & Row, 1986.

Gelb, Arthur, and Barbara Gelb. *O'Neill.* New York: Harper & Brothers, 1960.

Gelman, Barbara, ed. *Photoplay Treasury.* New York: Crown, 1973.

Gilbert, Julie. *Opposite Attraction.* New York: Pantheon, 1995.

Hadleigh, Boze. *Hollywood Lesbians.* New York: Barricade Books, 1994.

Hale, Georgia. *Charlie Chaplin: Intimate Close-Ups.* Edited by Heather Kiernan. Metuchen, N.J., and London: Scarecrow Press, 1995.

Hamilton, Ian. *Writers in Hollywood 1915–1951.* London: Minerva, 1990.

———. *In Search of J. D. Salinger.* New York: Random House, 1988.

Harris, Warren G. *Sophia Loren: A Biography.* New York: Simon & Schuster, 1998.

Hartnoll, Phyllis. *The Concise Oxford Companion to the Theatre.* Oxford and New York: Oxford University Press, 1972.

Hay, Peter. *Broadway Anecdotes.* New York: Oxford University Press, 1989.

Holdon, Anthony. *Behind the Oscar.* New York: Simon & Schuster, 1993.

Holmes, Richard. *Footsteps.* London: Penguin Books, 1985.

Isherwood, Christopher. *Diaries Volume One: 1939–1960.* Edited by Katherine Bucknell. New York: HarperCollins, 1997.

Jarvis, Everett G. *Final Curtain.* New York: Citadel Press, 1992.

Karney, Robyn, and Robin Cross. *The Life and Times of Charlie Chaplin.* London: Green Wood Publishing Company, 1992.

Koszarski, Richard. *Hollywood Directors 1914–1940.* London: Oxford University Press, 1976.

Lewis, Robert. *Slings and Arrows: Theatre in My Life.* New York: Applause Books, 1984, 1996.

Lloyd, Norman. *Stages.* New York: Limelight Editions, 1993.

Loggia, Marjorie, and Glenn Young. *The Collected Works of Harold Clurman.* New York: Applause Theatre Books, 1994.

Loney, Glenn. *Twentieth Century Theatre.* New York: Facts on File Publications, 1983.

Loos, Anita. *Kiss Hollywood Good-by.* New York: Ballantine Books, 1974.

Maland, Charles J. *Chaplin and American Culture.* Princeton, N.J.: Princeton University Press, 1989.

Mansfield, Stephanie. *The Richest Girl in the World.* New York: G.P. Putnam's, 1992.

Manvell, Roger. *Chaplin.* Boston: Little, Brown, 1974.

Mast, Gerald. *A Short History of the Movies.* New York: Pegasus, Bobbs-Merrill, 1971.

Matthau, Carol. *Among the Porcupines.* New York: Random House, 1992.

McCabe, John. *Charlie Chaplin.* London: Robson Books, 1978.

McDonald, G., M. Conway, and Mark Ricci. *The Films of Charlie Chaplin.* New York: Bonanza Books, 1965.

McDonald, Gerald. *The Picture History of Charlie Chaplin.* New York: Nostalgia Press, 1965.

Michael, Paul. *The Academy Awards: A Pictorial History.* New York: Bonanza Books, 1964.

Michael, Paul, et al., eds. *The American Movies Reference Book: The Sound Era.* Englewood Cliffs, N.J.: Prentice-Hall, 1969.

Milton, Joyce. *Tramp: The Life of Charlie Chaplin.* New York: Harper-Collins, 1996.

Mordden, Ethan. *The Fireside Companion to the Theatre.* New York: Simon & Schuster, 1988.

Nurnberg, Maxwell, and Morris Rosenblum. *What to Name Your Baby.* New York: Collier Books, Macmillan Publishing Company, 1984.

Parrish, Robert. *Hollywood Doesn't Live Here Anymore.* Boston: Little, Brown, 1988.

———. *Growing up in Hollywood.* New York: Harcourt Brace Jovanovich, 1976.

The Plays of Eugene O'Neill. New York: Random House, 1955.

Quigly, Isabel. *Charlie Chaplin: Early Comedies.* New York: Studio Vista, Dutton Pictureback, 1968.

Quinlan, David. *Quinlan's Illustrated Registry of Film Stars.* New York: Henry Holt, 1991.

Quintero, Jose. *If You Don't Dance They Beat You.* Boston: Little, Brown, 1974.

Robinson, David. *Charlie Chaplin: Comic Genius.* New York: Discoveries. Harry N. Abrams, 1996.

———. *Chaplin: His Life and Art.* New York: McGraw-Hill, 1985.

Ross, Lillian. *Moments with Chaplin.* New York: Dodd, Mead & Company. 1978.

Sandford, Christopher. *Bowie: Loving the Alien.* London: Little, Brown, 1996.

Saroyan, Aram. *Trio.* New York: Linden Press/Simon & Schuster, 1985.

Schickel, Richard. *Intimate Strangers.* New York: Fromm International, 1986.

Schroeder, Alan. *Charlie Chaplin: The Beauty of Silence.* New York: Franklin Watts, a division of Grolier Publishers, 1997.

Sheaffer, Louis. *O'Neill: Son and Artist.* New York: Paragon House, 1973.

———. *O'Neill: Son and Playwright.* New York: Paragon House, 1968.

Sinden, Donald. *The Everyman Book of Theatrical Anecdotes.* London: JM Dent, 1987.

Sokoloff, Alice Hunt. *Cosima Wagner.* New York: Dodd, Mead & Company, 1969.

Spada, James. *Peter Lawford: The Man Who Kept the Secrets.* New York: Bantam Books, 1991.

Stallings, Penny, with Howard Mandelbaum. *Flesh and Fantasy.* New York: St. Martin's Press, 1978.

Stapleton, Maureen, and Jane Scovell. *A Hell of a Life.* New York: Simon & Schuster, 1995.

Stasz, Clarice. *Vanderbilt Women.* New York: St. Martin's Press, 1991.

Stern, R., G. Gilmartin, and T. Mellins. *New York 1930.* New York: Rizzoli, 1994.

Thomas, David. *A Biographical Dictionary of Film.* Third Edition. New York: Alfred A. Knopf, 1996.

Vaillant, George E. *The Wisdom of the Ego.* Cambridge, Mass.: Harvard University Press, 1993.

Vanderbilt, Gloria. *Black Knight, White Knight.* New York: Alfred A. Knopf, 1987.

———. *Once Upon a Time.* New York: Alfred A. Knopf, 1985.

Viertel, Salka. *The Kindness of Strangers.* New York: Holt, Rinehart & Winston, 1969.

Warren, Patricia. *British Film Studios: An Illustrated History.* London: BT Batsford, 1995.

Wiley, Mason, and Damien Bona. *Inside Oscar.* New York: Ballantine Books, 1986.

Wilmeth, Don B., and Tice L. Miller. *Cambridge Guide to American Theatre.* New York: Cambridge University Press, 1993.

Winters, Shelley. *Shelley II.* New York: Pocket Books, 1989.

Yost, Elwy. *Magic Moments from the Movies.* New York: Doubleday, 1978.

ACKNOWLEDGMENTS

In my childhood I was a moviemaniac and worshipped, indiscriminately, male and female film stars. Although my tastes in the latter generally ran to chirrupy MGMers of the June Allyson, Jane Powell, Debbie Reynolds sort, I found Oona O'Neill Chaplin, a non-actress, utterly intriguing. She was pretty, she was elegant, and she was the daughter of Eugene O'Neill, whose plays I read almost as fervidly as I devoured *Modern Screen* and *Photoplay*. I didn't quite understand Oona's marriage and remember staring at photos of the Chaplins trying to reconcile what I saw with what I, in my childish way, believed was *normal* for married couples—a man and woman a *lot* closer in age. But they seemed so happy and looked at each other with such obvious love that I decided, somewhat uneasily, it was okay.

My devotion to movies has endured, but my ardor for movie magazines (and for O'Neill, too, except for *Long Day's*

Journey into Night) ended in my early teens and with it my obsession with movie stars. Other than being aware that she was living in exile in Switzerland, I had no idea what had become of Oona Chaplin until I saw the headline announcing her death. At once everything was brought back, and I was inspired by those memories to do this book.

Although I have written eight biographical works, this is the first done in my own voice rather than through the assumed voice of another. It was an exhilarating and terrifying experience, one that I would have abandoned on any number of occasions had it not been for the help and support of many people, whom I now gratefully acknowledge:

The late Louis Sheaffer gave me a much-needed vote of confidence by allowing me to read his correspondence with Oona Chaplin and by telling me to proceed slowly and never to appear too eager for information. (I followed the first directive to the letter.)

George Beecroft, a generous and ever-helpful colleague, was a key link in unraveling Oona's story. He is my hero.

Jeff and Kathy Heim, each an invaluable source of information regarding Point Pleasant, steered me into troves of material.

Roxanna Lonergan ably assisted me in starting the research and was a lovely, supportive presence.

Annalee Newman told me not to work so hard, but by putting me in contact with others who knew the Widow Chaplin, made it necessary for me to work even harder.

Without ever betraying the Chaplin family's desire for privacy, and with obvious affection and admiration for Oona, Betty Chaplin Tetrick has been a beneficent and cheerful supporter.

Chuck Adams, oft-time editor and always friend, introduced me to author Scott Eyman, a spirited and erudite film expert who provided me with needed material. Walter Bernstein spoke candidly and illuminatingly on his and Oona's relationship. At the beginning and toward the end of my research, Claire Bloom kindly shared some of her personal memories and observations. Sam Cohn talked about his meetings with Oona and of the classes he took with Eugene O'Neill Jr. at Princeton. I am indebted to Jim Delaney's nephew, Frank Conley, and his wife, Pat, for their hospitality and generous assistance. Alistair Cooke talked to me about the Chaplins and sent me a copy of his essay on Charlie. Jan and Jeremy Geidt, dear friends of long standing, were of immeasurable help from the outset. My thanks to Arthur Gelb for a most enlightening O'Neill-filled conversation with a little Maureen Stapleton thrown in. Debbie Gilbert and Mike Ryan sent me to Peggy and Norman Lloyd, who received me in their home and willingly shared their collective memories. Michael Lonergan was ever available and helped particularly in the selection of photographs. Diane Loughran read and ably critiqued my manuscript. Justin Kaplan showed me notes from his scuttled Chaplin biography, and he and Anne Bernays wholeheartedly shared their remembrances. During an interview ostensibly regarding Maureen Stapleton, Carol Matthau disarmingly threw in a bit of commentary about her childhood friend Oona. One afternoon Joyce Milton shared some of her thoughts on the Chaplins gleaned from her research. I thank Esther Newberg for her efforts and expertise. Sheila O'Neill discussed her family openly and tenderly. And on an early fall morning at their Sag Harbor home, Kathy Parrish and her husband, the late Robert Parrish, were both welcoming and giving. In Switzerland Pamela Paumier encouraged me to continue and cautioned that I would meet with resistance. She was right! I wish "Grace Penington" had let me use her real name, but I thank her nonetheless. Bill Phillips took me through his personal collection of *Oonamabilia*. David Robinson's biography of Charlie

Chaplin was of immense help, as was his in-person discussion. I thank Greta Schultz for her guided tour of Vevey and her anecdotes about her neighbors. The late Frankie Schuman's articulate, wry, and compassionate observations brought into focus Oona's final years. Martin E. Segal charmingly and discreetly recalled his times with the Chaplins. Louis Sheaffer's niece, Michelle Slung, kindly let me look at further documents and granted me persmission to use the Sheaffer/Chaplin letters. Dr. Lora Heims Tessman's astute insights into Oona's troubled relationship with Eugene O'Neill were revelatory. Alexander Walker graciously took time from his busy schedule to tell me of his personal encounters with Oona. Jed Wheeler had much to say about his brief but memorable encounters with Lady Chaplin. As ever, Jeannie Williams was more than willing to help out a fellow author and opera lover. And during an afternoon tea at his London home, Francis Wyndham offered me firsthand Chaplin data—not to mention delectable scones.

Thanks also to: Phyliss Adams, John Aherne, Piers Allen, Vance Alleyne, Mikki Ansin, Jeannie Bach, Charles Rowen Beye, Nancy Blackmun, Jane Clancy Bockius, Erika Bolton and Jane Quinn, Mary Carswell at The MacDowell Colony, Albert Clifton, Jose Correa, Jane Donahue, Sophie Geidt, David Gothard, Beverly Sills Greenough, Muffy Greenough, Peter Greenough, Fred Guiles, Walter Hance, David Henry at Cinema Books/London, John Hodgman, Marilyn Horne, Oren Jacoby, John Kois, David S. Korzenik, Morad Koufane, Michael Kustow, Orna Kustow, Anna Kythreotis, Sonia and David Landis, Robie Lanz and Sherlee Weingarten Lanz, Izzy Lenihan, Kathy Levine, Iris Love, Susanna Margolis, Frank Marino, Laura Marshall, Elizabeth Perinchief, Charles Pierce, Nancy Robertson, Cynthia and Steve Rubin, Chen Sam, Louis Schumaci, Rex Smith, Maureen Stapleton, Sheila Starr, Ted Tetrick, Eliza

Thorne, Louis Ufland, Brenda Watkinson, Judy Wolfberg, Brian Zeger, Mel Zerman, and Two Gentlemen from London who wish to remain anonymous.

Special thanks to Bryan Rogers, curator of the Sheaffer-O'Neill Collection at Connecticut College, who graciously steered me through Louis Sheaffer's wealth of photographs.

I am grateful to the obliging staff members of the British Film Institute, the New York Public Library, and the Library of the Performing Arts at Lincoln Center. Cheryl Leibold, archivist—Pennsylvania Academy of Fine Arts, sent me material on Teddy Boulton; and Joanne Koch, executive director of the Film Society of Lincoln Center, was most helpful in my search for photographs. Joyce Pavetti, curator of the Eugene O'Neill Theater Center, and Lois MacDonald, associate curator, escorted me on an enlightening tour of the Monte Cristo Cottage in New London, Connecticut. Whatever his shortcomings as a parent, Eugene O'Neill deserves recognition for his literary achievements, and thanks to the Theater Center he is being honored.

I am most appreciative of the help given by Ellen Cordis, Yale University; Norman Currie, Corbis/Bettmann; Gary Deckelneck, *Asbury Park Press*; Terry Geesken, MOMA; Howard Mandelbaum, Photofest; Scott Miller and Kristine Krueger, Academy of Motion Picture Arts and Sciences; and Lisa Nelson, AP Worldwide. In London, Matthew Somorjay, Katz Pictures; Rebecca Willetts, BAPLA; Fiona Jackman, Kobol Collection; Sara Varley and James Stevenson, Hulton Getty; and Lester Middlehurst, the *Daily Mail*, were all wonderfully responsive, as was Bonnie McCord, editor-in-chief, *Limelight*, the quarterly newsletter of the Charlie Chaplin Film Company.

My sincere thanks to a very special person, Susan Ginsburg, for her inestimable help in getting my solo writing venture off the ground.

I am tongue-tied in expressing appreciation to Robert Stewart for his wise counsel, total encouragement, keen observations, and treasured friendship.

I am fortunate to have children who are ever willing to assist, advise, and sometimes dissent, and that is why this book is dedicated to Amy, Lucy, and Billy Appleton, each of whom, in one way or another, made certain that the Matke stuck with it. Shelley Welton, too, remains a major ally in my writing efforts, and this is a cumulative as well as current thank you.

Last, I am forever grateful to my editor, Jamie Raab, whose constructive, intelligent, and gentle criticism, not to mention her patience and enthusiasm, guided me through to the end.

J. S.

INDEX